# BLOOD OF THE CAESARS

Also by Stephen Dando-Collins

*Caesar's Legion: The Epic Saga of Julius Caesar's
Elite Tenth Legion and the Armies of Rome*

*Nero's Killing Machine: The True Story of
Rome's Remarkable Fourteenth Legion*

*Cleopatra's Kidnappers: How Caesar's Sixth Legion
Gave Egypt to Rome and Rome to Caesar*

*Mark Antony's Heroes: How the Third Gallica
Legion Saved an Apostle and Created an Emperor*

# BLOOD OF THE CAESARS

## HOW THE MURDER OF GERMANICUS LED TO THE FALL OF ROME

STEPHEN DANDO-COLLINS

WILEY

John Wiley & Sons, Inc.

# CONTENTS

# CONTENTS

# ATLAS

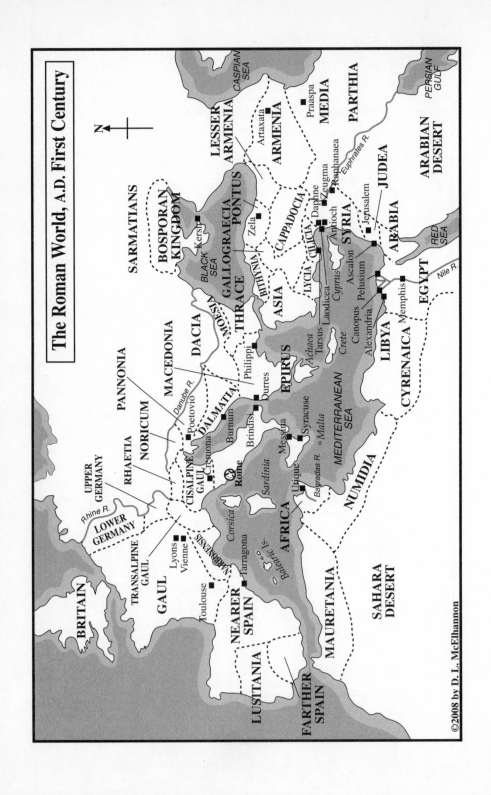

The Roman World, A.D. First Century

©2008 by D. L. McElhannon

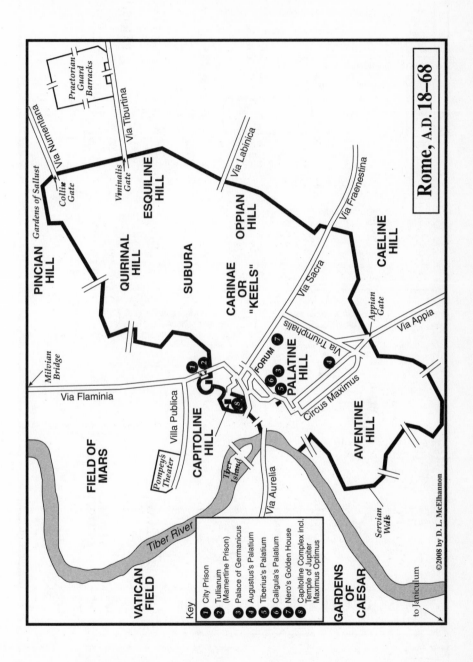

**Rome, A.D. 18–68**

Key
1. City Prison
2. Tullianum (Mamertine Prison)
3. Palace of Germanicus
4. Augustus's Palatium
5. Tiberius's Palatium
6. Caligula's Palatium
7. Nero's Golden House
8. Capitoline Complex incl. Temple of Jupiter Maximus Optimus

Praetorian Guard Barracks

Via Numentiana
Via Tiburtina
Via Labinica
Via Fraenestina

Gardens of Sallust
Collina Gate
Viminalis Gate

PINCIAN HILL
QUIRINAL HILL
ESQUILINE HILL
SUBURA
OPPIAN HILL
CARINAE OR "KEELS"
CAELINE HILL
AVENTINE HILL
CAPITOLINE HILL

Via Sacra
Appian Gate
Via Appia
Via Triumphalis
FORUM 7
PALATINE HILL
Circus Maximus

Milvian Bridge
Via Flaminia
Villa Publica
Pompey's Theater

Tiber Island
Via Aurelia
Tiber River

FIELD OF MARS
VATICAN FIELD
GARDENS OF CAESAR

Servian Walls
to Janiculum

©2008 by D. L. McElhannon

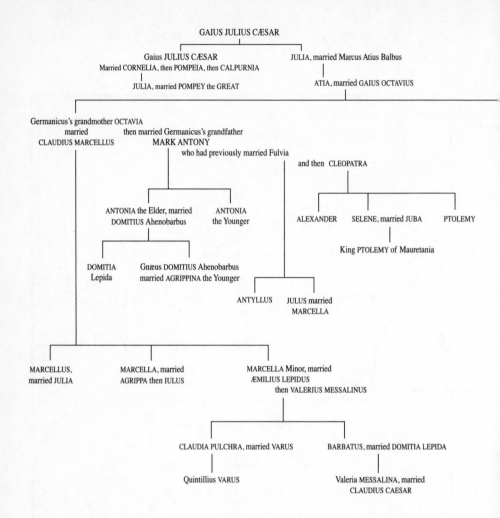

GAIUS JULIUS CÆSAR

Gaius JULIUS CÆSAR
Married CORNELIA, then POMPEIA, then CALPURNIA

JULIA, married POMPEY the GREAT

JULIA, married Marcus Atius Balbus

ATIA, married GAIUS OCTAVIUS

Germanicus's grandmother OCTAVIA
married
CLAUDIUS MARCELLUS

then married Germanicus's grandfather
MARK ANTONY
who had previously married Fulvia

and then CLEOPATRA

ANTONIA the Elder, married
DOMITIUS Ahenobarbus

ANTONIA
the Younger

ALEXANDER    SELENE, married JUBA    PTOLEMY

King PTOLEMY of Mauretania

DOMITIA
Lepida

Gnæus DOMITIUS Ahenobarbus
married AGRIPPINA the Younger

ANTYLLUS    JULUS married
MARCELLA

MARCELLUS,
married JULIA

MARCELLA, married
AGRIPPA then IULUS

MARCELLA Minor, married
ÆMILIUS LEPIDUS
then VALERIUS MESSALINUS

CLAUDIA PULCHRA, married VARUS

Quintillius VARUS

BARBATUS, married DOMITIA LEPIDA

Valeria MESSALINA, married
CLAUDIUS CAESAR

# BLOODLINE OF THE CAESARS

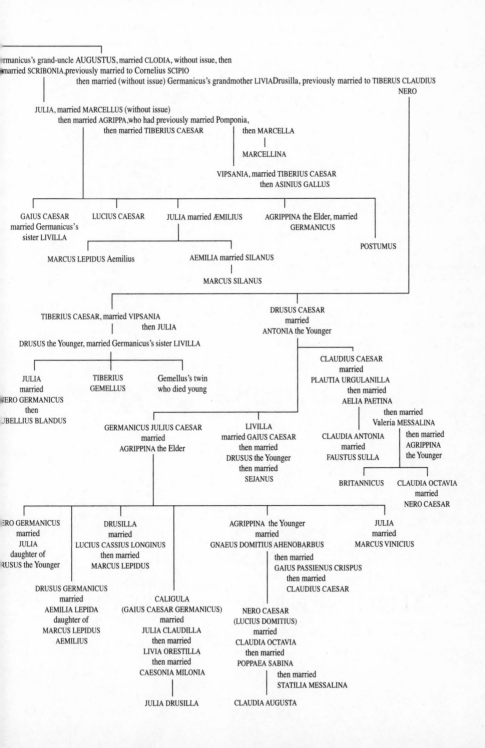

Germanicus's grand-uncle AUGUSTUS, married CLODIA, without issue, then married SCRIBONIA,previously married to Cornelius SCIPIO

then married (without issue) Germanicus's grandmother LIVIADrusilla, previously married to TIBERUS CLAUDIUS NERO

JULIA, married MARCELLUS (without issue)
then married AGRIPPA,who had previously married Pomponia,
then married TIBERIUS CAESAR

then MARCELLA

MARCELLINA

VIPSANIA, married TIBERIUS CAESAR
then ASINIUS GALLUS

GAIUS CAESAR
married Germanicus's
sister LIVILLA

LUCIUS CAESAR

JULIA married ÆMILIUS

AGRIPPINA the Elder, married
GERMANICUS

POSTUMUS

MARCUS LEPIDUS Aemilius

AEMILIA married SILANUS

MARCUS SILANUS

TIBERIUS CAESAR, married VIPSANIA
then JULIA

DRUSUS CAESAR
married
ANTONIA the Younger

DRUSUS the Younger, married Germanicus's sister LIVILLA

CLAUDIUS CAESAR
married
PLAUTIA URGULANILLA
then married
AELIA PAETINA

JULIA
married
NERO GERMANICUS
then
UBELLIUS BLANDUS

TIBERIUS
GEMELLUS

Gemellus's twin
who died young

then married
Valeria MESSALINA

GERMANICUS JULIUS CAESAR
married
AGRIPPINA the Elder

LIVILLA
married GAIUS CAESAR
then married
DRUSUS the Younger
then married
SEJANUS

CLAUDIA ANTONIA
married
FAUSTUS SULLA

then married
AGRIPPINA
the Younger

BRITANNICUS

CLAUDIA OCTAVIA
married
NERO CAESAR

NERO GERMANICUS
married
JULIA
daughter of
DRUSUS the Younger

DRUSILLA
married
LUCIUS CASSIUS LONGINUS
then married
MARCUS LEPIDUS

AGRIPPINA the Younger
married
GNAEUS DOMITIUS AHENOBARBUS

JULIA
married
MARCUS VINICIUS

then married
GAIUS PASSIENUS CRISPUS
then married
CLAUDIUS CAESAR

DRUSUS GERMANICUS
married
AEMILIA LEPIDA
daughter of
MARCUS LEPIDUS
AEMILIUS

CALIGULA
(GAIUS CAESAR GERMANICUS)
married
JULIA CLAUDILLA
then married
LIVIA ORESTILLA
then married
CAESONIA MILONIA

NERO CAESAR
(LUCIUS DOMITIUS)
married
CLAUDIA OCTAVIA
then married
POPPAEA SABINA
then married
STATILIA MESSALINA

JULIA DRUSILLA

CLAUDIA AUGUSTA

# ACKNOWLEDGMENTS

Over the decades that I spent researching ancient Rome for my series of histories of the legions of Rome, the character of Germanicus Julius Caesar loomed larger and larger in my consciousness. The more I learned about this charismatic character, this pivotal yet virtually unknown figure in Roman history, the more I wanted to know. The mystery of Germanicus's death, with its fatal implications for so many members of his family, the family of the Caesars, began to exercise my thoughts very early into my research. But it would be many years before the evidence began to take shape, before the mystery unraveled and the scenario of how the murder was conceived and carried out fell into place, and until I was able to determine who had killed Germanicus, and why.

Often, historical forensic works such as this credit a small army of helpers. Indeed, my American history about a nineteenth-century legal case involving Native American chief Standing Bear lists a number of sources without whom I could not have written that book, from leading figures within his Ponca Indian tribe to Native American researchers and a hugely helpful Omaha newspaper publisher. While I have been aided by many kind people dealing with Roman history at libraries, universities, and historic sites over the decades, this particular book is all my own work. Its theories and conclusions are entirely my own, formed on the back of my many years of research into the history of ancient Rome and using what modest skills as an interpretive historian I may have developed over those years.

My grateful thanks go to my all-conquering New York literary agent, Richard Curtis, who originally steered me onto the legion history path, for encouraging me to explore the Germanicus case and its historical repercussions. My thanks, too, to Stephen S. Power, my editor at Wiley for a number of years now, who saw the potential for the book and helped me focus on the essential elements and the implications for Rome of the murder of Germanicus. Thanks, too, to production editor John Simko and copy editor Bill Drennan for their usual thorough work on the typescript.

My special thanks, as always, go to my inspiration, my wife, Louise. We two are great walkers. For decades, on our walks, I have told Louise stories that had not been widely told before, stories I have found buried in history. Stories about soldiers and emperors, tribal chiefs and presidents, millionaires and idealists, scientists and politicians, sea captains and revolutionaries. Stories in which ambition sometimes clouded otherwise clever minds, and in which brave men and stalwart women stood up for what they believed in, even if they were wrong. For years, Louise was the only one who listened. Her story, of her faith and support, is the greatest one of all.

# INTRODUCTION

T he fall of Imperial Rome has been ascribed to many things. Some say the fall was generated from without, blaming the invasions of the Visigoths, Huns and others from the east, with the fifth-century sacking of Rome by the Vandals serving as a prelude to the final collapse. Others say it had an internal cause during this same period, blaming weak emperors, or overly ambitious and jealous propraetors and generals who rent the empire with civil wars that sapped it of its manpower, wealth, and cohesion for centuries, leaving it incapable of meeting the outside threats.

There are those who blame the rise of Christianity for the fall of Rome. They claim that where veneration of the Roman pantheon had been just one brick in the foundation of Roman life, Christian leaders sought to make the new faith the sole foundation, to the exclusion of the other factors that had previously made Rome great.

Some say that the western half of the empire was doomed from the moment when Constantine turned his back on Rome in the fourth century and made the future Constantinople his capital.

I take the view that the fall began earlier than all of these manifestations. Much earlier. Julius Caesar ignited the imperial period, and Augustus shaped it. In Augustus, Rome was blessed with a leader unique in history. In all things—military, political, commercial, architectural, and artistic—Augustus created the master plan for his successors to follow. He intended that his grandson Germanicus Julius Caesar would be one of those successors, following a brief interlude with Tiberius on the throne, apparently believing that not even

1

Tiberius could do much damage to the foundation he had laid. In Germanicus, Augustus saw himself. An astute young man with immense talent. A learned man with artistic sensibilities. A diplomat who could win over foreign rulers. A soldier of unquestionable bravery and skill. A general of genius who led from the front. These were all qualities that Augustus shared with his grandson. In the early decades of his reign, Augustus personally led the legions of Rome in its wars with external enemies. It would be another hundred years before there was another emperor, Trajan, who did the same. Tiberius, Caligula, Claudius, and Nero all left the soldiering to underlings. Not even Vespasian or his son Titus, both of them successful generals, took to the field once they were on the throne, and Titus's successor, Vespasian's youngest son, Domitian, had neither the experience nor the inclination to pick up a sword.

Like ordinary Romans of the time, Augustus could see greatness in Germanicus. Germanicus would have been, like Augustus, a soldier emperor. But more than that, Germanicus had a quality that set him above even Augustus, and Augustus knew it. Few Roman emperors could genuinely claim to have been loved by the Roman people. Some were admired, some were respected. Many more were loathed, or feared. But even though Titus was much lamented after his short, benevolent reign, not one emperor was loved. Germanicus was loved. As emperor, he would have been unique. Adored by the Roman people and admired by foreigners, Germanicus the soldier, Germanicus the diplomat, Germanicus the charismatic leader would have taken up where Augustus left off.

But with the murder of Germanicus, which in turn touched off a series of unnatural deaths that rent and within fifty years destroyed the Julian family, the Caesar dynasty, the foundation laid by Augustus was irretrievably fractured. Instead of experiencing a continuation of the Augustan golden age and an expansion of Rome's greatness, with Germanicus gone Rome lurched onto the first stage of the road to ruin. In expectation of seeing a new Germanicus on the throne, Romans welcomed Germanicus's son, his brother, and his grandson to the throne, and each time were sorely disappointed. The addled Caligula, the female-dominated Claudius, the tortured Nero—none of them was equipped for the task, none of them shared Germanicus's qualities.

Yes, there was the occasional pause along the declining road. Vespasian briefly applied a brake. Trajan even expanded the empire's borders, only for them to contract as soon as he died. Marcus Aurelius was a soldier emperor, but he spent most of his reign away from Rome fighting desperately to hold back the invading Germans. Once Marcus had gone, the pressures from both the north and the east proved irresistible, despite brief expansionist interludes under the likes of Septimius Severus.

History has taught us that all empires decline and fall. Would Germanicus, as emperor, have wrought a different outcome for the Roman Empire? There can be no doubt that the emperor Germanicus would have cemented the foundations created by Augustus and built on them. And had Germanicus reached the throne, it is highly unlikely that Caligula, Claudius, or Nero would have become emperor. The family of the Caesars would have continued to reign. Galba, Otho, Vitellius, Vespasian, Titus, Domitian, Nerva, Trajan, Hadrian, and their successors all would have remained merely high officials or generals.

What if Germanicus had become emperor? It is one of history's great what-ifs. Perhaps the Roman Empire of Germanicus would have produced a military or a diplomatic solution that defeated or incorporated the invading hordes. Perhaps the invasion might have been reversed, with Europeans sweeping east under Germanicus's leadership. Perhaps the Roman Empire would have spread to every continent. And perhaps from China to Australia, Africa to the Americas, we would all be speaking Latin today and naming our sons Germanicus.

With the death of Germanicus and the subsequent demise of the Caesar family, Rome was robbed of its founding dynasty. With the death of Germanicus, Rome was consigned to a future dominated by mostly second-rate rulers sitting on rocky foundations, men who were unable to cope with greedy neighbors battering at its doors.

Rome never again saw the likes of the Caesar dynasty, or the like of Germanicus. And it was all thanks to the myopic and ultimately lethal ambitions of just two people, the murderers of Germanicus Julius Caesar.

# I

# THE MURDER OF
# GERMANICUS CAESAR

**A** murder is in progress. The most famous Roman of his day, heir apparent to Rome's imperial throne, lies on his bed, racked with pain and convinced that he has been poisoned. Thirty-three-year-old Germanicus Julius Caesar, grandson of Mark Antony, brother of Claudius, father of Caligula, grandfather of Nero, nephew, adopted son, and heir apparent of the emperor Tiberius, is a handsome, principled, dashing young Roman general adored by the Roman people. According to one Roman authority, Germanicus was seen as potentially the equal of Alexander the Great as a soldier and as a man.[1] Talented, courageous, and kind, he was, to many, the hope of Rome. And here he is just hours away from meeting his death.

It is early October in the year A.D. 19, twenty-three years after the birth of Christ. We are in the grand palace at Daphne (sometimes called Epidaphna), on the Orontes River, five miles west of Antioch, capital of the Roman province of Syria. That province takes in most of modern-day Syria plus Lebanon and part of Turkey. In A.D. 19, the palace at Daphne, along with temples to Jupiter, Apollo, and Diana, sat amid ten shaded and sacred square miles of tall cypress trees, cool ponds, and rippling streams. This October day, beyond lofty, pillared halls and lush courtyard gardens with their tumbling, perfumed fountains and sweet-smelling flowers, all attention is focused on the bedchamber of the dying young general.

At the bedside kneels Germanicus's attractive thirty-two-year-old wife, Agrippina, granddaughter of the late emperor Augustus and

5

daughter of Augustus's loyal lieutenant Marcus Agrippa. She is alternatively giving Germanicus sips of water and dabbing his flushed face
with a damp cloth. His redheaded young chief of staff and five of his
best friends—generals and Roman senators—cluster around the bed.
Some of them are looking worried, others, angry. Anxious servants
hover in the background.

Germanicus Caesar's multifaceted fame has spread beyond the borders of the Roman Empire, as far as Parthia, Rome's traditional enemy
farther to the east in latter-day Iraq and Iran. The Parthians know that
as a youthful colonel Germanicus had played an important role in putting down a five-year revolt in the Balkans, leading flying columns that
tracked down and eliminated rebel forces in Dalmatia. As Roman
commander in chief on the Rhine he led massive counteroffensives
against German armies led by Arminius—or Hermann, as the Germans called him—after the three Roman legions of General Publius
Quintilius Varus had been notoriously wiped out by Hermann in Germany's Teutoburg Forest. Sweeping into central Germany, Germanicus had defeated the Germans in three major battles, and had kept
the German hordes east of the Rhine. After recapturing two of the
three sacred golden eagle standards of the legions of Varus destroyed
by Hermann, Germanicus had consecrated those standards at Rome.
In doing so, he gave Romans back their pride.

The Senate had voted Germanicus a Triumph for his achievements
in Germany. When he drove through the streets of Rome in a golden
four-horse chariot on his triumphal procession on May 25, A.D. 17,
those streets were lined with as many as a million cheering Romans,
many seated in the massive Circus Maximus, through which the Triumphal procession passed, others seated on the temporary wooden tiers
erected along the broader city streets for Triumphs. That day, too,
Germanicus had done something quite unique. Prior to this, generals
celebrating a Triumph had shared the chariot with just a driver and an
attendant. On the day of his Triumph, Germanicus had shared his
chariot with his then five children, including four-year-old Caligula
and even his youngest daughter, two-year-old Agrippina the Younger.

Sent by the emperor Tiberius to become commander in chief of
the Roman East that same year, Germanicus had sailed across the
Mediterranean, landed in southern Turkey, and marched into Armenia, a country tussled over by Rome and Parthia for centuries, to de-
throne one king and make another. The king of Parthia, Artabanus,

had made his son king of Armenia, but Germanicus had other ideas. He hadn't gone into Armenia with an army. He went with just his personal staff. After crossing treacherous mountains and trekking hundreds of miles, he had entered the Armenian capital of Artaxata as the Parthian-installed ruler fled ahead of him. There, Germanicus had crowned the son of the king of Roman ally Pontus as Armenia's new King Artaxias, allying the country to Rome.

Half a century before, Germanicus's grandfather Mark Antony had achieved a similar result in the face of Parthian resistance, but he had taken a hundred thousand Roman soldiers into Armenia to do it. According to the Roman historian Tacitus, King Artabanus of Parthia— the King of Kings, as he was styled—was in dread of Germanicus,[2] and in dread of the possibility that the reputedly unbeatable Germanicus would lead his legions on an invasion of Parthia. To pacify Germanicus, the Parthian king had sent envoys with gifts of crowns of gold for the prince of Rome. And then he had come himself to the bank of the Euphrates River, the border between Parthia and Roman Syria, to meet with Germanicus and seal a peace treaty with Rome.

No Roman had ever before brought the Parthians to heel like this; certainly no Roman who marched without an army at his back and who achieved success purely on the strength of his reputation and his personality. Running out of honors for Germanicus, the Senate voted him an Ovation, a form of Triumph where the recipient rode through the streets of Rome on horseback on his triumphal progress rather than in a chariot.

Even before he came to the East, Germanicus, said the Roman biographer Suetonius, had won such popular devotion that he was "in danger of being mobbed to death whenever he arrived at or left Rome."[3] No Roman before or after Germanicus won such popularity. From comforting his wounded soldiers at their bedsides to talking with people in the city streets, in the words of first-century Jewish historian Flavius Josephus, Germanicus had never let his royal dignity "prevent him being familiar with them all, as if they were his equals."[4]

Germanicus's charismatic image was enhanced by his gutsy, much-admired wife, Agrippina, herself a member of the royal family of the Caesars, who devotedly went everywhere with her husband. Imagine a glamorous pair of young royals today who were also movie stars—such was the status achieved by Germanicus and his Agrippina in their day and long after it. If there had been celebrity magazines in those times, young Germanicus Caesar and Agrippina would have dominated their covers year in, year out.

Now Germanicus is dying. And he knows it. Weeks before, in September, he had been hit by the first violent symptoms. News of his sudden illness, which quickly laid him low, swept around the Roman Empire. At that time, the government courier service, the *Cursus Publicus Velox*—literally "the State's very fast runner"—could take news to Rome from the farthest edge of the empire in just ten days via its express riders and fast stage coaches. At Rome, when the news of Germanicus's serious illness arrived late one day in the early fall, people rushed in their thousands to the temples on the Capitoline Mount with burning torches in their hands and leading sacrificial animals. According to Roman biographer Suetonius, the crush of devotees was so great that the gates to the Capitoline complex were nearly torn down.[5]

The next day, says Tacitus, the courts of Rome were deserted. Shops closed down, business ceased.[6] Barges lay idle at the Tiber River docks. Streets were eerily deserted. Private houses, which usually only closed their outer doors at night, left their doors shut and bolted throughout the day. People would not venture out unless it was to seek the latest news of Germanicus's condition or to make offerings at temples for his recovery. Rome had come to a standstill; the city had never before experienced a paralysis like it.

When a merchant ship from Syria soon after arrived at Ostia, the port of Rome, with the news that Germanicus had recovered, the word spread rapidly and the city rejoiced. Tacitus says that people ran through the streets shouting the news—Germanicus is alive and well, thanks be to the gods![7] Suetonius says that the emperor Tiberius was awoken by crowds in the city below his Palatine Hill palace singing that all was well again at Rome now that their Germanicus was well again.[8] Life went back to normal.

But the rejoicing had been premature. Even as Romans returned to their daily lives believing that their prince had fully recovered, at Daphne, within weeks of the first attack, Germanicus's symptoms had returned, only worse than before. Vomiting racked Germanicus's strong body until he had no strength left. This was a man who had never been seriously ill in his life. He was a soldier—young, fit, and athletic. Suetonius says that when Germanicus was a youth his legs were weak but he deliberately strengthened them with regular exercise. He trained every day; marched hundreds of miles; and, unlike many

Roman generals, fought the enemies of Rome hand-to-hand at the head of his troops. No one had been fitter than Germanicus Caesar. Surviving carved marble busts of him depict Germanicus as big-boned, with a square face, jutting jaw, Roman nose, and the same thick neck as his grandfather Mark Antony. "Germanicus is described everywhere as being of outstanding physical and moral stature," Suetonius was to say.[9] Unlike most wealthy Romans, the prince did not even employ a personal doctor.

Now, on his deathbed, Germanicus himself has become convinced that he had been poisoned, and equally convinced that he knows who is responsible. Ever since he'd arrived in the East, he'd been hindered by the new propraetor, or imperial governor, of Syria, Gnaeus Calpurnius Piso. Appointed by the emperor Tiberius at the same time that Germanicus received his posting, Piso, in late middle age, is a former consul of Rome who had previously governed the provinces of Africa and Farther Spain under the emperor Augustus. Germanicus's unique appointment as commander in chief of the entire eastern half of the empire—it would be centuries before a similar division of power would be made by a Roman emperor—made Piso the prince's subordinate.

Provincial governors usually had free rein in their provinces, to rule as they pleased, being answerable to no one but the emperor at Rome. More than once, this virtually unrestricted power tempted a corrupt or vicious governor to plunder his subjects or treat them cruelly. But here in Syria, Piso had to give way to the emperor's nephew and adopted son. All Piso's administrative decisions in the province, civil and military, were subject to Germanicus's approval or overrule. Nor was Piso the most senior judge in his own province; while the governor of Syria had previously presided in major court cases, now Germanicus sat in judgment, as his seniority dictated. Even before he arrived in Syria, the haughty Piso had been notorious for respecting no one, not even the emperor himself. And to compound the governor's humiliation, Germanicus, his superior, was half his age.

From the commencement of his appointment, Germanicus had allowed Piso to govern without interference, deliberately leaving Antioch, the provincial capital, to Piso, and taking up residence outside the city at Daphne so that their paths crossed only when absolutely necessary. This Daphne palace that Germanicus made his home had frequently been used in the past by his grandfather Mark Antony, and also had been visited by the likes of Antony's lover Cleopatra and

Antony's close friend King Herod the Great. Yet, over the two years since taking up his post, whenever Germanicus was away, Piso had deliberately and provocatively ignored or reversed his orders in a variety of matters, particularly in relation to the legions in Syria and the annexed subprovince of Judea, whose governor, the prefect of Judea, reported to the much more senior propraetor of Syria in Antioch. At official dinners attended by both Germanicus and Piso, Piso had done his best to embarrass Germanicus. Clearly, Piso had been bent on making life difficult for Germanicus.

After Germanicus had fallen ill for the first time, the prince had been reminded that at a banquet shortly before, Piso had occupied the position beside him on the dining couch, as his rank required, giving him the opportunity to introduce poison to Germanicus's food or drink. To compound suspicions, since Germanicus had become ill, Piso and his wife, Munatia Plancina, were known to have been delighted. What was more, Piso had audaciously sent members of his staff to disrupt the religious observances of locals who were making vows at the temples of Antioch for Germanicus's recovery.

When he heard this, Germanicus had sent Piso a letter, terminating their friendship, such as it was, using a traditional formula, and ordering the governor home to Rome. After the furious, humiliated Piso had set sail in a small fleet of ships with his wife, son, adherents, and hundreds of slaves, Germanicus had sent men to search the vacated governor's palace, which occupied an island in the middle of the Orontes River at Antioch. There at Piso's former palace, hidden under the floor and in the walls, the investigators had found the remains of unidentified bodies taken from tombs, and cinders smeared with blood. On lead tablets they found the name of Germanicus engraved, as well as incantations and spells.[10] This all cried witchcraft, with which, it was now rumored, Piso's wife, Plancina, had been involved. Now, too, envoys from Piso began to arrive at the palace at Daphne, asking about the current state of Germanicus's health.

Those present at Germanicus's palace in his final weeks and days would say that he'd become angry when these "spies" were detected in his palace. According to them, Germanicus had said, "If my doors are to be besieged, if I must breathe my last breath under the gaze of my enemies, what hope is there for my grieving wife and my little children?" Piso, he observed, seemed to be in a hurry to regain control of Syria and its garrison of twenty thousand Roman legionaries. "But

Germanicus is not yet dead," said the dying prince, "nor will the murderer keep his reward for the fatal deed, if I do die."[11]

With his first recovery, Germanicus's spirits had been buoyed, and he had thought himself safe. But now, even though every precaution had been taken at the palace to make sure his food and drink were untainted, this time the poison seemed even stronger than before, its symptoms plainly more violent. Somehow Germanicus's enemies had circumvented the security, and with an increased dosage were achieving with a new batch of poison what they'd failed to do the first time. The usual treatment for poisoning during Roman times involved using purgatives to induce the victim to vomit. This was supposed to remove the poison from the body. But a major symptom of all of the most deadly plant poisons was vomiting, so more often than not, all the use of purgatives achieved was the further weakening of the patient.

The actual poison administered to Germanicus would never be identified by Roman authorities. Roman physicians did occasionally conduct autopsies on the dead. One such famous autopsy following the assassination of Julius Caesar in 44 B.C. indicated that only one of twenty-three stab wounds received by Caesar, that to the heart, had been fatal. But the science of forensics was not sophisticated in those times, and there was no test in existence to identify a particular poison in the system of a murder victim.

The best-known poison of classical times was hemlock. This was the poison famously used by Greek philosopher Socrates to take his own life in 399 B.C. There are two types of hemlock, and both have similar symptoms and results. Water hemlock is found naturally in northern temperate regions, and in Roman times was imported from Europe to Syria by apothecaries and physicians, who used deadly poisons in small doses as purgatives. This habit of using poisons as purgatives would continue until the present day in various parts of the world. In the same way, arsenic, which is deadly if ingested, is used today in small quantities as a skin treatment. Poison hemlock, the other variety of hemlock, was native to North Africa, and likewise was imported into Syria. The notoriously fatal plant poisons foxglove and larkspur are also, like water hemlock, temperate plants. Another deadly plant, belladonna, was found in both Europe and Asia, and was commonly available in Syria.[12] For a variety of reasons that will later become apparent, belladonna was most likely the poison used on Germanicus.

Roman historian Tacitus was to describe Germanicus's dying moments, his final words. "If I were dying a natural death," Germanicus says slowly, swallowing with difficulty as he lies on his deathbed, "I would have grounds to complain even against the gods for tearing me away, so young, by an untimely death, from my parents, my children, my country." His eyes fall on his friends, men who range in age from the thirties to the fifties. "Now cut down by Piso and Plancina, I leave you with my final wishes. Tell my father [the emperor Tiberius] and my brother [Drusus the Younger] how I was torn by persecutions and entrapped by plots, and ended my life by the worst of deaths. Those who were touched by my bright prospects and by family ties, even those who were once envious of me, they will weep when they learn that this once prosperous survivor of so many wars has perished by a woman's treachery."[13]

Germanicus believes that Governor Piso's wife, Plancina, has somehow introduced the poison to his palace. He must have assumed that she had accomplices among the servants at his palace, for she herself had left Syria with her husband by the time Germanicus became ill a second time.

"You will have the opportunity," says Germanicus now to his friends, talking in gasps, "to lay a murder complaint before the Senate, of an appeal to the laws. It isn't the chief duty of friends to tearfully follow the dead man's body, but to remember his wishes, to fulfill his commands. Even strangers will shed tears for Germanicus. Vengeance must come from you, if you have loved the man more than his position. Show the people of Rome the granddaughter of the divine Augustus, my companion in life." He grasps the hand of his wife. "Place before them my six children. Sympathy will be on the side of the accusers. Those who hide behind the excuse that they were only following orders will be neither believed nor forgiven."[14]

One by one, the friends of Germanicus kneel beside him and take his right hand. Even the Parthians believed the grasping of right hands to be a solemn gesture. And so, gripping his right hand, each of Germanicus's friends now swears that they would sooner die than fail to avenge him.

Once all his companions have given their sacred oath—and Romans believed that they would be cursed by the dead if they failed to keep to such an oath—Germanicus looks up at a now teary-eyed Agrippina. Knowing that she can be "rather excitable,"[15] he urges her:

"When you return to Rome, honor my memory, and honor our children, by laying aside your ferocious pride. Accept what fortune throws at you. Don't stir up political rivalry, or antagonize those who are more powerful than you." He pulls her close and whispers a few words more. And then he closes his eyes.[16]

Had Germanicus been poisoned by water hemlock or foxglove he would have now gone into convulsions. With poison hemlock, he would have gone completely blind. Poisoned by larkspur, he would have suffered uncontrollable itching and respiratory distress. On the other hand, those who ingest belladonna and a number of other plant poisons slip into a coma before death claims them.[17] Roman historian Tacitus's account of Germanicus's death says that he passed away "soon after" whispering to Agrippina. There is no mention of convulsions, itching, or respiratory distress.[18] "Soon after" could refer to minutes; hours; or, at the outside, days, suggesting that Germanicus may well have lapsed into a coma before dying. Coma preceding death is a symptom of belladonna poisoning. Probably slipping into a coma then, and after lasting for several more hours, perhaps through the night and into the next day, Germanicus continued to breathe at most for an unconscious day or so, and then died.

Tacitus would say of Germanicus that he had been a dignified man whose greatness shone from him. Inspiring reverence by both his appearance and his voice, he said, Germanicus had avoided the hatred generated by arrogance.[19] Another Roman historian, Cassius Dio, writing two hundred years later, also would lavish praise on Germanicus, saying that he had never acted oppressively or shown jealousy, that while he had been the bravest of men against the enemy, he had been the most gentle of men with his fellow countrymen.[20]

The devastating news that brave and gentle Germanicus had been assassinated galloped toward Rome in the carriages of the *Cursus Publicus Velox* courier service and plowed west aboard merchant ships driven by the summer winds, to stun, stagger, and enrage the people of the empire and to bring Rome to the brink of revolution.

# II

# THE IMMEDIATE AFTERMATH

The incredible news that Germanicus Caesar was dead swept throughout the ancient world. "His death," Jewish historian Josephus was to say, "was lamented by all men everywhere." This was not the kind of fake sorrow produced to flatter rulers, Josephus added, but the real thing. "Everybody grieved at his death, as if they had lost someone close to them."[1]

Suetonius says that barbarian nations that were at war with Rome immediately made peace, "as if a personal tragedy had afflicted the entire world." Some foreign princes, he said, even went so far as to shave their own beards and their wives' heads to show their extreme grief. In Parthia, Rome's traditional enemy in the East, King Artabanus canceled his banquets and his royal hunt to observe a period of mourning for a man he had feared yet respected.[2] Josephus was to say that Germanicus was a man the Parthian ruler had come to admire, after being affected, like so many other foreign sovereigns who had met him in the East, by the graceful and gracious way in which Germanicus had received him when the pair had conferred and sealed a peace treaty beside the Euphrates River two years before.[3]

The most violent reaction to the prince's death occurred at Rome. Once the news reached the capital, the population erupted. Suetonius wrote that tens of thousands of people stoned temples and upset altars because their prayers for Germanicus had been ignored. Running riot, people threw statues of their household gods into the street and, incredibly, refused to acknowledge their newly born children.[4] The

emperor Tiberius tried to calm the situation by issuing official proclamations, but neither edicts nor official expressions of grief could console the people.[5] It became clear that the general public would not be
easily reconciled to the idea that the prince they had idolized had been
taken from them. Many Romans were baying for blood.

It was the Roman custom to swiftly cremate the bodies of the dead.
This was supposed to take place outside the walls of a city or town, as
funeral rites were said to pollute the dwelling places of the living. The
ashes and bones of the deceased were then interred in cemeteries or in
roadside tombs, beyond city walls. Once before, this convention had
been flouted for political purposes. Prior to the cremation of Julius
Caesar in 44 B.C., his body had been displayed in the Forum at Rome
by Germanicus's grandfather Mark Antony, to show off Caesar's stab
wounds and his bloodied clothing and so inflame the people against
his assassins.

Now Germanicus's widow, Agrippina, herself a descendant of the
Caesars, used an identical tactic. She had the corpse of Germanicus
carried in solemn procession along the long, straight east–west axis
road from Daphne to Antioch. The road, lined at that time by grand
villas, was crowded all the way into Antioch by a grieving population.
Antioch was then a great metropolis with as many as six hundred
thousand residents, which ranked it third among the cities of the empire after Rome and Alexandria. Today barely a trace remains of Antioch. In October A.D. 19, the entire shocked population of Antioch,
Roman citizens, slaves, and foreigners alike, and people from many
nearby towns and villages thronged the city streets to see the cortege
of Germanicus Caesar pass by.

In the Forum of Antioch, where a sea of closely packed, silent
mourners stood to honor the prince, Agrippina displayed the naked
body of Germanicus on a funeral pyre for the entire world to see.
Countless thousands filed past the corpse. "That poison was the cause
of his death" was revealed by the condition of his body, says Cassius
Dio.[6] Tacitus was to write that there were conflicting accounts of the
state of the body, that those who pitied Germanicus and suspected
Governor Piso of his murder positively testified that the body showed
signs of poisoning, while those who were inclined toward Piso claimed
it displayed no such signs.[7]

Others were more certain. Suetonius was to write, "Because of the
dark stains covering his body and the foam on his lips, poison was

suspected." He added, theatrically, that after the cremation of Germanicus his heart was found intact among his bones. Suetonius was also to comment that a heart filled with poison could not, according to superstition, in which the Romans were steeped, be destroyed by fire.[8] So prone to exaggeration and sensationalizing was Suetonius in his biographies of the Caesars that if he lived in our era, he would probably write pulp fiction or TV soap operas. His claims about the state of Germanicus's body can be taken with a grain of salt. Nonetheless, most classical authors were convinced that Germanicus had been poisoned and that Governor Piso had been involved. "His life was taken away by the poison given to him by Piso" declared Josephus, writing several decades after the event.[9]

The preponderance of evidence points to poison having been used to kill Germanicus, and that there was at least one telltale sign of it. Suetonius's supposed foam on the lips, and the talk of the heart that survived the flames, are without doubt his inventions. But often, where there's smoke, there's fire, as the Romans were the first to say. Most of the plant poisons mentioned in the previous chapter leave no visible external signs. But one particular plant poison, a poison readily available in the Middle East, does leave its mark on the skin.

The skin of a person who dies after ingesting this poison goes blue. In fact, the lips can go particularly blue. This bluish skin discoloration, called cyanosis, is the result of a lack of oxygen in the blood caused by this poison in the system, and this could account for Suetonius's reference to dark stains covering the body of Germanicus. The poison in question is belladonna. In addition to cyanosis, belladonna's predeath symptoms include dryness of the skin, dryness in the mouth and throat, difficulty swallowing, flushing of the face, nausea, vomiting, slurred speech, and coma followed by death.[10]

It is difficult to imagine Agrippina displaying the naked body of Germanicus, a shocking thing in itself by both ancient and modern standards, merely to emphasize the fact that he was dead. With his dying words, Germanicus had called on his wife and his friends to avenge him in a trial at Rome. His body was soon consumed by the flames of the funeral pyre, but the memory of his unnatural bluish skin would remain. Almost certainly, Germanicus did exhibit cyanosis, and this very public cremation in the center of Antioch, in defiance of one of the most sacred of Roman customs, which required that cremations take place outside the city, was Agrippina's way of making sure that no one could dispute the fact once his corpse, and the evidence, had been destroyed.

While Agrippina made plans with her husband's redheaded young chief of staff, his quaestor, Publius Suillius Rufus, to return to Rome with Germanicus's ashes and charred bones as soon as possible, to deposit them in the Mausoleum of Augustus beside those of the late emperor, members of Germanicus's entourage turned their attention to more immediate matters. It was agreed that a new governor of Syria should be appointed from among them at once, someone who would ensure order in the province and supervise a murder investigation. There was a contest for the job between the two most senior of the late general's friends, Vibius Marsus and Gnaeus Sentius. Both were former consuls, and both were in their forties. After some debate Marsus yielded to Sentius as the better qualified. Sentius would remain in Syria as acting governor, until the emperor either confirmed his appointment or sent a replacement from Rome. Marsus would return to Rome with Agrippina and the remainder of Germanicus's associates.

But before Agrippina's party set off back to the capital, there was detective work to be done. Once Sentius had taken on the role of propraetor, two other generals among Germanicus's friends then in Syria both immediately took it on themselves to investigate the crime, assemble evidence, and prepare an indictment against Governor Piso for a murder prosecution at Rome. One of these investigators was Publius Vitellius, who had held the rank of legate, the equivalent of a modern brigadier general, and commanded the 2nd Augusta Legion during Germanicus's campaigns in Germany. The other was a former praetor, or major general, Quintus Veranius, whom Germanicus had appointed governor of Cappadocia and who had come hurrying down to Syria at the first news of Germanicus's illness. Playing the role of investigators now, Vitellius and Veranius questioned the staff at the governor's palace at Antioch and those at Germanicus's palace at Daphne. They quickly established that Governor Piso's wife, Plancina, had made a suspicious friend in the province, a woman named Martina, who had a reputation as a sorceress and maker of poisons. At the request of Vitellius and Veranius, Acting Governor Sentius had Martina located and arrested.

Meanwhile, the former governor Piso and his wife, Plancina, had halted their little fleet at the Greek island of Cos to await news of the state of Germanicus's health. When centurions loyal to Piso began arriving by ship, informing the couple that Germanicus was dead, Piso and his wife were overjoyed. Piso made offerings of thanks at the local temples. Plancina, meanwhile, had been wearing black in mourning for the recent death of her sister. Now she threw off her mourning gowns and wore bright, colorful garments in celebration of the death of the prince.

The centurions who came to Cos urged Piso to return to Syria and reclaim the governorship of the province, implying that the legions of the Syria-Judea garrison, the 3rd Gallica, 4th Scythica, 6th Ferrata, 10th, and 12th Fulminata, would support him. But Marcus, Piso's son and quaestor, or chief aide, advised him to return to Rome at once. Unlike his father, Marcus Piso appreciated how enormously popular Germanicus was with the Roman people, and how angry they would be at the news of his death. What was more, he had not approved of the way his parents had acted toward the prince.

Tacitus was to describe a conversation that now took place on Cos between Marcus Piso and his father. "So far," Marcus told Piso Sr., "you haven't done anything that would suggest that you are guilty of murder. And vague rumors are nothing to worry about. Perhaps your confrontation with Germanicus deserves public detestation, but it doesn't deserve your punishment. But if you return to Syria, and Sentius resists you with force, it will mean that you have launched into civil war. In that case, you won't retain the support of the centurions or the soldiers, who will be powerfully influenced by the memory of their general [Germanicus] and their deep-rooted affection for the Caesar family."[11]

On the other hand, a member of Piso's party, Piso's friend the senator and former general Domitius Celer, argued that the emperor had appointed Piso, not Sentius, to govern Syria, and Piso should return and take control of the legions there now that Germanicus was out of the way. "Should we hurry to reach Italy at the same time as the ashes of Germanicus," said Celer, "only to permit you to be rushed to ruin, unheard and undefended, as a result of the wailings of Agrippina and the gossip of an ignorant mob?" He added a telling reminder: "You have on your side the complicity of Livia [the emperor's mother] and the favor of the emperor himself, even if it is secret."[12]

Piso, who wanted above all to regain his governorship and the power that went with it, embraced Celer's view. He quickly wrote a letter to the emperor at Rome in which he accused the now dead

Germanicus of luxury and arrogance. Piso wrote to Tiberius that he was going to retake command of the legions in Syria in the same spirit of loyalty to Tiberius as when he had previously held it. Piso sent Celer ahead in a speedy, triple-banked war galley of the Roman navy that had brought centurions to him. Celer was told to take the fast but dangerous direct route across the open sea. Once he reached Syria he was to take charge of the legionary troops in the province and bring them to meet Piso when he landed. As Celer departed on his mission, Piso turned his fleet around and headed back toward Syria via the slow but safe route used by merchant shipping, which followed the Turkish coastline. The usual practice for sailing ships of the day, "coasting" allowed sailing ships to duck into safe anchorages should storms or pirates threaten, rather than be caught on the open sea.

The legions in Syria had just gone into their various winter bases throughout the province—as Rome's legions throughout the empire did every year in the third week of October—and would not ordinarily come out of them again until the following spring, so Piso's envoy Domitius Celer knew precisely where to find them. Celer believed that of all the units in the province, the 6th Ferrata Legion would be the most likely to swing its allegiance behind Piso, possibly because several of its centurions were particularly loyal to Piso and had been among those who had come to Piso at Cos. Landing at Laodicea, Syria's principal port, west of Antioch, Celer set off for the base of the 6th at Raphinaea, on the Euphrates in southeastern Syria. But the commander of the 6th, General Pacuvius, was expecting just such an attempt by Piso to win over the loyalty of his troops, and, remaining loyal to the memory of Germanicus, the general arrested Celer as soon as he appeared on the scene.

Piso's fleet, in the meantime, was coasting around southern Turkey, heading back east. En route, it was intercepted by the westbound fleet carrying Agrippina and the ashes of Germanicus to Rome. Aboard the ships of both fleets, men rushed to arms and prepared for battle. As the fleets came together, both sides held their fire but not their tongues, hurling insults rather than missiles at each other across the waves. Now Vibius Marsus, seniormost officer on Agrippina's flagship, called out to Piso, "You are going the wrong way, Gnaeus Piso. You must go to Rome, and defend yourself there."[13]

"I'll be there," Piso yelled back with a laugh in his voice, "as soon as the praetor who tries poisoning cases fixes a date for the trial."

Roman law provided that a citizen accused of a crime be brought to trial at Rome before one of fifteen current praetors, the senior judges of Rome. Just as there were praetors for crimes such as extortion, bribery, and treason, there was also a praetor *de sicariis et veneficus* who heard cases where defendants were accused of murder "by blade and poison." But Piso was sailing away from Rome and a trial before a praetor, not toward it.

The two fleets separated. Agrippina and her supporters continued on for Italy. Piso's ships plowed on east a little longer, before Piso came ashore in southern Anatolia, which was then the Roman province of Cilicia, west of Syria. There he occupied the clifftop Cilician fortress of Celenderis and began making preparations for war. To create the foundation of an army, he sent messengers to Rome's allied potentates in the East such as the king of Nabataea and the king of Emesa, and to Rome's regional governors, ordering them to send him troops.

Against his better judgment, Piso's son Marcus was now actively engaged on his father's behalf. Roman conscripts marching through Cilicia bound for Syria to join the 4th Scythica Legion and the 6th Ferrata, both of which would be undergoing their twenty-year discharge and reenlistment in the new year, were intercepted by the young quaestor and ordered to join Piso's force. Piso armed his hundreds of slaves with farm implements—sickles and hay forks—and welcomed deserters from the legions in Syria who had come up to Cilicia in the hope of financial rewards from the wealthy ex-governor. Only one local commander, the governor of Cilicia, obeyed Piso's summons—a unit of Cilician-based auxiliary light infantry arrived, bringing Piso's motley force to some five thousand men. Piso would need these men if he was to regain control of Syria. A letter was brought by courier from General Sentius, acting governor of Syria, informing Piso of the arrest of his friend Celer by the commander of the 6th Ferrata Legion, and warning Piso not to make any further attempts to interfere with the legions of the region.

Word had soon reached Antioch that Piso had locked himself away at Celenderis, and as the year was drawing to a close, General Sentius assembled a task force at the port of Laodicea. Soon after, Sentius and his task force arrived off Celenderis in a fleet of ships. Sentius landed with the officers most loyal to the memory of Germanicus plus General Pacuvius's 6th Ferrata Legion and cohorts from several other of the legions based in Syria. Once ashore, Sentius lined up his ten-thousand-man army at the bottom of the slope below the Celenderis fortress. In response, Piso brought out his ad hoc army and lined his men up on the rocky heights looking down at Sentius's troops. Sentius's legionaries were hardened professional soldiers, many of them veterans of close to twenty years' service, and all of them were heavily armed—legionaries were actually called "heavy infantry" in their own day because of their weighty armor and array of weapons. Piso's pitiful, hastily thrown-together force was an army in name only, with little armor among them, and only light weaponry.

Piso addressed his men, urging them to hold their ground, assuring them that Sentius lied if he said that Piso had murdered Germanicus, and also assuring them that the legionaries on the other side would soon flock to his banner, for only recently they had been calling him the "father of the legions." He then addressed Sentius's army, its men standing rock solid and eerily silent behind curved shields emblazoned with the charging bull symbols of their units. Piso called down to individual soldiers of the 6th Ferrata and 10th legions by name, promising them rich rewards if they changed sides. When a standard-bearer of the 6th ran from the lines with his silver open-hand standard held aloft and climbed the hill to join Piso's force, General Sentius acted quickly to prevent any further defections.

On the general's order, the trumpets of the legions and horns of reserve auxiliary units sounded "Charge." With a cheer, Sentius's troops rushed forward. Piso's men had neither heart nor hope, and, seeing the wave of legionaries coming determinedly up the slope toward them, they turned and fled back into the fortress. Piso had no choice but to join them. As Sentius's men re-formed in their ranks and files on the landward side of the fortress, the general gave new orders. Scaling ladders were sent for, and the bravest volunteers from among the cohorts were chosen to mount them in a full-scale attack on the walls of Celenderis.

Artillery was also ordered up from the rear—every legion was equipped with fifty rapid-firing Scorpion catapults, which fired large metal-tipped "bolts," or spears, for antipersonnel use, and ten heavy stone-throwing catapults for battering down emplacements and pulverizing flesh and bone. As the artillery was positioned, plenty of ammunition was loaded onto pack mules and brought up from the beach where Sentius's force had landed—arrows, rounded stones the size of baseballs and bowling balls, and firebrands dipped in tar.

Seeing these earnest preparations going on below his ramparts, seeing the determination of the legions to obey Sentius's orders, and seeing the fearful looks on the faces of the men around him, Piso at last appreciated the folly of resistance. Encouraged by his son, begrudgingly he now called down to Sentius and sought peace terms. He asked to be allowed to remain in the fortress if his men surrendered their arms, while envoys were sent to Rome to seek the emperor's decision on who should govern Syria. But Sentius refused. All he would allow Piso was a few ships for his family and himself and some of their attendants, and only then on condition that Piso gave his word to return to Rome at once to face charges.

Piso, who had done his cause absolutely no good by his obstinate and doomed attempt to regain power here, and had only made himself appear all the more guilty of complicity in the death of Germanicus, was forced to accept the humbling surrender terms. Piso and his wife and son boarded the offered ships for a somber voyage home.

# III

# THE RETURN
# TO ROME

**B**y late January A.D. 20, word that the fleet carrying Agrippina and the ashes of Germanicus was soon to arrive in southern Italy had reached Rome. All of Italy was still in mourning for Germanicus. Not even the Saturnalia, the festival of Saturn in late December, had lifted the gloom. Normally the Saturnalia, forerunner of the later Christian Christmas celebrations, was a time for gift-giving, a time when slaves were given special privileges, and when all Romans could legally gamble on things other than chariot races, for four festive days. (The festival was later increased to five and then seven days.) But this year there had been no reason for joy.

Since the death of Germanicus the Senate had voted one honor after another for the late prince of Rome. An official song was ordered to celebrate his exploits. Chairs of state were to be dedicated to him wherever members of the Augustales priesthood, of which he'd been a member, served temples to the deified emperor Augustus throughout the empire. An ivory bust of Germanicus was now to be carried at the head of the commencement procession every time festival games and races were held at the circus. Triumphal arches were to be erected to him in stone and inscribed with his achievements—one was to be sited at Rome; another on the bank of the Rhine where he had served with such distinction; a third on Mount Amanus in Syria, the province where he had died. A cenotaph was to be built in his honor at Antioch, on the very spot in the Forum where his body had been cremated.

A tall earth mound dedicated to him was to be raised at Daphne, where he had breathed his last breath.

Following the lead of the Senate, other honors to Germanicus were created in Rome and across the empire by the grieving Roman people. The Equestrians, the Roman order of knights, decided that in every drama theater in every city and town around the empire where rows of seats were reserved for them, these seats, previously called "the juniors," were now to be known as "Germanicus's benches." And countless statues were voted to Germanicus in cities and towns the length and breadth of the empire. Tacitus was to say that many of the honors initiated in Germanicus's memory would still be in place in his day, seventy-five years later.[1]

Yet honors could not bring Germanicus back, and the angry determination of the population to see their hero avenged had not abated. But first the people wished to pay their final respects. Agrippina had asked that the fleet carrying her, and Germanicus's ashes, pause for several days at the Greek island of Corfu. This was designed to give Agrippina time to compose her mind, says Tacitus. Germanicus's widow was, he said, "wild with grief."[2] The pause also allowed time for people in their tens of thousands to gather at the southern port of Brundisium, today's Brindisi.

Among those who flocked to Brindisi were Agrippina's intimate friends and most of the senior military officers who had served under Germanicus. One of those officers would have been Albinovanus Pedo, who, as a prefect, or young colonel, had served as deputy commander of cavalry during Germanicus's German campaigns. A talented writer of verse and a friend of the famous poet Ovid, Pedo would write an epic poem about Germanicus's exploits that would quickly become a best seller. Only a fragment of Pedo's epic, describing one of the campaigns against Hermann, has survived. Also marching down from Rome came two cohorts, or companies, of the elite Praetorian Guard. These two thousand guardsmen had been ordered by Tiberius to escort his adopted son's remains back to the capital.

When February arrived, so did the remains of Germanicus. At Brindisi, word quickly spread that Agrippina's fleet had been seen on the horizon. People rushed to vantage points. They crowded onto boats in the harbor, filled open windows, lined the city walls, and perched on rooftops. Each asked the other whether they should remain respectfully silent when Germanicus's ashes were carried ashore, or whether they should give voice to their emotions—their grief, their anger, their pity for Agrippina and her children. Normally when Roman warships came into port, the paid freedmen who made up their crews waved, smiled, and called to those on the shore. But not today. Not a smile or a wave was to be seen or a word heard as the war galleys came slowly into the harbor to the steady, monotonous beat of their timekeepers' hammers and the slow rise and fall of their dripping oars. The members of the huge crowd made not a single sound, almost as if it would have been sacrilegious to speak.

In this eerie silence, the flagship tied up in the military section of the Brindisi dockyard, which was shaped like a deer's antlers. A crowd of sad-faced passengers appeared at the flagship's rail. A gangplank was quickly put in place by scurrying deckhands, and the passengers formed up at the head of the gangway. Without delay, down the gangway came the young widow Agrippina, dressed in mourning black. For many in the crowd, this was their first sighting of the famous wife of Germanicus, daughter of Agrippa and granddaughter of Augustus. While not tall, she possessed a neat figure. She had a boyish face, with large eyes and a small, pert mouth just like her father. Her fashionable hairdo, labored over by her personal hairdressing staff before her ship docked, featured the elaborate use of curling tongs for the front and top; more hair trailed down the back of her neck in a braided ponytail.

Today, Agrippina was looking pale as, clutching her husband's funeral urn and with her eyes fixed on the ground, she walked down the gangway. According to Tacitus, two of her children accompanied her as she landed at Brindisi.[3] One was her youngest child, Julia Livilla. Born on the island of Lesbos when her parents had been on their way to the East, Julia was now two and a half years of age.

Suetonius says that the other child was Caligula,[4] who was now a seven-year-old. Suetonius is the only classical author who says that Caligula went to Syria with his parents. Artists down through the centuries have picked up on this reference and painted Caligula into the story of Germanicus's death—Nicolas Poussin in his 1627 *The Death of Germanicus*, and Benjamin West in his 1768 *Agrippina Landing at Brundisium with the Ashes of Germanicus*, for example. Twentieth-century British novelist Robert Graves, in his influential 1934 novel *I, Claudius*, also mirrored Suetonius's reference and suggested in his novel that Caligula was in Syria with his parents and was an evil child who had something to do with his father's death.[5]

There is no other evidence that Caligula did in fact go to the East with his mother and father. Tacitus, who provides by far the most detailed account of Germanicus's life and death, makes absolutely no reference to Caligula being in Syria. It is quite probable that Suetonius was in error—in the same stanza that he speaks of Caligula being in the East with his parents, he says that after his mother was removed from his life, years later, Caligula went to live with his great-grandmother Livia. But Livia was dead by that time. So if he could be wrong in one thing, he was probably wrong in this.

If Caligula's parents followed their previous policy of always keeping their then youngest with them, the second child coming off the ship at Brindisi would have been three-year-old Drusilla. Not that it matters. Even if Caligula was that second child with Agrippina as she came off the ship, there is absolutely nothing to connect the boy in any way with the murder of Germanicus in Syria. And all classical references to Caligula in his childhood paint him as an adorable child loved by everyone, from the emperor Augustus down to the lowliest legionary. It would be years later, under the influence of Tiberius, that Caligula would find the vices that changed his ways and polluted his reputation.

The sight of Agrippina carrying Germanicus's ashes as she stepped onto the stone jetty, says Tacitus, generated a groan from those watching. Then the sight of Agrippina's black-clad female attendants following after her with tears streaming from their red eyes brokered a general explosion of grief. Tears flowed from the eyes of complete strangers to the family, just as they did from those of relatives of Germanicus and Agrippina. Men and women were equal in their mournful cries. Never, said Tacitus, had the country known a universal grief like it.[6]

Also on board one of the ships that had come from Syria was the prisoner Martina, the arrested sorceress and maker of poisons. She was quietly, discreetly placed in a safe house at Brindisi, heavily guarded by staff of Germanicus and Agrippina. There, it was intended, she would stay until it was time to bring her up to the capital to testify at a murder trial.

Within days, the funeral procession set off from Brindisi for Rome. Germanicus's twelve lictors, his official attendants as a former consul, led the way. Each carried the fasces, the standard of a Roman judge comprising a bundle of whipping rods surrounding an ax, symbol of a judge's power to order both punishment and execution. Now each fasces was reversed, as a symbol of mourning. Next in the cortege came the two Praetorian Guard standard-bearers, wearing their lion capes

and carrying their silver hand standards bare, without the usual consecrated ribbons, again as a sign of mourning. In two lines, two thousand
grim-faced Italian-born Praetorian guardsmen followed, fully armed
with shields and javelins. The troops both led and flanked the funeral
bier, a wooden platform onto which was fastened the funeral urn. In
rotation, the bier was carried on the shoulders of the two tribunes and
twenty centurions of the two Praetorian cohorts. Agrippina, her children, her kinfolk, her attendants, and the friends of Germanicus
walked behind the platform that bore the prince's ashes.

This journey on foot across half of Italy could have been avoided.
Agrippina could have docked at Ostia, the port of Rome, at the mouth of
the Tiber River, and transferred to small craft for the last stage of the
journey up the river to the capital. But Agrippina had deliberately landed
at Italy's southernmost port. It was her intention to walk all the way to
Rome with her husband's remains, covering hundreds of miles, as a political statement. She was determined to stoke public anger at the death of
Germanicus with every step. At slow walking pace, then, the solemn funeral cortege set out from Brindisi and made its way along the Appian
Way, a long, straight, stone-paved military highway, heading north toward Rome through the regions of Calabria, Apulia, and Campania.

At every population center they encountered, the population lined
the road. Men and women wore black mourning clothes; members of
the Equestrian Order wore their state robes. The magistrates of every
town had been ordered by Tiberius to honor Germanicus, and as the
prince's remains passed by, they burned vestments and incense and
conducted funeral rites at the roadside. From towns off the route came
a flood of residents and official deputations to crowd crossroads, build
temporary altars, and pay their respects. As the public shed tears and
wailed in their grief, priests from each town sacrificed animals to Germanicus's memory.

Day after day the procession made its slow, painful progress, stopping at various towns overnight before setting off again the next day at
dawn. It took weeks for the procession to reach Tarracina, today's Terracina, then a low-lying town surrounded by marshes, forty miles
southwest of Rome. Here it was met by a vast crowd from Rome
headed by Rome's most senior office-bearers, the two current consuls,
Marcus Valerius and Gaius Aurelius. With the consuls came Germanicus's biological brother, twenty-eight-year-old Claudius, who, with his
clubfoot and stammer, was considered something of a fool, and

Germanicus's thirty-one-year-old cousin and adoptive brother, Drusus, who was now Tiberius's heir apparent. In the brothers' care came Germanicus's four remaining children—the eldest, fifteen-year-old Nero Germanicus, as well as thirteen-year-old Drusus Germanicus and four-year-old Agrippina the Younger, plus either Caligula or Drusilla, depending on which version of who went east with their parents we accept. Here at Terracina, at last, a tearful Agrippina and all six of her children were reunited for the first time in almost three years.

A vast number of people thronged the road, says Tacitus, with everyone in tears. But, he added, this was genuine public sorrow—this astonishing outpouring of grief wasn't just for effect to impress the emperor. Just the contrary—it was Tacitus's belief that "everyone knew that Tiberius could barely hide his joy at the death of Germanicus."[7] This public display was directed as much against Tiberius as it was for the late prince.

The last time that Germanicus had returned to Rome had been following his victories in Germany. According to Suetonius, on that occasion most of the population of the city had flooded north for twenty miles to meet him, and each of the cohorts of the Praetorian Guard had gone out to greet him and escort him home, despite orders that only two of the then nine cohorts were to do so.[8] Now, in the second half of February A.D. 20, only the ashes and bones of Germanicus were coming home.

As for the emperor himself and his mother, they were now conspicuous by their absence. Their faces were not seen, in the city or outside it. This was because "Tiberius and Livia were thoroughly pleased at the death of Germanicus," says Cassius Dio,[9] supporting Tacitus's view. Tacitus was to conjecture that Tiberius and Livia either felt it below their dignity to mourn openly, or feared that their hypocrisy would become apparent if they were to appear in public and pretend to be grief-stricken when they were not.[10] In contrast, almost three decades earlier, in 9 B.C., the then emperor Augustus had personally gone many miles out of Rome in the middle of winter to meet the body of Drusus Caesar (Drusus the Elder), the brother of Tiberius and father of Germanicus, when it was returned to Rome from Germany, even though Drusus was only Augustus's stepson.[11]

Surprisingly, to many, Antonia, the mother of Germanicus, did not make an appearance either as her son's remains neared the capital. Tacitus was to speculate that perhaps she was ill at the time. "But I can more easily believe," he was to write, "that Tiberius and Livia, who didn't leave the Palatium [the imperial palace on the Palatine Hill at Rome], kept her inside with them." He was of the opinion that they did this to make it look as if their sorrow was equal to that of Antonia's, so that the grandmother and uncle of the deceased prince would be thought to be following his mother's example by staying home.[12] Antonia would later show herself to be a very feisty and independent woman, but she would always obey the emperor. Were he to command her to stay at the palace with his mother and himself rather than go out to meet Germanicus's funeral cortege, she would have done so.

Followed by thousands of people, the cortege moved on from Terracina, continuing along the Appian Way at the slow march. Several days later, in the last week of February, the procession entered Rome via the Appian Gate. Here, at the capital, the entire populace was, says Suetonius, "still stunned and distressed" by Germanicus's death.[13] On the evening of the following day, Germanicus's simple funeral took place on the Campus Martius, the Field of Mars, beside the Tiber River on the northern outskirts of Rome. The city streets thronged with people who crushed out the northern gates to attend the funeral in groups representing all the traditional voting tribes of Rome. The Field of Mars was ablaze with burning torches, and the roadways on the campus were lined by all the cohorts of the Praetorian Guard and the German Guard, the emperor's bodyguard, each man fully armed with shield and javelin; inside the city proper they were only permitted to bear swords.

People were heard to exclaim repeatedly, "The commonwealth is ruined! No hope remains for us!"[14]

Of Tiberius, still there was no sign, but he would have had many a spy in the crowd, and they would report back to the Palatium with tales of the outpourings of grief and the popular sentiments they heard expressed. Tiberius would have been particularly concerned to hear that men spoke out in favor of Germanicus's widow. Many were describing Agrippina as the glory of Rome because she was the sole surviving descendant of Augustus and the last connection with the golden Augustan era. Looking up to heaven, people prayed to the gods that Agrippina and her children would continue to be safe and would outlive their enemies.[15]

On Tiberius's orders, there was no official state funeral; Germanicus was to receive none of the pomp and circumstance that would have involved. At the state funeral of his father, Drusus the Elder, two hundred eulogies had been delivered. For Germanicus, there was not a single eulogy, not even a statue of the deceased carried before the bier, as was the usual practice with a Roman funeral. And people resented it. It was clear to the man in the street that Tiberius was deliberately trying to play down the importance of his adopted son's death. It was well remembered that in October, when the Senate had proposed a giant golden shield to the memory of Germanicus, a typical tribute to great Roman authors, in recognition of Germanicus's poetical works and plays, Tiberius had vetoed it, saying that such an honor was too much.

In the dark of night, at the massive, circular Mausoleum of Augustus on the Field of Mars, the urn containing the remains of Germanicus was reverently placed beside that of the emperor Augustus. As Agrippina and her children returned to the palace of Germanicus on the Palatine Hill, calls for justice and revenge rang around the streets of Rome.

Tiberius heard those calls, and also heard the criticisms leveled at him for failing to give Germanicus a state funeral.

The day after Germanicus's remains had been interred in the Mausoleum of Augustus, Tiberius issued a new proclamation from his palace on the hill. This time, Tiberius told the Roman people that while many a famous Roman had died in the service of his country before, no death was the subject of more passionate regret than that of Germanicus. But the observances for Germanicus that were being carried out in the humble homes of ordinary people did not befit a prince of the imperial family, said the emperor. Enough tears had been shed, he said. It was time to move on, just as Rome had moved on and left behind its grief following the death of Julius Caesar's only daughter, and following the death of other grandchildren of Augustus. Often in the past, said Tiberius, the Roman people had endured the defeat of its armies, the death of generals, the extinction of noble families. And endure they must again. "Princes are mortal; the State is everlasting," said the proclamation.[16]

Tiberius told Romans that they must now get back to living their lives, must enjoy the annual spectacles of the Matronalia, the festival dedicated to the "Great Goddess" Juno, principal deity of Roman women, which was due to begin on March 1. Tiberius declared that with the coming of the Matronalia, people should begin again to enjoy themselves.[17] The law courts, suspended for many weeks due to the death of Germanicus, now reopened, and business resumed. But no amount of proclamations or festive diversions could take the public mind off the desire to punish Germanicus's murderer. There was by now, says Tacitus, universal eagerness to exact vengeance on Piso.[18]

# IV

# PISO RETURNS

**G**naeus Piso was in no hurry to return to Rome. He had given his word to Governor Sentius that he would go home to the capital, and he intended to keep his word. But instead of going directly back to Rome, he had lingered in the ports of Asia and Greece on the way west. Then he had landed in the Balkans, from where he sent his son Marcus on to Italy to seek an interview with the emperor at Rome. Young Marcus was given the mission of clearing the way for his father's return without recriminations.

Piso himself had made his way, accompanied by his wife, Plancina, up into the Roman province of Illyricum in the Balkans, hoping for a meeting with Tiberius's son, Drusus the Younger. Tiberius had sent Drusus back to his post as Roman commander in the region immediately following Germanicus's funeral. Piso was hoping, says Tacitus, that Drusus would be kindly disposed toward him because, with Germanicus out of the way, Drusus was now Tiberius's heir apparent.[1] Drusus's twin sons, born only weeks before to his wife, Livilla, who was the biological sister of Germanicus, were now next in the line of succession, ahead of the sons of Germanicus, who otherwise would have been first in the line of imperial succession after Drusus.

Piso's wife, Plancina, would have assured Piso that he could bank on the support of the Palatium once he returned to Rome, for she had connections with the emperor's mother, just as Piso's friend Celer had reminded him. But Piso seems to have doubted that he genuinely enjoyed the favor of the Palatium. By taking this sidetrack to Illyricum, he was looking for the moral support of Drusus, the new heir apparent. At the same time, he was trying to forestall the inevitable; back at

Rome, proud Piso knew, he would face the humiliation of criminal charges proffered by the friends of Germanicus. To delay his return and to delay the inevitable court case, he would pursue any diversion.

Piso was received by Drusus at his headquarters, at Burnum, today's Kistanje in Croatia, not far from the Adriatic Sea. Drusus, two years younger than Germanicus, was Germanicus's complete opposite. He possessed a reputation for heavy drinking and for violent rages, and to date had shown little interest in public administration. Yet he and Germanicus had been very close, partly because of Germanicus's sweet nature and partly because Drusus had married Germanicus's sister. In early A.D. 17, Germanicus and Drusus had teamed up in the Senate to jointly sway senators to their way of thinking and ensure the promotion to the vacant post of praetor of a relative of Germanicus's wife, Agrippina. Germanicus had even stopped off in Illyricum on his way east later in A.D. 17 to pay Drusus and Livilla a brotherly visit before he launched into the next, and last, stage of his career.

For all his affection for Germanicus, Drusus was, according to Tacitus, firmly under the control of his father, Tiberius. When Piso arrived at his door, Drusus said to him, quite publicly, for all to hear, "If certain insinuations are true, I would be the first to resent you. But I prefer to believe those insinuations are false and without grounds. The death of Germanicus need not be the ruin of anyone."[2] It was just the sort of supportive statement that Piso was looking for.

Drusus the Younger, said Tacitus, was a man who normally displayed all the simplicity and candor of a boy, yet suddenly here he was speaking with all the cunning of an old and experienced politician. Tacitus was to remark that when Drusus's words were reported at Rome, men were certain that this response had been drafted for him by Tiberius, or his advisers.[3] Yet even though Drusus benefited directly and substantially from the death of Germanicus by replacing him as Tiberius's principal heir, no classical author was to suggest that Drusus had been involved in his adoptive brother's murder. Drusus, who had never shown any interest in becoming emperor, was apparently only interested in a hedonistic life. Drusus was guilty of a failure to demand justice for Germanicus and failing to pursue his murderers, and of betraying his memory, but beyond that he seems to have been innocent of any crime against his adoptive brother. In all probability, Drusus suspected his own father of complicity in Germanicus's death. Perhaps now fearful for his own life, Drusus did as he was told.

Following his meeting with young Drusus, Piso and his party crossed the Adriatic Sea and landed in eastern Italy at the port city of Ancona. From there they headed along the Flaminian Way, a broad, paved military highway like the Appian Way, heading toward Rome. The Piso party soon encountered the five thousand troops of an entire legion on the march, heading in the same direction. This was the 9th Hispana Legion. Usually based at Sisak (today's Siscia) in Pannonia, the unit had been ordered by the efficient Palatium to transfer temporarily to the province of Africa, today's Tunisia in North Africa. The resident 3rd Augusta Legion was having trouble in Africa countering a revolt in Numidia led by Tacfarinas, a native Numidian and former prefect of Numidian auxiliaries in the Roman army who had raised a large rebel army that was raiding towns and road convoys and harassing the province's garrison.

To reach North Africa, the legionaries of the 9th Hispana had marched along paved military highways from Pannonia into northeastern Italy. Their course would take them on to Rome, where they would camp on the grass of the Field of Mars. For the majority of the legionaries of the 9th Hispana, who had been recruited in Spain, this would bring their first ever sight of the capital. From Rome, where they would be reprovisioned, they would march on down to the western coast of Italy to Reggio, to board ships that would ferry them to Messina in Sicily. From Messina they would march along the northern coast of Sicily to Marsala, and there they would take ships to the province of Africa, landing near Carthage. This was how Rome quickly deployed its legions, using its military highways and fleets to move thousands of men and all their equipment, in this case from eastern Europe to North Africa, in just weeks.

Piso, being an ex-consul, which gave him the military rank equivalent to a lieutenant general today, was welcomed by the officer leading the 9th Hispana, its deputy commander, who was a "tribune of the broad stripe" in his late twenties. Also called a "military tribune," this rank was the equivalent of a modern-day colonel. The Piso party now linked up with the army column. At the rear of the long military column, Piso's hundreds of slaves joined the legion's baggage train, which comprised scores of wagons and upward of a thousand pack mules— one mule for every eight-man squad of the legion, and many more besides. Piso and Plancina traveled up front in their slaveborne litters, with the mounted officers. Piso, ignoring the rumor that he had been responsible for the death of Germanicus, says Tacitus, repeatedly "displayed himself to the soldiers" on the march.[4]

At the riverside town of Narnia in the Apennine Mountains just northeast of Rome, Piso and his wife and some of their attendants left the legion column. Here at Narnia, Piso hired a riverboat. After transferring to the boat, the Pisos sailed down the Nera River and joined the Tiber River, following it into Rome. Rather than sneak into the city in darkness, the pompous Piso had the boat tie up in broad daylight opposite the Mausoleum of Augustus, as if thumbing his nose at the remains of Germanicus resting there. Going ashore, and followed by a large retinue of dependants and staff, Piso and Plancina paraded along the streets of the Field of Mars and entered the city with broad smiles on their faces. Once in the city proper, they headed for the Piso mansion, which happened to be among the homes of the elite on the lower slopes of the Palatine Hill, not far from the imperial palaces, overlooking the Forum.

Gnaeus Piso Jr., Piso's and Plancina's eldest son, had remained in the family home at Rome while his parents were in the East. In expectation of their imminent return, he had decked out the house with floral decorations for the Festival of Juno. These decorations were still in place when Piso arrived at the house. Piso promptly gave orders for a large banquet. He made no attempt to keep the fact that he had returned to the capital a secret; Piso wanted it publicly known that he was back in town and hiding from no one. The news that awaited him was both good and bad. His younger son Marcus, sent ahead to Rome by Piso, had been granted the requested interview with the emperor. Tiberius had courteously received the young man, in the same way that he would receive any son of a noble family. According to Tacitus, this was because Tiberius was striving to make it appear that he was totally impartial in the matter of Germanicus's death.[5]

But at the same time, Tiberius, anxious to clear himself of any suspicion of involvement in the death of the prince, told Marcus Piso that he wanted a prosecution to be commenced against the young man's father as soon as the former governor returned to Rome. Tiberius knew he must act before the public demands for revenge for Germanicus's death exploded into riots in the streets, or brought the legions of the Rhine armies marching down from the north to avenge their former commander in chief. Like it or not, Piso was about to be put on trial for murder.

# V

# MOTIVES FOR MURDER

I n the first century, Roman writers identified five potential suspects whom they believed had been involved in the murder of Germanicus. In the murder scenarios spun by their proponents, often two or three of those suspects were accused of working together to achieve Germanicus's death. The emperor Tiberius figured in most of these murder scenarios. Suetonius was to write that, "according to the general verdict, Tiberius cunningly orchestrated the death of Germanicus, using Gnaeus Piso as his middleman and agent."[1] But was that truly the case?

There was a question in Roman law that prosecutors still ask to this day: *Qui bono*? (Who benefits?) To pinpoint a murderer, find a motive. That motive often becomes apparent when it is established just who benefits when a person dies in suspicious circumstances. The emperor Tiberius seemingly had much to gain from the death of Germanicus. The broad public belief was that he was jealous of Germanicus, that he feared his popular adopted son would depose him, and as a consequence wanted Germanicus out of the way. But did the insecure Tiberius really want to kill his own adopted son, the agreeable, self-effacing son of a brother whom Tiberius had adored, and in the process potentially stir the empire into revolt against him?

To understand the intricacies of Roman imperial family politics at this time, and to comprehend why Germanicus was so hugely popular with the Roman public and correspondingly such a perceived threat to

Tiberius, it is necessary to do a short crash course on the complex family relationships of the Caesars.

When he was alive, Germanicus Julius Caesar was addressed as "Caesar." This was because, at the beginning of the imperial era, Caesar was a family name, not a title. The Roman imperial family of the Caesars was established by Gaius Julius Caesar Octavianus, the great-nephew of Julius Caesar. He became sole ruler of Rome in 30 B.C. by finally defeating Antony and Cleopatra. In 27 B.C. he officially took the title of Augustus (meaning "revered"), the name by which we know him as the first emperor of Rome. The family that Augustus created was a blend of the Julian and Claudian bloodlines. In this royal family created by Augustus, marriage between cousins was common. The adoption of nephews as sons further complicated matters. In the case of Germanicus Julius Caesar, both of these factors applied. Through adoption by his uncle Tiberius following the death of his father, Drusus Caesar, Germanicus's first cousin Drusus the Younger became his brother. And because Drusus the Younger married his cousin and Germanicus's sister Livilla in one of the many incestuous political marriages arranged by Augustus, Livilla was both Germanicus's sister and his sister-in-law.

Because Tiberius had made Germanicus his son by legally adopting him on Augustus's orders, Germanicus was the heir apparent to the Roman throne after Tiberius, and ahead of Drusus, who was several years younger than he. And, with the lineage of his wife, Agrippina—she being the last surviving biological grandchild of Augustus Caesar—the children and grandchildren of Germanicus and Agrippina were considered special people by Romans. The future of the Caesar dynasty rested with them. Ultimately, with the death of Germanicus's grandson the emperor Nero, forty-eight years after the death of Germanicus himself, the Caesar family would disappear. Future emperors would adopt the name Caesar as part of their title, and later again the title Caesar would denote heirs apparent to the Roman throne, but none of these emperors and potential emperors shared the Caesarian bloodline.

Germanicus's mother, Antonia the Younger, was the daughter of Mark Antony and Octavia, the second of Antony's three wives—after Fulvia and before Cleopatra (if he did indeed officially marry Cleopatra). Octavia was the sister of Octavian, who became the emperor Augustus, and was from the same bloodline as Julius Caesar. This made

Antonia's sons, Germanicus and Claudius, grandsons of Mark Antony as well as great-nephews of Augustus and distant relatives of Julius Caesar.

Antonia, "famous for her beauty and discretion" according to first-century Greco-Roman historian Plutarch,[2] married Drusus Caesar (or Drusus the Elder, as he would also be described by later historians), eldest son of Tiberius Claudius Nero, who had been Julius Caesar's onetime quaestor, or chief of staff, and a successful admiral during Caesar's 47–46 B.C. battle to conquer Egypt. Antonia's husband, Drusus, was handsome, a brave soldier, and a born leader, yet possessed the same sweet nature displayed by his eldest son, Germanicus. Drusus had, like his younger brother Tiberius, become the stepson of the emperor Augustus when their mother, Livia, divorced Tiberius Claudius Nero and married Augustus. The two boys had been raised by their father until his death, and Drusus and Tiberius had formed a close bond, with Drusus apparently looking out for the younger Tiberius as they grew to manhood.

Well liked by the Roman public, Drusus the Elder enjoyed the same birthday as his late father-in-law, Mark Antony, and suffered a similarly tragic fate. Germanicus had been just six years old when his father died while on campaign in Germany—Drusus was seriously injured when thrown from his horse. Apparently contracting gangrene, he was dead thirty days later, dying in the arms of his devoted brother Tiberius, who had galloped all the way from northern Italy to be at his bedside. Antonia had never remarried, despite the urgings of Augustus. Instead, much respected for choosing to do so, Antonia had led a chaste life at Rome, helping to raise her grandchildren.

In a marriage arranged by Augustus, Germanicus had, in about A.D. 5, wed Agrippina, the intelligent, feisty daughter of Augustus's troublesome daughter, Julia, and Augustus's loyal right-hand man, the talented general and admiral Marcus Vipsanius Agrippa. Agrippina would bear Germanicus nine children, two of whom died at birth, with a third dying in infancy. Unlike many of the husbands and wives in other arranged royal marriages, Germanicus and Agrippina gave every appearance of genuinely loving each other, and were inseparable.

When in his twenties, Germanicus demonstrated both military skill and leadership qualities, first in the Dalmatian War and later serving under Tiberius in several campaigns in Germany. By A.D. 14, Germanicus had been appointed by Augustus to replace Tiberius as

Roman commander in chief on the Rhine. Ignoring the convention that generals' wives stayed home in Rome while their husbands served on the frontiers, young Agrippina had joined Germanicus on the Rhine, living at his headquarters in the city of Cologne. Their elder children had remained in Rome, in the palace that Augustus had permitted Germanicus to build on the Palatine Hill. It sat below the emperor's own palace, the Palatium, a title from which came our word "palace."

As the years passed, the couple had the habit of always keeping their youngest child with them at Germanicus's headquarters, a natural habit for loving parents. In this way, their third son, Gaius, spent his early years at the Rhine army base. A legion tailor made a little red legionary's tunic for the popular child; a legion cobbler crafted him a pair of small *caligulae*, the military sandals worn by legionaries. As a result, the boy had gained the nickname Caligula, or Little Boot. It was a nickname that would resonate down through history, although in his own time Caligula was generally, and officially, known as Gaius.

During the winter of A.D. 13–14, when Agrippina was pregnant with her eighth child, the infant Caligula stayed at Rome with his grandfather the emperor Augustus. Caligula was so well liked by his father's troops, who saw him as something of a good-luck charm, that in the spring of A.D. 14 the couple had sent to Rome for Caligula to join them on the Rhine. In May, elderly emperor Augustus, who had become extremely fond of the child, wrote to Agrippina, who was about to rejoin Germanicus at Cologne from where she had wintered in Gaul:

> Yesterday I made arrangements for Talarius and Asillius to bring your son Gaius [Caligula] to you on the 18th of May, if the gods will it. I am sending one of my slaves with him, a doctor, [to serve as Caligula's physician] who, as I have told Germanicus in another letter, need not be sent back to me if he proves to be of use to you.
>
> Farewell, my dear Agrippina. Stay well on the return to your Germanicus.[3]

Within three months of writing that letter, Augustus was dead—from pneumonia, it seems—after a reign of more than forty years. Augustus had been grooming his elder grandsons, Agrippina's brothers Lucius and another Gaius, as his heirs, but they both passed away prematurely—officially one died from battle wounds, another from illness, although historian Tacitus was to express suspicions that Augustus's wife, Livia, had played a role in their deaths, perhaps via poisoning.[4] Hugely fond of his stepgrandson Germanicus, whom he considered a model of manliness and virtue, Augustus in his last years contemplated naming Germanicus his heir. But under pressure from Livia, Augustus had named her surviving son, Tiberius, as his chief heir in his will. At the same time, he had made Tiberius adopt Germanicus, making Germanicus Tiberius's heir in preference to Tiberius's own son, Drusus the Younger. In this way, Augustus established a line of succession that satisfied his wife yet that was designed to also make Germanicus emperor, even if that would occur later rather than sooner.

The problem was, Augustus never formalized that succession plan. His will certainly made Tiberius the chief beneficiary of his estate, but nowhere had Augustus written his intent that Tiberius should succeed him as emperor. After Augustus passed away at Nola near Naples on August 19, A.D. 14, Tiberius had not immediately claimed the throne. One potential rival for the throne, Marcus Agrippa Postumus, another of Augustus's grandsons, was promptly decapitated on the Italian island where he had been held prisoner by Augustus for a number of years. Suetonius was to speculate that the order for that execution was either written previously by Augustus, to be enacted on his death, or was issued by Tiberius or by his mother, Livia. In his defense, Tiberius had appeared both angry and upset at the news of the execution of Postumus. Disavowing any knowledge of the execution order, he threatened to punish the Praetorian tribune in charge of guarding Postumus, who had carried out the young man's beheading and then reported to Tiberius and presented him with the severed head. Yet Tiberius never did follow through on that threat.[5]

Even after Postumus Agrippa's execution, and after Tiberius had announced Augustus's death to the Senate, Tiberius hesitated to claim the vacant throne. There was, Tiberius believed, another, more powerful rival to contend with: his own nephew and adopted son, Germanicus. Much of his paranoia about Germanicus can be attributed to the commander of the Praetorian Guard, Lucius Aelius Sejanus. Praetorian Prefect Sejanus was able to convince Tiberius that Germanicus wanted the throne for himself. And while Sejanus brought Tiberius the support of the Praetorian Guard—a sort of military police force not unlike today's carabinieri in Italy—plus the imperial bodyguard unit, the German Guard, totaling twelve thousand men, Germanicus commanded eighty thousand crack legionary and auxiliary troops on the Rhine who were extremely loyal to him; some of his troops had even offered to make Germanicus emperor, using their swords as their authority.

If Germanicus chose to march on Rome with even half those men to make himself emperor, not even the self-confident Praetorians would be able to stop him, not that there was any guarantee that the rank-and-file Praetorians would want to stand in Germanicus's way. As they were to prove in late A.D. 16, when every cohort of the Guard went out of the city to meet Germanicus on his victorious return from Germany—when only two cohorts had been ordered to do so—the Praetorians also revered Germanicus, and would almost certainly have refused any order to resist him.

In August A.D. 14, just prior to Augustus's death, Germanicus was away from his troops, making the annual tax collection in Gaul. In his absence, the legionaries of eight Roman legions, or regiments, on the Rhine had gone on strike at the news of the passing of Augustus. Germanicus had galloped back to Cologne, where Agrippina waited with two-year-old Caligula, to find that the four legions there had killed some of their officers and thrown out the rest. The troops were making various demands, but most of all they wanted the length of their military service reduced. Several years before, Augustus had extended their period of service from sixteen years to twenty. If the original sixteen-year enrollment had still been observed, thousands of these men would have been in retirement by that time; instead, they were faced with several more years in the ranks.

Addressing the assembled troops, Germanicus had agreed to let the men who had served sixteen years or more retire. After restoring order, he had dashed up the Rhine to Mainz, to calm the four mutinous legions there. But at both legion bases, the troops had clamored for Germanicus to take the Roman throne for himself, promising to back him to the hilt. But Germanicus knew that Augustus had intended that his adoptive father, Tiberius, become the next emperor. Angrily, Germanicus resisted all calls from the troops for him to take the throne, telling them that he would rather take his own life than be disloyal to his "father." To take his troops' minds off the throne, Germanicus had immediately led them in a surprise assault across the Rhine into Germany, to punish the German leader Hermann—or Arminius, as the Romans called him—and his German allies, for wiping out Rome's general Publius Quintilius Varus and the 17th, 18th, and 19th legions in the Teutoburg Forest east of the Rhine five years before.

Once it was clear that Germanicus was more interested in being a general than an emperor, Tiberius had ascended the throne. But he had never entirely trusted his nephew/adopted son. Praetorian Guard commander Sejanus would have told Tiberius that no one with the popular support attracted by Germanicus could be that honorable or that trustworthy, and would have warned him that eventually Germanicus must point his legions toward Rome.

Each year for three years, Germanicus drove across the Rhine with well-organized Roman invasion forces and utilizing well-conceived and quite complex battle plans. Sweeping through central Germany using carefully coordinated pincer movements, he had destroyed numerous German strongholds, towns, and villages and put the tribes on the run. In three major set-piece battles his professional soldiers had defeated Hermann's undisciplined German warriors every time, using good intelligence to avoid ambushes and inflicting tens of thousands of casualties on the enemy. Hermann himself just managed to avoid capture, and became a fugitive, but his pregnant young wife, Thusnelda, fell into Germanicus's hands and was sent to live in Italy under house arrest; there, Hermann's son was born, into Roman captivity.

As, each year, news of Germanicus's successes reached Rome and his fame blazed brighter than ever, Tiberius became all the more suspicious of him. The new emperor had a good friend, a general named Seius Tubero, serving on Germanicus's military staff, someone who could keep him posted on what Germanicus said and did. In A.D. 15 he had also sent a former consul, Lucius Apronius, supposedly to give Germanicus the benefit of his experience, but in reality to spy on him. Germanicus had left Apronius in charge of a fort in his rear, where he could spy on nothing more than an empty forest.

The following year, Tiberius had sent two thousand men of the Praetorian Guard to join Germanicus's army. This was unheard of. Praetorians never usually left the emperor, and many Romans would suspect that the Praetorian officers had orders from their commander at Rome, Sejanus, to assassinate Germanicus in the heat of battle and so eliminate him as a threat to Tiberius's throne. Well aware of that possibility, Germanicus had deliberately led these Praetorians in the vanguard of a charge against a vast German emplacement, the Angrivar Barrier. What's more, he removed his helmet and went into battle bareheaded, so that he was easily recognized and no Praetorian officer could put a sword into him with the excuse of mistaken identity.

To the disappointment of his army and of the Roman people in general, just as Germanicus was preparing to invade Germany again, in A.D. 17, on a campaign he believed would bring final victory against the Germans and expand the Roman Empire as far as the Elbe, Tiberius had recalled him to Rome. Various excuses were offered by the Palatium for this recall. Tiberius wanted Germanicus to become a consul for the second time. He wanted him to take the Triumph voted him by the Senate. He had a new assignment for him. Tiberius had also hinted that he wanted Germanicus's adoptive brother Drusus the Younger to share some of the glory by sending him with the Rhine legions on the next campaign against the Germans. But while there would be the occasional punitive Roman raid into Germany in future decades, once Germanicus left the Rhine, the legions were never again sent on a major invasion of Germany, and the Rhine became the northeastern border of the Roman Empire.

To many, then and now, it would seem illogical that Tiberius would want to prevent his best general from capitalizing on what Germanicus had achieved in Germany over the past two and a half years, in the process expanding the empire. But Tiberius was clearly jealous of his adopted son. A decade before, Tiberius himself had led an army of fifteen legions—almost twice the size of Germanicus's army—on harrowing campaigns in Germany, and had achieved little apart from peace treaties with some of the German tribes that, subsequently, had gone to war with Rome under the leadership of Hermann. Germanicus, with fewer troops than Tiberius and with less difficulty, had defeated the Germans in a number of major battles. He had destroyed their major centers and sent hundreds of thousands of German refugees streaming east. He had captured numerous German leaders. He had retrieved two of the three captured golden eagle standards of General Varus's vanquished legions. And unlike Tiberius, a man without an ounce of personal charisma, Germanicus had been hailed as a hero by the Roman people. To the increasingly paranoid Tiberius, the final defeat of Hermann and the occupation of Germany by Germanicus Caesar would only raise the young general's reputation to the point where he would be catapulted onto the throne—Tiberius's throne—by the adoring Roman people.

Yet Germanicus remained loyal to Tiberius. He obeyed orders, gave up his plans for one final German campaign in A.D. 17, and returned to Rome, receiving a tumultuous welcome home from citizens and soldiers alike. Once Germanicus took his Triumph in the streets of

Rome, Tiberius had ordered him to take charge in the Roman East, granting him *imperium*, which gave him supreme command over all Roman troops and officials in all eastern provinces of the empire. This would put thousands of miles between Germanicus and Rome, and even more distance between Germanicus and his loyal legions half a world away on the Rhine.

There were seven legions in the East—four based in Syria, one in Judea, and two in Egypt. But their legionaries only knew Germanicus by reputation, and it would take time for him to build the no-questions-asked loyalty that he had won for himself among his troops on the Rhine. To deliberately complicate matters for Germanicus, Tiberius had also appointed a new provincial governor to Syria, where Germanicus would be based, having recalled the existing governor, Creticus Silanus. Retiring governor Silanus was a friend of Germanicus—his daughter was engaged to marry Germanicus's eldest son, Nero—not the future emperor Nero, but his great-uncle Nero Julius Caesar Germanicus.

The new governor appointed by Tiberius was Gnaeus Calpurnius Piso. Certainly, Augustus had thought highly of Piso—under Augustus he had been in charge of the imperial mint at Rome, had been made a consul, had governed the senatorial province of Africa for a year in 3 B.C., and, in A.D. 9 had been made governor of Farther Spain. Yet despite Piso's broad experience, to outsiders, Piso's Syrian appointment was unusual, for Piso was no friend of Tiberius. Arrogant, self-opinionated, and argumentative, son of a noted opponent of Julius Caesar, Piso despised Tiberius, even though he had shared the consulship with him in 7 B.C. In his sixties now, Piso had respected no man apart from the emperor Augustus, who had been his close friend. Piso had even gone against Tiberius in the Senate in A.D. 16, arguing that the House should be able to sit and conduct business if the emperor was away from Rome, even after Tiberius had said he thought it should not. Tiberius had won the argument, but only after heated debate in the Senate between Piso and senators close to Tiberius.

Piso's wife, Plancina, a woman of noble birth and of great independent wealth, was on good terms with the emperor's mother, Livia. It was generally believed that Livia had recommended Piso's appointment to the governorship of Syria, one of the highest-paid Roman gubernatorial postings, as a favor to her friend Plancina. Piso's irascible nature would have finally influenced Tiberius's choice. As the astute

Praetorian commander Sejanus would have noted, prickly Piso could be expected to make life very difficult for Germanicus in the Roman East.

Germanicus made just one misstep in his career, and that was while he was in the East. Importantly, it was a misstep that could only antagonize Tiberius and exacerbate his fears about his adopted son's ambitions. At the beginning of the summer of A.D. 19, hearing that Egypt was experiencing a famine, Germanicus had hurried down through Judea to the Egyptian capital, Alexandria, to supervise relief operations. Some modern historians and authors have speculated that Germanicus took Agrippina and two of his children with him on this excursion, as he rarely if ever traveled without his family in friendly territory. No classical author confirms that Germanicus took his family to Egypt with him on this trip. Tacitus, who describes a solo visit,[6] says that on arrival in Alexandria, Germanicus promptly opened the government granaries and reduced the price of grain to help the Egyptian populace recover from the drought. He also implemented a number of other measures that received great popular approval.

The problem was that Germanicus's visit to Egypt broke the law. Augustus, at the beginning of his reign, had introduced a law that extended a practice first introduced by Julius Caesar. This law of Augustus decreed that no Roman of senatorial rank could enter Egypt without the emperor's personal approval. This was because Egypt's lush fields of the Nile Delta supplied so much of Rome's grain for its daily bread that Egypt was called "Rome's breadbasket." If a rival to the emperor were to take charge of Egypt, he could literally starve Rome into submission and wrest the throne away from the incumbent. As a result, not even the governor of Egypt was of senatorial rank—he was only a knight, with the title of prefect. Likewise, the commanders of the two legions stationed in Egypt were not legates, or brigadier generals, men of senatorial rank, as they were almost everywhere else throughout the empire. This was because legion commanders could not take orders from a governor who was of lower rank than themselves. In Egypt, as in Judea, the legions were commanded by colonels—tribunes of the broad stripe, who would only later enter the Senate on their next step up the promotional ladder of the Roman civil service.

That no Roman of senatorial rank could enter Egypt was literally written in stone, and Germanicus knew full well that he was breaking this law. Yet he seemed to think that the law did not apply to him.

This was apparently not through arrogance, a characteristic never ascribed to Germanicus, but through an innocent, almost naive belief that because he had no evil intent and was indeed going to Egypt to help his people there, it would be overlooked in this instance.

At Alexandria, Germanicus would have stayed at the vast palace of the Ptolemys, the kings (or pharaohs) of Egypt for hundreds of years until Julius Caesar terminated their reign and made Egypt a Roman province. This palace's last royal occupant had been Queen Cleopatra. Now the palace was home to the Roman governor, the prefect of Egypt. In A.D. 19, that governor was the prefect Gaius Galerius, who had taken up his appointment in A.D. 16, apparently after the death in office of his predecessor, Seius Strabo, father of Praetorian Guard commander Sejanus. To reflect the importance of this post in Egypt, although Galerius was only a knight he was paid as much as the most senior governors of other provinces, all former consuls—400,000 sesterces a year. This was a fortune, especially to a knight. A net worth of 400,000 sesterces was required for knights to qualify for and maintain membership in the Equestrian Order, and here the prefect of Egypt was paid his net worth every year. And with the new emperor Tiberius showing a reluctance to replace his governors once they were installed, Galerius could look forward to many profitable years in Egypt.

Living with the prefect Galerius at the Alexandrian palace were his wife, Marcia, and his twenty-two-year-old nephew, Lucius Annaeus Seneca Jr. Seneca, born at Córdoba in the Roman province of Baetica, or Farther Spain, was the son of Lucius Annaeus Seneca Sr., a Spanish-born Roman knight who had served as a provincial procurator and had gained some fame as an author and teacher of rhetoric at Rome before retiring to his home city of Córdoba. Young Seneca had been educated at Rome, but after being afflicted with a serious health problem—he seems to have suffered from severe asthma and possibly also tuberculosis—his aunt Marcia had brought young Seneca to live with her husband, Prefect Galerius, and herself. That aunt would have been a sister of either Seneca's father or his mother, Helvia.

Germanicus was already acquainted with the prefect Galerius—like all the Roman governors and allied potentates of the East, the prefect and his nephew Seneca would have traveled to Daphne to pay their respects to the prince, the prefect's new superior in the East, on Germanicus's arrival in the region in A.D. 17. For young Seneca, there would also have been the added element of curiosity in this visit—a desire to make the acquaintance of Germanicus and Agrippina, the most famous couple in the Roman Empire.

At Alexandria eighteen months after Germanicus had taken up the command in the East, Galerius and Marcia made the visiting prince welcome. Germanicus would have reviewed the two Roman legions then based at Alexandria, the 3rd Cyrenaica Legion and the 22nd Deiotariana Legion, also enjoying the sights of this well-laid-out metropolis of upward of a million inhabitants beside the Mediterranean, and which was then considered the most beautiful city in the world. Germanicus would have visited the famous library of Alexandria, the world's largest, viewing some of the hundreds of thousands of books in its collection and speaking with Greek scholars who worked at the library. He would have gone to see the city's mausoleum of Alexander the Great, where Alexander's remains were reputedly interred. And without doubt he would have gone to see the mausoleum of Cleopatra, where the remains of his grandfather Mark Antony lay beside those of Cleopatra. And as a Roman priest, he would have performed religious rites in Antony's memory.

Tacitus says that Germanicus also took the opportunity to play tourist by visiting the Egyptian antiquities along the Nile, the same antiquities that attract tourists to this day. Removing his military uniform and putting on the sort of simple Greek tunic that Mark Antony had himself favored when off duty here in Egypt, Germanicus had hired a riverboat and, leaving behind his military escort, journeyed up the Nile from Canopus as far as Elephantine and Syene, then the limit of the Roman Empire—which would later extend to the Red Sea. At Thebes, which was ancient even in those times, Germanicus the tourist took in the vast ruins. There, says Tacitus, an elderly local priest translated inscriptions about the pharaoh Rhamses and his military adventures for the visiting prince. Germanicus also marveled at the statue of Memnon, and at the pyramids of Giza "rising up like mountains in almost impassible wastes of shifting sand," says Tacitus.[7]

When word reached Rome that Germanicus was in Egypt, Tiberius was furious. He wrote a letter to the Senate containing mild disapproval of Germanicus's dress and manners while in the country, but expressing sharp censure for his visiting Alexandria without the emperor's permission—in contravention of the regulations of Augustus. Only when Germanicus returned to Syria did he learn how much he was "blamed" by Tiberius for his expedition to Egypt.[8]

This innocent Egyptian sojourn, a combination of drought relief mission and sightseeing trip by Germanicus, would be taken by Tiberius, and particularly by his influential chief adviser, Sejanus, as proof that Germanicus was prepared to flout the law and thumb his nose at Tiberius and his authority. If Tiberius had not previously considered eliminating Germanicus, now his fear of his adopted son, accentuated by this unwise Egyptian episode, and fanned by the manipulative suggestions of Sejanus, could well have caused him to authorize his murder.

Several classical authors were to suggest another, allied motive for Tiberius to remove Germanicus. During the first five years of his reign, up until the death of Germanicus, Tiberius acted with restraint. He was generally fair in his rulings regarding Roman law, and rarely ordered anything, instead making suggestions to the Senate and senior officials rather than issuing them with instructions. As the Roman saying went, a word is enough for a wise man. If the recipients of this "advice" were wise, they acted on it and benefited accordingly. Following Germanicus's death, now that Tiberius no longer had "a rival awaiting his chance" to take the throne, in the words of Dio,[9] he became increasingly autocratic and arbitrary. His change in conduct, which previously had been marked by caution and moderation so that Germanicus could have no excuse to act against him, was obvious to all. Now, said Dio, "his rule became cruel."[10]

Suetonius took the same line as Dio—that Tiberius had been restrained by Germanicus's presence. Suetonius reasoned that if Tiberius acted autocratically while Germanicus was alive, there would have been a public outcry for his replacement by Germanicus. "Everyone believed," Suetonius was to say, "with good reason, that respect for Germanicus had alone kept Tiberius from showing the cruelty of his wicked heart," which, he said, soon showed itself after the death of Germanicus.[11]

So if we accept that Tiberius did finally decide to murder Germanicus, five years into his reign, to remove both a powerful rival and to remove inhibitions to his rule, how would he have gone about achieving his adopted son's death? Of course, he could not arrest Germanicus on some trumped-up charge and have him executed by the Praetorian Guard, the usual method employed by many Roman emperors for the removal of rivals. Such an act would have brought about a revolt against Tiberius by both the public and the military; Tiberius would have been signing his own death warrant. A murder was required, a surreptitious murder. For Tiberius to escape blame for the crime, Germanicus's death would have to be seen to be an accident, or, preferably, to have a natural cause. Poisoning was the obvious solution. But who, on the spot in Syria, would carry out the act? Suetonius, like many other Romans, was convinced that, in Suetonius's own words, "Tiberius cunningly orchestrated the death of Germanicus, using Piso as his middleman and agent."[12]

But where was the proof? And would Tiberius's middleman have been so inept as to use a poison such as belladonna that left a calling card? Surely, the point of the exercise, if Tiberius was behind it, was to make the poisoning of Germanicus look like a natural death, so that no accusing fingers were pointed Tiberius's way? Tiberius was an obvious murder suspect, and he knew it. Would such a paranoid ruler have risked being implicated in the murder of Germanicus? Would Tiberius really have put his own neck on the line by risking a revolt by the people and the soldiers of Rome, a revolt that was still a very real possibility when Gnaeus Piso returned to Rome to face his accusers?

Gnaeus Calpurnius Piso had done little to make himself appear innocent of complicity in the death of Germanicus, either before or after the prince's demise. Piso's arrogance was born of a belief that he was superior to every man alive, including the emperor Tiberius. Tacitus was to say that there had been a report that Augustus, just prior to his death, had been musing about who, apart from his relatives, had both the ability and the ambition to succeed him as emperor. One story had Augustus numbering Piso among three senior senators whom he considered fitted into this category. Piso, said Augustus, was "not unworthy" of the throne, and, if offered it, would have accepted it.[13] Piso obviously also thought himself worthy of the throne.

Following his appointment as propraetor of Syria, Piso had left Rome to head for the East, some little time after Germanicus and Agrippina had made their departure. Piso sailed from Italy in a fleet of merchant ships carrying his wife, Plancina; their youngest son, Marcus Piso, who was in his late twenties or early thirties and who would serve as his father's aide; and hundreds of slaves, staff members, and friends, including the senator Domitius Celer. Piso in fact took a veritable royal court with him to the East.

Agrippina was well into her ninth pregnancy when she and Germanicus sailed from Italy, and after stopping at Actium in Greece to silently view the site where her grandfather Augustus had defeated Germanicus's grandfather Antony and Queen Cleopatra in the famous Battle of Actium, Agrippina and Germanicus had paused at the Greek island of Lesbos. There Agrippina gave birth to their last child and third daughter, Julia Livilla. Germanicus was in no hurry to reach Syria. Possessed of an insatiable curiosity, he took his time coasting around western Greece and eastern Turkey, all part of the Roman Empire, with his wife and newborn child, inspecting various cities as he went. At every city and town they visited on their royal tour, the famed young prince Germanicus and his equally revered wife were welcomed enthusiastically by the populace and fawned over by local officials. At Colophon in the province of Asia, Germanicus had visited a famous oracle who had, according to Tacitus, predicted, in verse form, an "early doom" for the prince.[14] Germanicus, never one to be superstitious, had made light of the prediction.

This leisurely eastward progress of Germanicus and Agrippina had allowed Piso to overtake the prince. Pausing briefly in Greece while on his way to take up the Syrian posting, Piso had given a bitter speech to the leading citizens of Athens in which he'd made indirect aspersions against Germanicus, who, he claimed, had derogated the Roman name by treating with excessive courtesy leading Germans whom he had taken prisoner in his German campaigns.

Piso's fleet caught up with Germanicus's fleet at the island of Rhodes. Arriving in a storm, Piso's ships, powered only by sail, were soon in danger of being swept onto the Rhodian rocks, until Germanicus sent oar-powered warships to throw them lines and drag them to safety. Without as much as a "thank you" to Germanicus for this act, which had saved his life and those of his family and entourage members, Piso set sail again within a day, determined to arrive in Syria well in advance of his new commander in chief. Once he landed in Syria, Piso quickly set out to establish regional control for himself and to systematically undermine Germanicus's power and authority. The battle of wits between Piso and Germanicus would last for the next two years, ending only with the removal of Piso and the death of Germanicus.

Why did Piso embark on this program of confrontation with Germanicus? What was the point? Roman authors would agree that Piso seemed to believe that he had the backing of someone well placed at the Palatium at Rome to implement his campaign to antagonize Germanicus and sabotage his government. Whether this approval was tacit or real would later become the subject of intense debate. But what would have been Piso's motive for going as far as murdering Germanicus? What did he have to gain from such an act? Certainly it would remove an annoying overlord and potentially give Piso a free hand in Syria. But surely Piso must have realized that he would become the chief murder suspect if Germanicus were to die in suspicious circumstances—following Piso's quite overt campaign against him?

Was the unfettered government of Syria a strong enough motive to murder the heir to the Roman throne? Did Piso in fact have the most to gain from the death of Germanicus? He certainly did not have as much to gain from it as the emperor Tiberius. There were others who also had more to gain than Piso. Much more. Germanicus's death would make Tiberius's biological son, Drusus the Younger, his heir apparent and potentially the next emperor. So Drusus would gain significantly from the death of his cousin and adoptive brother. Not that any Roman author ever suggested that Drusus had ambitions for the throne or wished Germanicus dead. Just the opposite—he was considered to be extremely close to Germanicus. Piso, then, had less to gain from Germanicus's death than either Tiberius or his son Drusus.

Could Piso have been compelled to engineer the murder of Germanicus? Many Roman writers were convinced that the man with the strongest motive, Tiberius, had been behind the murder, using Piso as his agent of death. Yet, while Tiberius would benefit from Germanicus's death, other possibilities would emerge, involving Piso but not necessarily implicating Tiberius.

There is no doubt that Piso arrived in the East determined to undermine Germanicus's authority. Before Germanicus even set foot in Syria, Piso immediately removed the older centurions and strict tribunes of each of the legions stationed in the province, replacing them with men he could trust or could bribe. He ordered a relaxation of discipline in the legions, allowing the troops to idle away their time in their camps without any duties and to do as they pleased in the towns, where they were not subject to Roman law. He also made sure the men knew that it was he they had to thank for this newfound freedom. In response, some soldiers began to call him "father of the legions." His wife, Plancina, had even watched the legions and the cavalry training at their Syrian bases—an unheard-of thing for a Roman lady to do. And the governor and his wife were on record as having openly made insulting remarks about Germanicus and Agrippina.[15]

According to Tacitus, a whispered rumor had quickly gained currency in Syria once Piso was in the province, to the effect that the emperor was not averse to these anti-Germanicus goings-on of the new governor.[16] Piso was infamously irascible, and it is not impossible that he set out to cause Germanicus problems simply because that was the nature of the man. Yet some Roman writers firmly believed that Piso had highly placed support at Rome for his campaign against Germanicus. Circumstantial evidence would later emerge to support that view, but following Germanicus's death, Piso did not act like a man operating on the emperor's orders. The amateur attempt to take control in Syria using force, then sending his son to Rome to seek the emperor's blessing for his return, while he himself diverted to the Balkans to seek the backing of Drusus the Younger, none of these were the actions of a man who believed that the emperor secretly but wholeheartedly supported him.

It should be remembered that Piso and Tiberius had not been on good terms just prior to Piso's appointment, with Piso challenging Tiberius's authority over whether the Senate should sit while the emperor was away from Rome. On the face of it, Tiberius was no friend of Piso's. So why would Tiberius employ Piso, a man who made a show of his opposition to him, against Germanicus? And why would the ultra-independent Piso agree to act for Tiberius, a man he despised, against Germanicus or anyone else?

Suetonius believed that Piso had decided he must make an enemy either of Germanicus or of Tiberius, although we aren't told what the reason for this might have been, and that was why he took every opportunity he could to provoke Germanicus. [17] Why would Piso have to make such a choice? Was he perhaps under threat—from Sejanus, for example—that if he did not act against Germanicus he would be considered Tiberius's enemy, and he and his family would suffer accordingly? Piso seems so strong-willed and contemptuous of everyone from the emperor down that he would have been unlikely to be influenced by or governed by threats from anyone. Whoever influenced Piso, they gave him the impetus and the confidence to take every opportunity to inconvenience Germanicus and even to put him in danger, seemingly without fear of repercussions. Was that influential person his wife, Plancina? Piso's wife seems to have been the principal influence in his life, if not the only influence apart from the late emperor Augustus.

When Germanicus landed in Cilicia in southern Turkey he had been met with news of Piso's activities, and the accompanying rumor that Tiberius approved of those activities. Brushing both aside, Germanicus had sent Agrippina on to Syria by sea, to take up residence at the palace at Daphne, while he headed for Armenia to crown a king loyal to Rome. In company with Agrippina, Germanicus had sent an officer with sealed orders for the governor Piso at Antioch—Piso was to march two legions into Armenia without delay and to meet him there. If Piso could not leave the province, said Germanicus's dispatch, then the governor was to deputize his son and quaestor Marcus to lead the legions north to meet up with Germanicus in Armenia.

Apparently setting off from Tarsus, the thriving capital of Cilicia, Germanicus had continued overland with a small retinue including his closest friends, the former generals Silius, Vitellius, Veranius, and Marsus, as well as Zeno, son of the king of Pontus, a Roman ally. Arriving in Armenia after crossing the mountains, Germanicus had waited in vain at the rendezvous point. There was no sign of Piso, Senior or Junior, and no sign of the ten thousand legionaries whom Germanicus had ordered sent north to meet him for his mission in Armenia. After waiting in vain for the troops to show up, Germanicus had continued on to Artaxata, the Armenian capital, in the far northeast of the country, with just his personal staff, and armed merely with bravado. He'd been welcomed into the city by the Artaxatans, who up to that point had been ruled by the Parthians. And there he had crowned Prince Zeno, naming him King Artaxias of Armenia, to the resounding approval of the Armenian people, who were mightily impressed by the famous Germanicus Caesar.

Subsequently, on the way down to Syria from Armenia, Germanicus had left his friend Quintus Veranius in charge in Cappadocia as its first Roman governor—Rome had recently annexed the kingdom on the death of its last king, making it a Roman province. In nearby Commagene, another former kingdom, another of Germanicus's friends, Quintus Servaeus, a man in his thirties who was a former praetor, remained behind as its new governor, again on Germanicus's instructions.

Just weeks later, the men of the guard cohort of the 10th Legion's winter base at Cyrrhus, just northwest of Antioch, would have rubbed their eyes with surprise when Germanicus Caesar rode up to their main gate with a small entourage. Germanicus took up residence at the base and sent for the governor. By the time Piso arrived, Germanicus had been primed by those of his staff members whom he'd sent ahead to Daphne with Agrippina—including his quaestor, Publius Suillius Rufus (commonly referred to by Roman writers by his middle name of Suillius). These officials had hurried to Germanicus at Cyrrhus with tales of Piso's exploits since he'd taken up the post of governor, exaggerating some episodes and inventing others to incite the anger of their normally genial general so he would rid himself of Piso before the man did too much damage.

Tacitus was to make the sweeping statement that Germanicus was a kindhearted man who never took a menacing stance with a fellow Roman.[18] Menacing he may not have been, but when Piso finally arrived at Cyrrhus—having taken his time to answer Germanicus's summons—Germanicus demanded to know why his orders had been disobeyed. Piso, says Tacitus, replied with "haughty apologies."[19] After this edgy conference at Cyrrhus, the pair parted in an atmosphere of restrained but undisguised mutual enmity, and each went his own way—Piso returning to Antioch, Germanicus reuniting with Agrippina and their two children at Daphne, which he went on to use as his residence and headquarters in the East.

From that first tense conference in Cyrrhus, the relationship of Germanicus and Piso progressively worsened. Whenever Germanicus sat in judgment of legal cases in his capacity of chief judge in the province, for example, Piso, who would otherwise have occupied the judge's seat, rarely bothered to attend court. If he did, it was wearing a sullen frown and showing signs of opposition to Germanicus's rulings with sighs and raised eyebrows.

At a banquet given by Germanicus in honor of the visiting king of Nabataea, a Roman ally on Syria's southeastern border that supplied a famous unit of auxiliary cavalry to the Roman army, Germanicus and Agrippina were presented with heavy golden crowns as gifts, with Piso and other Roman officials given lesser crowns by the king. Piso had thrown his crown to the ground in disgust. Jumping to his feet, Piso had declared, "This adornment is given to the son of a Roman emperor, not the son of a Parthian king!" He had then launched into a long speech against luxury. Germanicus, while no doubt privately riled by Piso's speech, had patiently suffered it in statesmanlike silence, rather than cause a scene or admonish a senior Roman official in front of a foreigner.[20]

Piso had particularly taken exception to Germanicus on another score. When Piso had arrived in Syria, he'd found that his predecessor as governor, Silanus, had been giving sanctuary to a Parthian prince, Vonones. This Parthian had been sent to Rome when a child by his father, as a hostage, and there he had been raised among Roman nobility. When Vonones's father died, the emperor Augustus had sent him back to Parthia to take his place as king. But Vonones had grown up with Roman habits, and the Parthians soon dethroned him, considering this Romanized Parthian too foreign for their tastes. He had then become king of neighboring Armenia, but he'd also become unpopular there and had been ejected from that country by its people, whose habits and tastes were very much like those of the Parthians. Vonones, the twice-dethroned king, ended up seeking refuge in Syria, which the governor Silanus had granted him.

Once Piso replaced Silanus, the extremely wealthy Vonones had showered expensive gifts on Piso's wife, Plancina, as he sought the new Roman governor's support in reclaiming the Armenian throne. How Vonones thought that Piso could put him back on the throne of Armenia we are not told. Perhaps Piso, to extract the gifts from Vonones, had let the former king think that he would lead the Roman legions based in Syria on an invasion of Armenia and reinstate Vonones. But while Germanicus had the authority to do such a thing, under Roman law the governor of Syria was not permitted to lead the troops under his command beyond the borders of his province.

Piso had been all for Vonones's restoration, but Germanicus was not of the same mind. Considering Vonones a man without a future, Germanicus had other ideas. First, Germanicus had made Zeno of Pontus the new king of Armenia, in opposition to Piso's support of Vonones. On top of that, in the peace treaty he sealed with King Artabanus of Parthia, Germanicus agreed to remove Vonones some distance from Syria so he was not living threateningly on Parthia's doorstep. Germanicus had sent Vonones to Cilicia, where he lived a comfortable life on a luxurious private estate, but under guard, a veritable prisoner in a gilded jail. Probably encouraged by Piso in secret communications, Vonones had not given up his ambitions to rule in Armenia. Before long, while on a hunting expedition in Cilicia, the former king had escaped. He had soon been recaptured on a riverbank, and was killed by one of his Roman guards, a retired legionary who claimed Vonones had again attempted to escape. When Vonones died, so, too, had Piso's ambitions to extend his power and influence in the region, as had Plancina's hopes of being the recipient of further rich gifts from Vonones.

So Piso had no love for Germanicus. That much Piso had made evident. That much was indisputable. More than that, Piso had acted in an insubordinate manner toward Germanicus, and Piso and his wife had behaved insultingly toward both Germanicus and Agrippina, members of the imperial family. On top of that, Piso had celebrated Germanicus's illnesses and had not tried to hide his delight when he heard that Germanicus had died. But despite all this, and despite the rumors and assumptions concerning his complicity, had Piso actually been involved in Germanicus's death?

Cassius Dio, writing in the third century and using the numerous Roman biographies and history books then available as his source material, including the writings of Tacitus and of Suetonius, was to form the view that the death of Germanicus occurred "as the result of a plot formed by Piso and Plancina."[21] But could Plancina have planned and carried out the murder of Germanicus with her husband or on her own?

Gnaeus Piso's wife, Munatia Plancina, was the daughter of Lucius Munatius Plancus, who had been a consul several times during the reign of Augustus. Plancus had been so rich that when Augustus had called on the wealthy patricians of his day to endow the city of Rome with grand buildings, and Marcus Agrippa had subsequently built the astonishing domed Pantheon, which stands to this day, Plancus used his own money to build Rome's Temple of Saturn, at the heart of the Roman Forum.

Raised amid wealth, luxury, power, and privilege, Plancina was a snobby aristocrat who counted among her friends Livia, influential widow of the late emperor Augustus and mother of the emperor Tiberius. It seems very likely that in private meetings with Livia at the Palatium, Plancina had lobbied for the prestigious and well-paid appointment of her husband as governor of Syria, and that as a result, Livia had persuaded Tiberius to give Piso the job.

Plancina is known to have shown intense dislike for both Germanicus and his beautiful and much-admired wife, Agrippina. Plancina knew that Livia was almost insanely jealous of Agrippina, her late husband's last grandchild, with whom she had no blood connection. Tacitus believed that this "feminine jealousy" was due to "Livia feeling the bitterness of a stepmother toward Agrippina"[22]; since Agrippina's mother, Julia, had been incarcerated, Livia had been in effect Agrippina's stepmother. But there was more to this than mere jealousy. Plancina knew that Livia would do almost anything to thwart Agrippina's ambitions to become wife of the next emperor of Rome, which would rank Agrippina above Livia, requiring Livia to pay court to her stepgranddaughter. What was more, many Romans believed that Livia had instructed Plancina to make life a misery for Agrippina and her husband in the East. Some believed that Livia had even encouraged Plancina to carry out the murder of Germanicus, to prevent Agrippina from becoming the next empress.

It should be remembered that according to Tacitus, Germanicus himself had seemed to suspect Plancina of being involved in his poisoning. So what had Plancina done that would incriminate her? What evidence is there to link Plancina to the murder of Germanicus? There can be no doubt that she had spoken rudely and slanderously about both Germanicus and Agrippina in Syria, and had reveled in the news of Germanicus's death. It was said that in Syria, Plancina had been known to have had contact with Martina, an infamous sorceress and maker of poisons. And evidence of sorcery had been discovered at the governor's palace on the island in the middle of the Orontes River at Antioch, the palace that Plancina had shared with her husband.

But had Plancina really organized, or participated in the organization of, the poisoning of Germanicus? The connection with Martina suggests that Plancina had access to poison. Yet how would she have administered it to Germanicus? Critics of Piso and Plancina would point out that Piso had reclined beside Germanicus at a banquet just prior to the prince's first illness, giving him an opportunity to poison Germanicus's food or drink. But they could not explain how Germanicus was poisoned the second time, or link that second poisoning to either Plancina or her husband. By that stage, Piso and Plancina were sailing away from Syria. By that stage, too, all of those around Germanicus would have been alert for further attempts to poison the prince.

Vitellius and Servaeus, the two generals who had collected evidence in Syria for the indictment against Piso, can be expected to have interrogated slaves at Germanicus's palace to find out if any of them had been employed by Piso or Plancina to administer the poison on either the first or the second occasion, or on both occasions. No confessions of guilt or statements implicating anyone in the crime were forthcoming from any person associated with Germanicus, Plancina, or Piso.

In summation, Plancina had two possible motives for Germanicus's murder: personal jealousy of Agrippina and the prince, and possibly the desire to please the emperor's mother. Plancina potentially had access to poison, and her husband had an opportunity to administer the poison to Germanicus prior to the first occasion Germanicus fell ill. But others also had motives, some of them much stronger than Plancina's. Anyone with enough money could acquire poison. And many others also had an opportunity to administer that poison to Germanicus. But there was no proof of Plancina's complicity. And there was no confession from Plancina or anyone connected with her, including Martina the poison-maker. The case for accusing Plancina of the murder of Germanicus, either acting on her own or linked with her husband, was based purely on slim circumstantial evidence, on her occasionally self-incriminating behavior, and on her odious personality.

The fact that Plancina and Piso were such obvious culprits should also be taken into account. It was almost as if someone had set them up, or had used them as their agents in the crime—knowing that the governor and his wife would be blamed for Germanicus's death. Were Plancina and Piso so arrogant and so stupid as to think that they would get away with murdering the most popular Roman figure of the day after having so publicly reviled and obstructed him? Perhaps they were that arrogant and that stupid. Many Romans thought so. Perhaps Plancina was emboldened by the belief that she would be protected by her friendship with Livia, the emperor's mother.

Yet an array of doubts seem to outweigh such a possibility. Where was the solid evidence against Plancina? And the proof that she was somehow in partnership with the emperor's mother?

Tiberius's mother, Livia Drusilla—who took the honorary title of Julia Augusta on the death of her husband, Augustus, but continued to be called Livia by most Roman writers—had a solid motive for wanting Germanicus killed. She was known to despise her stepgranddaughter, Germanicus's ambitious wife, Agrippina. By repute, Livia had been prepared to do anything to ensure that her son, Tiberius, came to the throne, and she would have wanted to see Tiberius's biological son, her grandson Drusus the Younger, rather than Germanicus, succeed Tiberius in due course. Most especially, she didn't want Agrippina to become empress.

Robert Graves, author of *I, Claudius*, would point out that the name Livia is connected with the Latin word that means "malignity,"[23] the quality of malevolence, spite, and unprovoked malice. Ambitious, manipulative, and spiteful all her life as Augustus's wife and Tiberius's mother, Livia would actively protect Plancina as the tide turned against Piso. Why? Tacitus was to say that rumors were rife in Rome at the time of Germanicus's death that Livia had conducted secret interviews with Plancina prior to Plancina and Piso going to the East, and that in these interviews she and Plancina had plotted Germanicus's death.[24] In the same vein, some would suggest that Livia subsequently protected Plancina because Plancina had murdered Germanicus on Livia's orders. Yet this was all unsubstantiated, all based on gossip.

Some would also assert that Tiberius had known nothing of the murder plot hatched by his mother. In support of this theory, Suetonius was to speculate that on the death of Augustus in A.D. 14, Livia may have ordered the death of Tiberius's rival Postumus Agrippa in Augustus's name, without the knowledge of Tiberius. Says Suetonius, Tiberius himself had appeared to know nothing about that murder before the event, and went to some length to disassociate himself from it afterward.[25]

Tacitus, too, felt that Livia had the capacity to murder. He had his suspicions about the deaths of Agrippina's brothers Lucius Caesar and Gaius Caesar when they were still only young men. Officially, one had died from illness while on the way to Spain, while the other had reportedly succumbed to a lingering battle wound while returning to Rome after leading a military campaign in Armenia. Tacitus was to ponder whether that pair had been cut down by fate "or by the treachery of their stepmother Livia."[26]

If we accept this line of thinking, it is possible to conceive that Livia did engineer Germanicus's murder, without Tiberius's knowledge. She had the motive and, through Plancina, an opportunity to carry out his assassination. But where is the proof? Just as there was no proof to link Livia with the deaths of Agrippina's brothers Lucius and Gaius, and only the suspicion that she ordered the execution of their sibling Postumus, there is nothing to directly link Livia with the murder of Germanicus. But that would not prevent many Romans from wishing to see her punished for the crime.

There was a fifth suspect in the Germanicus murder in the first century. Praetorian Guard commander Lucius Aelius Sejanus was the son of a soldier and the nephew of a soldier. His father, Lucius Seius Strabo, was a knight of the Equestrian Order and a tribune in the Roman army who rose to become joint commander of the Praetorian Guard. Sejanus's mother, Strabo's wife, was a member of the distinguished Cornelii Lentuli senatorial family. Sejanus's uncle, Quintus Junius Blaesus, was a former consul, lieutenant general, and provincial governor—he had been governor of Illyricum at the time of the A.D. 14 Illyricum Mutiny, which Sejanus put down with Drusus the Younger and elements of the Praetorian Guard and German Guard.

Late in the reign of Augustus, Sejanus became joint commander of the Praetorian Guard together with his father—Augustus had established the convention that there should be two Praetorian prefects at any one time, to limit the power of the position, a convention observed on and off by later emperors for hundreds of years to come. Sejanus, himself a member of the Equestrian Order of knights like his father, but not a member of the senatorial class, had as his patron the senator Marcus Gabius Apicus, a wealthy spendthrift. Sejanus also had been a friend of Germanicus's father, Drusus the Elder, and it is likely that Sejanus had served under Drusus during his German campaigns, in which case he would have then been a prefect, commanding a cavalry or auxiliary light infantry unit attached to one of Drusus's legions on the Rhine.

Within a year of Sejanus's appointment as joint Praetorian Guard prefect, Strabo was sent by Tiberius to Egypt to become its new governor. Strabo seems to have died in Egypt within the next twelve months or so, to be replaced by Gaius Galerius. Sejanus was then left as sole prefect of the Praetorian Guard. At his instigation, the then nine one-thousand-man Praetorian cohorts and three fifteen-hundred-man City

Guard cohorts were brought from separate barracks throughout the city and consolidated in a new headquarters on the northeastern edge of Rome, a massive new fortress called the Castra Praetoria, on a site today occupied in part by Italy's national library. From this point on, the consolidated Praetorian Guard was used by Sejanus as, in effect, his private army.

The order to execute the exiled Postumus Agrippa in August A.D. 14 had to pass through the hands of Sejanus, as commander of the Praetorian Guard, for it was a Praetorian tribune who had charge of Postumus, and he would take orders only from his superior, the Praetorian prefect. Classical authors Tacitus and Suetonius would speculate about whether that execution order came from Tiberius or from his mother, Livia, but it is not impossible that Sejanus issued the order of his own accord, to clear the way to the throne for Tiberius. Sejanus had formed a close relationship with Tiberius, probably while serving under him on the Rhine after Tiberius replaced his brother Drusus as commander of the Rhine legions. In the confusion following Augustus's sudden death, this execution order, from Sejanus, would not have been questioned by the tribune in charge of Postumus's exile.

According to Cassius Dio, Sejanus quickly became Tiberius's senior and most influential confidant, his adviser and his assistant in all things.[27] In A.D. 20, following the death of Germanicus, Tiberius promoted Sejanus from the rank of knight to that of praetor, automatically entitling him to sit in the Senate. This was the equivalent promotion from the rank of colonel to that of a modern-day major general. It may have been coincidental that this spectacular promotion came in the wake of Germanicus's death. It was a reward for Sejanus; of that there can be no doubt. Many Romans and later historians would ask themselves whether this could have been Tiberius's reward to Sejanus for eliminating Germanicus.

Could Sejanus have engineered Germanicus's death at Tiberius's request or suggestion? Or did Sejanus orchestrate Germanicus's death of his own accord, to please Tiberius and to solidify both their positions, just as he may possibly have ordered the execution of Postumus five years before? And if the latter was the case, had he only informed Tiberius of what he had done after the event, receiving his reward accordingly? This reward gave Sejanus the confidence to advance his own ambitions. He began an affair with Germanicus's sister, Livilla, the wife of Germanicus's adoptive brother, Drusus the Younger, who had become Tiberius's heir apparent. Sejanus was considerably older than Livilla. His past friendship with her late father, Drusus the Elder, a father Livilla barely could have remembered, would have enhanced Sejanus's access to the young woman. By all accounts the younger Drusus was initially unaware of this affair between his wife and the Praetorian commander.

In early A.D. 20, just as Agrippina was returning to Italy with Germanicus's ashes, Livilla gave birth to twin boys, who became next in line for the Roman throne after Drusus the Younger, sidelining Germanicus's sons. There is no way of knowing when Sejanus's affair with Livilla had commenced, but it is possible it began before Germanicus's death and that, as novelist and Roman scholar Robert Graves would suggest in I, Claudius, Livilla's twins were fathered by Sejanus, not by her husband, Drusus.[28]

As later events were to show, following the death of Germanicus, Sejanus set in motion a long-term scheme to eliminate Drusus as well as Agrippina and her three sons, the sons of Germanicus, removing them from the line of succession. Sejanus was not doing this for Tiberius. As events would prove, and as later Roman writers would record, Sejanus was setting himself up to eventually overthrow Tiberius and make himself emperor of Rome.

Sejanus was a master at manipulating others to do his dirty work for him. Do his bidding, and you won his favor and support. As Tiberius grew older, he would rely on Sejanus more and more. Ultimately, with Tiberius in semiretirement on the isle of Capri, off the western coast of Italy near Naples, Sejanus came to rule the empire by proxy. That stage was still some years off, and Sejanus's first provable murder of an heir to the throne was, in A.D. 20, three years away. His insinuations against Agrippina and her boys, meanwhile, had already begun by the time Agrippina arrived back in Italy with Germanicus's remains. Sejanus would press his campaign against everyone associated with Germanicus without relent in the coming years, as he set out to destroy the wife and sons of the murdered prince.

It was not beyond the bounds of possibility that in A.D. 19 it was Sejanus, not Tiberius and not Livia, who had orchestrated the murder of Germanicus, as his first step down the road to his ultimate goal of gaining the throne for himself. It is possible that he used Piso, Plancina, or both to carry out the murder. Then again, perhaps he involved neither of them, but used someone else in Syria as his agent. Who might that agent have been? As an example of how far Sejanus's tentacles could reach, in years to come it would transpire that one of Germanicus's closest friends was a secret associate of Sejanus. This was Quintus Servaeus, the former praetor appointed by Germanicus to govern Commagene in A.D. 17. This was the same Servaeus who, in partnership with Publius Vitellius, was now, in the spring of A.D. 20, preparing the indictment against Piso. It is Tacitus who reveals Servaeus's "discreet" friendship with Sejanus.[29] Unfortunately, he fails to tell us whether Servaeus's friendship with the Praetorian commander began before the death of Germanicus or after it.

It is probable that Servaeus quietly joined the Sejanus camp following the death of Germanicus. Sooner or later, most of Germanicus's former friends would abandon Agrippina in the wake of Germanicus's death. They would do so as an act of self-preservation, as it became obvious that Agrippina was a marked woman as far as the Palatium was concerned. One or two of them, such as Servaeus, went farther and cultivated the friendship of Sejanus to ensure their career advancement. Perhaps Servaeus's friendship with Sejanus did only begin following the death of Germanicus. But if he had been Sejanus's friend prior to Germanicus's death, it is possible that he had been brought into Sejanus's murder plot, if such a plot existed. Servaeus had been in Commagene when Germanicus fell ill the first time, but apparently was at Daphne when Germanicus died. Perhaps Piso had administered the first dose of poison while reclining beside Germanicus at the last banquet they shared, and perhaps Servaeus had administered the second dose.

Countering this proposition is the fact that Servaeus received no further promotion, appointments, or honors following the death of Germanicus, unlike other friends of Sejanus. If he had been Sejanus's murder accomplice, some reward could have been expected—a consulship, perhaps, followed by a well-paid governorship. Instead, Servaeus's career ground to halt, like those of so many genuine friends and supporters of Germanicus. But at least Servaeus was not caught up in the purges instituted by Sejanus in the subsequent decade. This would suggest that Servaeus cultivated the friendship of Sejanus following the death of Germanicus—perhaps some years after, as the need for self-preservation took hold. Yet there are those who would say that even if Servaeus had not betrayed Germanicus, this does not mean that Sejanus did not use someone else close to Germanicus to carry out the murder of the prince.

Sejanus rounds out the list of five murder suspects whose names exercised the minds of Romans in the spring of A.D. 20, when the calls for justice and revenge for the death of Germanicus rang throughout Rome and around the empire. Tiberius, Piso, Plancina, Livia, and Sejanus. Alone, or in combination, these were the potential murderers who were the subjects of earnest and often heated conversation at every dinner table, at every tavern counter, on every barber's stool. All of Rome had an opinion about who the murderer was. The scene was set for a murder trial that would grip Rome and Romans throughout the known world.

# VI

# THE MURDER TRIAL
# BEGINS

I t was March A.D. 20. The Matronalia, the Festival of Juno the
Great Goddess that celebrated Roman motherhood, had passed.
Piso was back at Rome, and his accusers had prepared a case
against him. Just a day after Piso had returned home to his house overlooking the Roman Forum, the Senate convened at the Curia, the
Senate House, on the northeastern side of the Forum, to decide
whether Piso should be called to answer charges in relation to the
death of Germanicus. As the Senate benches filled before dawn, Piso
took his place with his fellow senators.

Once this preliminary hearing got under way with the sun rising
behind the Capitoline Mount and the Senate's water clocks beginning to trickle into the first hour of the day, the senator Fulcinius Trio
came to his feet. Trio, an experienced lawyer, was infamous as a man
who informed on his fellow senators, telling Tiberius if he overheard
them speaking treasonously, or betraying them if they committed
adultery or any number of other crimes. Tacitus also described Trio as
a man who liked notoriety and who recklessly made enemies in the
process.[1] Trio now sought permission from the presiding consul, Aurelius Cotta, to launch a prosecution against Gnaeus Piso for the murder
of Germanicus.

The senators Publius Vitellius and Quintus Veranius, the two generals and friends of Germanicus who had been in the East with him,
quickly objected, and were supported by other friends of Germanicus.
This prosecution was not Trio's role, they declared. They said that

they intended to report to the House that they had instructions from Germanicus, received from him on his deathbed, to personally pursue a trial of Piso for murder, and to personally give evidence in that trial as men who had been with Germanicus at the time of his death. How, they asked, could Trio possibly conduct a prosecution when he had not even been in Syria at the time of the murder?

In the light of this objection, Trio now withdrew his original request and sought the consul's permission to conduct a prosecution against Piso for crimes he would allege Piso had committed while governing Farther Spain earlier in his career. This sounded odd and unnecessary, but the consul Cotta proposed that the emperor be asked to undertake an inquiry into whether any prosecution should be launched against Piso, be it for the murder of Germanicus or on the charges brought by Trio. Not even Piso objected to this, and the Senate unanimously voted in favor of the proposal. The consul duly wrote to the emperor to advise him of the Senate's resolution.

When Tiberius received the Senate's request, he summoned the accusers, the accused, and a small number of his own most intimate friends from among the senators, to attend a meeting at his palace. Tacitus says that this suited Piso, as he felt he would receive a fairer hearing from a single judge than from hundreds of senators. He was also confident that Tiberius would support him, because, in Tacitus's words, Tiberius was "entangled in his mother's complicity."[2] Tacitus believed that both Piso and Livia had played a role in the murder of Germanicus, but he was not convinced that Tiberius was also guilty.

There was a chamber within the Palatium complex standing high on the Palatine Hill overlooking the bustling city where Tiberius conducted audiences and hearings. This semicircular imperial basilica would survive, as a shell, to modern times. Here, seated on a raised tribunal, Tiberius listened to the accusations leveled against Piso by the companions of Germanicus, and to a plea of innocence from Piso himself. Tacitus says that Tiberius was well aware of the rumors that he himself was implicated in the murder.[3] With these rumors in mind, he decided to send the case back to the Senate, recommending that the Senate conduct a trial, with charges to be preferred against Piso for defying Germanicus's orders, for making civil war, and for murdering Germanicus. In addition, Piso's wife, Plancina, was to be charged as Piso's accomplice in the murder of Germanicus, and Piso's son Marcus was to be charged with making civil war in Cilicia alongside his father.

As Cassius Dio was to write, in this way, by bringing Piso and members of his family to trial in the Senate, Tiberius set out to clear himself of the suspicion that he had been involved in the destruction of Germanicus.[4]

A trial in the Senate meant that it would be held out of the public gaze. In criminal trials held before a panel of judges in the Julian Basilica, Rome's courthouse, the public galleries of the four adjoining courtrooms were always packed with onlookers, male and female. Many of these audience members sitting in the mezzanine galleries were paid by one side or another to applaud or heckle the various advocates. Now, with a trial in the Senate House, the emperor would be able to control proceedings, for there was no public gallery in the Senate. Members of the general public were banned. This also allowed Tiberius to personally attend its sittings. Now, too, every senator could share the responsibility and the blame for this murder trial that the people had been baying for, and could share responsibility for the verdict.

Tiberius decreed that the prosecution be given two days to present its case, and, after an adjournment of six days, the defense would occupy three days. As was usual practice, the Senate would sit on each of those days from dawn until dusk. Critics of the emperor would wonder why Tiberius had given the prosecution less time than the defense. The defense was presumably being allocated more time because there were three defendants, and because two different prosecutions were to level charges against Piso—in addition to the Germanicus case, the emperor also was permitting Senator Trio to make his case about Piso's alleged improprieties in Spain. But it was generally believed that two days should be enough to prove the case for murder against Piso.

Torches glowed throughout the city. In the Forum, it was as if daylight had come. The sun had yet to rise, yet the day on which Piso's trial was to commence had begun. Not just all of Rome but also all of Italy was talking about the trial, which, says Tacitus, was conducted "amid the excitement of the entire country."[5] No business would be conducted in the city while the trial was in progress. Rome had once more come to a standstill.

In the torchlight, the Forum was packed with tens of thousands of people, all facing the squat, rectangular Senate House below the

Capitoline Mount. The Senate House of A.D. 20 still stands today. It had been rebuilt by Julius Caesar after its predecessor had been burned down in riots leading up to the civil war that brought Caesar to power. Centuries later it would be given a face-lift by the emperor Diocletian, but the Curia we see today still looks much as it did on the day the Piso trial began.

The Praetorian Guard was out in force. Its job included providing security to the Senate on sitting days, keeping the public out of the Senate House, and searching every senator for weapons before allowing him to enter its portals. The Guard's stony-faced Italian soldiers surrounded the Senate House in solid ranks, each man with one hand on the hilt of his sheathed sword, the breeze of the last days of winter ruffling their blood-red cloaks. A hush hung over the crowd. Many citizens were moodily silent; others spoke in hushed voices, sharing "secret whispers against the emperor," says Tacitus.[6]

Inside the Senate House, the senators, wearing their official purple-bordered white togas that came out only for official occasions, were taking their places. No females were present; all senators were male. They were talking animatedly, their voices echoing around the shiny marble floor and soaring walls. This practical building was 220 feet long and 80 feet wide, with small windows set high in its tall brick walls to admit light. A series of large double doors, closed now, were set in three of the four walls. The Curia's ornate wooden ceiling, built in a checkerboard pattern, hung 100 feet above the senators' heads. Three low marble tiers rose to the left and to the right of the central walkway. These tiers were occupied by the benches of the members of the House.

The first row of benches on each side was occupied by former consuls, who were the first to speak in debates. Among these front-bench men today was Germanicus's friend Vibius Marsus. Less senior senators, praetors, and other middle-ranking officials sat in the second row. The least senior members of the House, men recently admitted to the Senatorial Order, occupied the back benches. Among the latter was the redheaded Publius Suillius Rufus, who had been Germanicus's quaestor. As a former quaestor, Suillius had automatically gained entry to the Senate after serving Germanicus.

On the highest of the three low tiers facing the main doors sat the marble curile chairs, the official chairs of the two consuls, who acted as presidents of the House. Between them today stood a handsome chair of gold and ivory, the emperor's chair, brought in earlier by Palatium staff. Here, too, were the Senate water clocks and their attendants. The clocks were elaborate devices of glass and wood that would mark the passing of the twelve hours of the Roman day, which began at dawn and ended at sunset, before the twelve hours of the night began. Roman water clocks were imprecise devices with floats descending in glass tubes as water seeped away, with the hours marked on the glass. The clocks served as a mere guide to the passing of time; to paraphrase a later saying, it was easier for all the water clocks of Rome to agree than for all its philosophers to agree, and even that would be something of a miracle.

Literate slaves were in place to note down every word said during the hearing, in Roman shorthand invented a century earlier by Tiro, secretary to the famous orator Cicero. The note-taking was for the official Senate record, the *Acta Senatus*, which would be kept in the Tabularium, Rome's 152-year-old archives building, just a stone's throw from the Senate House at the foot of the Capitoline Mount. That building is also still in existence today; the records, which would be consulted by later Roman historians including Tacitus, would not survive to modern times.

Julius Caesar had admitted as many as a thousand men to the Senatorial Order. Augustus had reduced the number to six hundred. With natural attrition, with forty or so senators absent commanding legions or governing provinces, and with others away on personal business or too infirm to attend, there were perhaps three hundred senators present for this, the most talked-about trial in Roman history. Germanicus's adoptive brother, Drusus the Younger, was among those sitting in the front row. Drusus had hurried across the Adriatic to Rome from his Balkan posting to be present at the trial, forgoing his right to enter the city by taking the Ovation voted to him by the Senate the previous year (an Ovation awarded more to please Tiberius than to praise Drusus), supposedly for Drusus's adept statesmanship when dealing with German tribes in a recent political crisis. According to Tacitus, Drusus looked genuinely sorrowful, as if the death of Germanicus had touched him deeply.

The three prosecutors in the Germanicus case were here, all close friends of Germanicus who had been with him at Daphne during his last hours and had taken his hand and promised to avenge him: Quintus Veranius, a former consul, the man appointed governor of

Cappadocia by Germanicus and now in his forties; Quintus Servaeus, the former praetor appointed governor of Commagene by Germanicus, close to forty, the man who would become, or perhaps already was, a secret friend of Sejanus; and Publius Vitellius, former commander of the 2nd Augusta Legion in Germany and companion to Germanicus in the East, in his late thirties, a member of Rome's illustrious Vitellius family. Of these three prosecutors, Vitellius had probably known Germanicus best, having fought beside him in campaign after campaign in Germany. He had seen Germanicus victorious at the Battle of Idistaviso, beside the Weser River, where Hermann's army of fifty thousand warriors had been crushed. Vitellius had seen Germanicus personally lead the Praetorian Guard against the Germans in the Battle of the Angrivar Barrier, and had heard Germanicus's firm command repeated through the ranks in the heat of that bloody, day-long battle: "Take no prisoners!"[7] Vitellius knew that while Germanicus may have acted kindly toward his fellow Romans, against the enemies of Rome he could be inexorable. Just as Vitellius and his colleagues had expressed their determination to be inexorable with the murderer of the prince.

Gnaeus Piso was here, sitting on a front bench. His sons Gnaeus Jr. and Marcus sat on back benches with the junior senators, in all likelihood looking worried and almost certainly being avoided by other members of the House. The three advocates for the defense were present, taking their places on the front bench. Piso had experienced considerable trouble finding qualified, respected senators who would represent him. Six senators had turned him down when he approached them, before three men known to be close to the emperor had agreed to represent him. One was Lucius Calpurnius Piso, a relative of the defendant, who had served as a consul five years before; it appears that he had a good tactical mind, for he was reputedly an avid player of *latrunculi*, Roman chess.[8] Another defense counsel was Livineius Regulus, a senator who would be made a consul by Tiberius. The third defense advocate was Marcus Lepidus Aemilius. Very rich, from the leading Aemilian family, and an able consul in A.D. 6, Lepidus was a man who possessed a "contemptuous indifference" to power, in the opinion of the late emperor Augustus,[9] while Tacitus was to describe Lepidus as a wise and highly principled man.[10] Lepidus also was a close friend and firm favorite of Tiberius.

Piso himself seemed calm, composed, and self-assured as the day of his trial dawned. He had been comforted, says Tacitus, by the fact that his wife, Plancina, had sworn to stand by him and to share his lot, whatever might come, and in the worst event even to share death with him.[11] Not that Piso was contemplating losing this trial. He had received assurances from Praetorian prefect Sejanus that the emperor would look after him.[12] Besides, he had some insurance: anyone who looked closely would have seen a rolled document beside Piso on the Senate House bench. The significance of this document, which Piso would occasionally take up but never open during the trial, would later become apparent.[13]

Before any business could be done in the House, augurs, or Roman priests who were to interpret signs from the heavens, had conducted a ritual animal sacrifice, checking the slain animal's entrails and certifying that they were clear, meaning the omens were consequently good for the sitting. The augurs also offered prayers to the gods for heavenly guidance for the senators in their deliberations. With those preliminary formalities out of the way, the senators now awaited the arrival of the emperor.

As dawn was breaking in the eastern sky, a herald bellowed an announcement. "Make way for the emperor!"

The senators fell silent and came to their feet as, preceded by his twelve lictors, official attendants in white robes and bearing his twelve fasces, Tiberius entered by the Senate House's front door. Behind him, tall, bearded auxiliary soldiers, Batavians and Germans from today's Holland and Germany, members of the emperor's German Guard bodyguard, took up positions at the door, looking uncivilized in their breeches, long hair, and trimmed beards—at that time in Roman history, Roman citizens shaved every day from the time they came of age at the end of their fifteenth year, but German troops in the Roman army did not.

Sixty-year-old Tiberius was tall and well built. Bald now that he was beginning down the road to old age, he had large eyes and fine features. Extremely pimply as a youth, he still suffered from poor skin. He walked, says Suetonius, with a stiff gait, and with his head poked forward.[14] Praetorian prefect Lucius Sejanus, a powerfully built man who affected a humble air, walked in the emperor's shadow, with several freedmen secretaries bustling along close behind. Tiberius walked down the center of the House to his raised chair, from where, with his staff arrayed behind him, he bade the senators resume their seats. Sejanus, now that Tiberius had granted him the rank of a praetor, also took his seat among the senators.

The doors around the Senate House walls were now all closed. Attendants would open them to allow senators to come and go as they slipped out to relieve themselves or to grab something to eat or drink as the day drew out, for Senate sittings went on without interruption until the sun went down. To learn how the trial was faring inside, the huge crowd outside would have to wait for word to be brought out to them by the coming and going senators, and many a senator would use the opportunity to make himself sound important as he regaled the crowd with the latest news from inside as the trial heated up.

With nervous coughs echoing around the chamber, Tiberius sought and received permission from the president of the House, Aurelius Cotta, the senior current consul, to address the honorable senators. As the emperor came to his feet, a secretary handed him a scroll containing a prepared speech. Tiberius was fluent in Greek as well as Latin, but, unlike other Roman leaders before him, including Julius Caesar, Tiberius preferred not to use Greek but addressed the Senate in Latin, the Roman tongue. He would go to great lengths to exclude even widely used Greek terms from his speeches. Both Caesar and Augustus had been excellent public speakers, but despite years of training as a youth and much practice since, Tiberius was not. He read this speech to the House in his usual slow and methodical manner.

"Senators, Piso was the representative and friend of my father [Augustus]," he began. "On the advice of the Senate, I appointed him to assist Germanicus in the administration of the East." In reality, the Senate had not had any influence in Piso's appointment. The emperor's gubernatorial appointments were always submitted to the Senate for rubber-stamping. In practice, the Senate always advised the emperor that it approved of his choice of governor. "It is for you to determine, with unbiased minds," Tiberius went on, "whether he provoked the young prince there through rivalry and willful opposition, whether he rejoiced at his death, whether he wickedly ended his life.

"Certainly, if a subordinate goes beyond the bounds of duty and beyond the bounds of obedience to his superior, and has been delighted by his death, and by my pain, I will despise him, and exclude him from my house. But I will avenge a *personal* wrong without resorting to my power as emperor. However, if it is found that a crime has been committed that should be punished, no matter who the murdered man is, it is for you to deliver just compensation to the children of Germanicus, and to us, his parents.

"Also consider this. Did Piso deal with the legions in a seditious, revolutionary manner? Did he seek popularity with the troops by underhand means? Did he attempt to retake the province of Syria using armed force? Or are these all fabrications put about by his accusers? As for those accusers—" he glanced briefly at the three prosecutors— "I am angry with their unrestricted zeal. Why did they strip Germanicus's corpse and expose it to the vulgar gaze, and circulate among foreigners the tale that he had been killed with poison, if this is all still doubtful and needs investigating?"

He paused, allowing his comments to sink in, before continuing. "Personally, I lament my son's death and always will. Yet, I wouldn't prevent the accused from producing any evidence that can prove his innocence or convict Germanicus of any unfair acts, if there were such acts. And I beg you not to take alleged charges as proven simply because this case is intimately linked with my loss."

He looked at Piso's three defenders. "You, whom blood ties or good hearts have made his advocates, help the accused in his time of peril, every one of you, to the full extent of your eloquence and diligence." He turned to the prosecutors. "I would urge the prosecutors to similar exertions and persistency."

Again he addressed the House as a whole. "In this, and in this alone will we place Germanicus above the laws, by conducting the inquiry into his death in this House instead of in the Forum, before the Senate rather than before a bench of judges. In every other respect let this case be tried as simply as any other. I want none of you to be influenced by Drusus's tears or by my own sorrow, nor by any stories you may hear that have been invented to discredit us."[15]

With that, the emperor took his seat, nodding to the consul Cotta, who then invited the prosecution to begin. But before Vitellius, Servaeus, or Veranius could open their mouths, Fulcinius Trio jumped up and was recognized by the consul. To the frustration of the prosecutors and many others in the chamber, Trio proceeded to level his irrelevant accusations against Piso, claiming that he had been involved in secret schemes and extortion of provincials when he had served as governor of one of the Spanish provinces during the reign of Augustus.

This seemed designed to waste the valuable time allocated to the prosecution, but the consul allowed Trio to expand on his allegations. Whether this was Trio's own contrivance, merely to win favor with Tiberius, or whether he had been put up to it by either Tiberius or Sejanus, we will never know. But he would later be among Sejanus's closest associates, eventually gaining a consulship via Sejanus's influence. By the middle of the day, after depriving the legitimate prosecution of precious hours, Trio finally completed his submission to the House and sat back down.

At last, a murder prosecution against Piso could commence. The prosecutors had to overcome several early hurdles. For one thing, there was Trio's time-wasting. Then there was Tiberius's insistence that he considered Piso innocent until proven guilty. In fact, the emperor's opening address had seemed to favor the accused. But worse than this, a key prosecution witness would not be appearing. Despite being kept under close guard at Brindisi, Martina, the Syrian maker of poisons, had been found dead in her quarters. Her body showed no sign of either murder or suicide, but a vial of unused poison had been found in a knot of her hair. Some would assume that she had used a second vial to kill herself, although no second, empty vial was located. Others would wonder if one of her guards had not poisoned her. No proof would emerge either way. Because no testimony had been forthcoming from Martina while she was alive—a written statement could not legally be presented in court, but witnesses could testify to what Martina had told them, if she had told them anything—the prosecution had to proceed without the one witness who might have shone light on how Germanicus died, and who could possibly have linked Plancina and/or Piso to the crime.

It was with these limitations that the prosecution of Piso, his wife, and his son began.

# VII

# PROSECUTION AND DEFENSE

With no witnesses to present other than themselves, the prosecutors Servaeus, Veranius, and Vitellius each addressed the Senate in turn, testifying to what they had seen and heard in the East as companions of Germanicus. According to Tacitus, Servaeus and Veranius were earnest and businesslike, while Vitellius was strikingly eloquent.[1] Not unlike in courtrooms today, Roman attorneys treated their courtrooms as their stage, and performed accordingly. It was not unusual for advocates to speak for five hours without a break, only occasionally pausing to take a sip of water. "You speak much and long, and with your head tilted back swill tepid water from a glass flask," the first-century Roman poet Martial was to say of one such legal advocate.[2]

The prosecution trio alleged that while in the East, Piso had displayed hatred for Germanicus and a desire for revolution against him, and had so corrupted the rank-and-file soldiery by relaxing discipline and by other means that the worst of them began calling Piso "father of the legions."[3] On the other hand, they said, Piso had treated all the best men, especially the friends and companions of Germanicus, with savage disdain, even cruelty. They gave numerous examples of Piso's contempt for and disobedience of Germanicus's orders, from his bribery of centurions to his performance at the banquet for the king of Nabataea, and, crucially, his failure to send the two legions into Armenia as ordered by Germanicus, an act that could have cost Germanicus his life at the hands of the Armenians or the Parthians.

The arrogant Piso, flicking his eyes around the benches opposite, would have seen anger and disgust registered on the faces of many a fellow senator. Some of his colleagues loudly interrupted the prosecutors to shake fists at Piso and voice their dismay at his actions as each instance of his disdain for and disobedience of Germanicus was detailed by the prosecutors. Tiberius's opening address would have given Piso heart, but now, seeing this fierce animosity being directed at him from around the benches, Piso must have begun to doubt the promises that Sejanus had made to him since his return to Rome, promises that he had nothing to fear.[4]

When the day's session ended and after the emperor had taken his leave, Piso's slaves brought his litter to a side door. He climbed in and drew the curtains. Escorted by an armed tribune, the commander of one of the Praetorian Guard cohorts, Piso was conveyed the short distance to his house. It would be variously rumored, Tacitus was to write, that the tribune was there to either guard Piso or ultimately to be his executioner.[5]

At home that night, Piso found his wife, Plancina, cool and withdrawn. After dinner, she announced to Piso that she had decided to conduct her defense separately from his. Earlier, while the case had been proceeding in the Senate, Plancina had been granted an afternoon interview with Livia, the emperor's mother, at the Palatium. And Livia had guaranteed to Plancina that she would be safe from punishment, but only if she withdrew her support for her husband and let him take all the blame for what had taken place in Syria.[6]

Stunned by his wife's desertion, Piso began to lose heart. The Palatium's public support of his wife could be, he knew, fatal for him. Seeing himself left as the scapegoat for Germanicus's death, and now fully aware of the public hatred for him, he thought seriously of throwing in the towel. But his sons Gnaeus and Marcus implored him to keep up the fight, which they were convinced he still could win. Strengthened by the support of his sons and clinging to the promises that Sejanus had made him, Piso decided to fight on.[7]

The next day, Piso again took his usual seat in the Senate as, once again, the benches all around him filled and a huge crowd gathered outside the Senate House for the second day in succession. As had been the case the previous day, no business would be done in the city while the trial proceeded. Once the emperor had arrived at the Senate House, carried down from the Palatium in his litter, the day's session, the last of the two days allocated to the prosecution, began.

Now the prosecutors came to the crux of the matter. They described how Germanicus had been poisoned; how he had died; and how, before he passed away, he had required them to swear to avenge him. Now they accused Piso of having personally destroyed Germanicus "by sorcery and poison." They spoke of Plancina's known association with Martina the poisonmaker, and particularly pointed out that just prior to Germanicus's first illness Piso had reclined to the immediate right of Germanicus in the place of honor at an official banquet at Germanicus's palace at Daphne. This, they said, would have given Piso ample opportunity to poison the prince's food or drink.[8]

According to Tacitus, Piso now glanced at Tiberius. Many sycophantic senators had grown to take their lead from the emperor when it came to debates; if the emperor nodded when a point was made, or smiled in the direction of an accused man, they knew what reaction he required from them. In this case, Tiberius had seemed, in his opening statement, to favor the defendant, but now Piso was shaken to see a cold expression on the face of the emperor. Registering neither pity nor anger, Tiberius seemed to be closing himself off, to be deliberately hiding any display of emotion or favoritism. With narrowed eyes, Tiberius looked away.[9]

Outside the Senate House, the crowd had grown restless. From within the House, the senators could hear increasingly raised voices beyond the building's walls. Impatient for a verdict, and beginning to fear that the senators would let Piso off under the influence of Tiberius, the people commenced to threaten violence should the Senate fail to convict Piso of Germanicus's murder. The unrest grew until large numbers of people flooded to where statues of Piso stood around the Forum—all ex-consuls were honored with statues. In this riotous atmosphere these statues were hauled down from their plinths and dragged to the Gemonian Stairs, which ran down from the Capitoline Mount on the northern side of the Forum. According to tradition, the bodies of traitors were thrown down these stairs, while the heads of men and women convicted of capital crimes and decapitated by the Praetorian Guard were displayed on the stairs, as gory yet indisputable proof that their punishment had been carried out. The angry mob began breaking up the statues of Piso so they could symbolically display the marble heads on the stairs.

The tumult outside caused Tiberius to suspend the trial's proceedings and to send messengers to find out what was going on. When news of the riot came back, Tiberius immediately commanded the Praetorian Guard to restore order and to rescue Piso's statues and return them to their plinths. Soldiers of the Guard swiftly obeyed. Hundreds of them peeled away from the Guard cordon around the Senate House and quickly headed for the Gemonian Stairs. As the members of the Senate waited in the Curia, the riot was broken up by the troops without bloodshed, and the damaged statues were reerected in their original locations.

After this delay, once news of the Praetorians' successful termination of the civil unrest had been delivered to Tiberius, the prosecution was authorized to resume. They returned to the evidence of sorcery found at the governor's palace at Antioch. As a prelude to Germanicus's death, the prosecutors now said, there had been the "ceremonies and horrible sacrifices made by himself [Piso] and Plancina,"[10] and they gave details of the macabre artifacts found in the search of the governor's palace. Finally, the prosecutors accused Piso of having threatened the Roman state with war, detailing his unauthorized orders to regional leaders and his foolish military exploits in Cilicia that had led to the brief and doomed stand at Celenderis. It was only after he had been defeated in battle, said the prosecutors, and had surrendered, that Piso could be returned to Rome to face trial and be meted justice for his monumental crimes. Having made this point, the prosecution rested.

All eyes turned to the emperor. Tiberius now gathered himself and came to his feet. After reminding the senators that the House would resume in six days' time to hear the defendants' cases, he turned to Piso's two sons and urged them to vigorously lead the defense of their absent mother when the hearing resumed. The trial was then adjourned,[11] and the emperor took his leave as the senators reverently stood in their places.

It had been an exhausting two days. These sittings of the Senate, where it acted as Rome's supreme court, were always exhausting for the participants. Eighty years later, after participating in a three-day Senate trial during which charges against another former governor of Farther Spain had been made and rebutted, the senator, legal advocate, and author Pliny the Younger would describe "the fatigue we experienced in speaking and debating for such a length of time, and in examining, supporting, and countering so many witnesses."[12]

In the darkness of early evening, Piso again went home in a closed litter and accompanied by the armed Praetorian tribune. He should have gone home in high spirits. As his defense team would have assured him before he left the Senate House, the prosecution had failed to make a convincing argument of his guilt on the major charge. Yes, the prosecution had successfully established that he had tampered with the soldiers in Syria and that he had insulted Germanicus, his superior. There was also no denying that Piso and his son Marcus had, in Cilicia, interfered with legion recruits, had illegally called auxiliaries to serve them, and had armed their own slaves, all with the intent of obtaining the government of Syria. Whether this amounted to civil war was disputable, but it would take considerable eloquence to convince the senators of Piso's claim that he had done this out of loyalty to Tiberius rather than through a selfish desire to regain the power of which Germanicus had deprived him.

It seemed certain that Piso could not avoid a conviction on the lesser charges, which could be expected to incur a punishment such as banishment. But on the capital charge of death by poisoning, the prosecution had fallen down. Unlike his wife, Piso had not been linked with poison or with a poisonmaker. As for the charge that Piso had personally administered poison to Germanicus at the Daphne banquet, it seemed absurd, his advocates were preparing to say in Piso's defense in six days' time, "that he would have dared to make such an attempt surrounded by strange servants and in full view of so many other guests."[13]

The defense advocates were right. It does seem highly unlikely that Piso could have or would have tried to poison the prince's food at this banquet in Germanicus's palace—in front of so many "unfriendly" witnesses. In classical times, only slaves sat down to eat. Free people lay on their stomachs on special dining couches, with three diners side by side on each couch, and three couches around each table so that the nine diners were all looking at each other across the low central table containing the food and drink. Diners did not eat from their own individual plates, as we do. Using their fingers, they selected items from all platters on the table, platters from which the other diners also took food. Even if Piso could have somehow managed to spread a poison on food right before the eyes of the eight other diners at his table and the numerous servants who were constantly coming and going, it is probable that others would have eaten the same food as Germanicus; yet no one else fell ill.

Poisoning Germanicus's drink was a more credible methodology. But with Germanicus's drinking cup sitting on the table in front of him, somehow Piso still had to put poison into the cup without being spotted, by either Germanicus himself, by other diners to the left and the right, or by Germanicus's numerous loyal servants, who were constantly bringing food and drink and taking away platters. And that seems improbable if not impossible.

"Besides," Tacitus was to write, "the defendant offered to allow his own slaves to be submitted to torture" for evidence that he had been involved in the murder of Germanicus. He had also insisted that the slaves on Germanicus's staff who had served the meal that night be tortured as well, to prove that he'd had nothing to do with the death of the prince.[14] It would seem to some that only a man truly confident of his innocence would do that. With such slim and contentious circumstantial evidence against him, there was a real chance that Piso would escape conviction on the murder charge.

Back at his home that evening, Piso sat down to write. His steward, a freedman, would later state that he assumed his master was working on his legal defense. Piso then sealed the document he had penned and handed it to the steward, without instructions. He then ate a meal and performed his toilet. His wife, Plancina, had gone to her own bedchamber when, late at night, Piso ordered the house's outer doors to be closed, and he withdrew into his bedchamber. At dawn the next day, Gnaeus Calpurnius Piso was found dead in his room, in a pool of blood. His throat had been cut. A sword lay on the tiled floor nearby.

The news that Piso was dead shocked Rome. Tiberius also seemed to be shocked. He called the Senate together immediately and, looking sad—although Tacitus felt it was a pretense of sadness—declared, unhappily and accusingly, to the assembled senators, "The purpose of such a death is to bring reproach on me!"[15] Tiberius seemed to be accusing Piso himself of taking his own life to make the emperor look bad, or accusing someone else, perhaps the friends of Germanicus, of engineering the murder of Piso before the man could be exonerated by the Senate of Germanicus's murder.

Rather than brush Piso's death under the mat, the emperor seemed determined to discover the truth about how he had died, for he proceeded to conduct an inquiry there in the Senate into the last day and night of Piso's life. He questioned, in front of the senators, the tribune charged with his escort, as well as Piso's two sons, and his steward. Some of the answers were cautious, others unwise, but none shed any real light on how or why Piso had died. Tiberius then read the Senate a letter he said had been written to him by Piso:

> Crushed by a conspiracy of my enemies and the hatred attracted by a false charge, since my truth and innocence find no place here I call on the immortal gods to witness that toward you, Caesar, I have acted loyally, with similar respect for your mother.
>
> I beg you to think of my children, one of whom, Gnaeus Piso, is not involved in my career in any way, such as it has been, seeing that he has been at Rome all this time. The other, Marcus Piso, strove to persuade me not to return to Syria. I wish that I had given in to my young son, rather than to his aged father. I therefore pray all the more earnestly that the innocent will not pay the penalty for my wickedness.
>
> With forty-five years of obedience, through my association with you in the consulate, as a person who previously won the esteem of your father, the Divine Augustus, and as one who is your friend and who will never again ask a favor of you, I beg you to save my unfortunate son.[16]

This letter, which, as Tacitus was to note, pointedly made no mention of Plancina, appeared to be the document that Piso had given his steward the previous evening. Taken in context, it had the hallmarks of the suicide note of a guilty man.

Yet in this note Piso had stuck firmly to his claim that he was innocent of the murder of Germanicus and had been falsely accused. Nor did he expressly say in the note that he was going to kill himself. Had Piso not been found dead, this letter, if genuine, would have been taken merely as a plea from Piso for leniency for his son Marcus prior to the commencement of the defense case in six days' time. Piso's friends would be adamant that he had not taken his own life. Tacitus was to say that in his own younger days he had personally spoken with aged senators who had told him they were convinced that Piso had not committed suicide, but had died at the hands of "a person sent to be his executioner."[17]

Did Piso take his own life? Suicide in the face of disgrace was a common course for Roman senators. Far from being cowardly, it was seen by Romans as a noble gesture, in the same way that many centuries later Japanese samurai would embrace and ritualize suicide in the form of seppuku, or hara-kiri, as an honorable alternative to defeat and dishonor. But the normal method used by Romans to take their own lives was to slice open the veins of the arms, and sometimes also the legs, so that they slowly bled to death. On the battlefield, a surrounded general might occasionally fall on his sword as a rapid last resort, as General Varus had done in the Teutoburg Forest in A.D. 6, rather than fall into enemy hands. Half a century later, the short-lived emperor Otho would commit suicide by stabbing himself in the throat with a dagger, and there were one or two instances of nobles ending their lives by slicing open their throats with a razor. But to cut one's own throat with a sword was a rare thing indeed. While it is not impossible that Piso did just that, the odds against him killing himself in this manner are high.

A possible scenario for what happened that night runs like this. On the instructions of his commander, Sejanus, the Praetorian tribune who escorted Piso home urged him to write a letter to the emperor begging leniency for his son, with the tribune promising to deliver it personally to Tiberius. Piso had duly written the letter and handed it to his steward, to be passed on to the tribune the next day. Then, in the early hours of the morning, Piso's hall porter, bribed by the tribune, or perhaps on the orders of Piso's wife, Plancina, opened the front door and admitted several Praetorian Guard centurions who wore civilian dress and carried sheathed swords beneath their cloaks. The assassins had then slipped into Piso's bedchamber, found him asleep, and slit his throat, leaving the bloodied murder weapon on the floor before they left.

Those same aged senators who had told Tacitus about the belief among Piso's friends that Piso had been murdered also told him about the mysterious document that Piso had kept by him during the two days of the trial. They told Tacitus that Piso's friends declared over and over again that this document was "a letter from Tiberius containing instructions referring to Germanicus, and that it was his intention to produce it in the Senate and embarrass the emperor."[18] The only reason Piso hadn't produced the letter, they said, was that he had been "misled by empty promises from Sejanus."[19] That incriminating letter had now disappeared, and would never again see the light of day. Once they had dispatched him, the murderers must have searched Piso's room to locate and destroy the letter.

Even though, just hours prior to his death, it had appeared that Piso could and would be found not guilty of the murder of Germanicus, Piso's sudden end very neatly brought the Germanicus murder case to a conclusion as far as the emperor was concerned. Tiberius now suggested to the Senate that Marcus Piso be acquitted of the charge of making civil war, on the grounds that the son could not refuse the orders of his father and military superior. Tiberius added that compassion was necessary in this case because of both the high rank of the Piso family and Piso's dreadful end. As for the role in Syria of the universally despised Plancina, Tiberius said it had been both shameful and disgraceful. However, he said, looking embarrassed, at the intercession of his mother, Livia, he called on the House to grant Plancina a full pardon.

A buzz ran through the Senate. "Secret complaints" from "all good men" about the emperor's mother were becoming more and more vehement, according to Tacitus. He quoted a typical covert complaint. "So, it was a grandmother's duty to look her grandson's murderess [Plancina] in the face, to speak freely with her, and to rescue her from the Senate?"[20] But in public, not a word of complaint was aired by the senators.

Now Tiberius called on the Senate to pronounce its verdict in the case. Normally, the presiding consul didn't cast a vote, but when the emperor was present in the Senate he did, so the consul spoke first. The consul Cotta announced that he believed that Gnaeus Piso Sr. was guilty on all counts, and moved that in punishment his name should be removed from the public register and that half his property be confiscated by the state, with the remainder given to his elder son, Gnaeus Jr., who must also change his first name so he had no association with his disgraced father. The younger Piso son, Marcus, the consul proposed, should be stripped of his senatorial rank and exiled for ten years with an allowance of 5 million sesterces. To show how little hardship this would have entailed for young Piso, a legionary earned 900 sesterces a year and received a pension of 12,000 sesterces after twenty years' service. A productive small farm could be had for 100,000 sesterces, while the going price for a large Italian farming estate owned by a senator was 3 million sesterces. Five million sesterces, even spread over ten years, was a small fortune. And finally, said the consul, in the light of the intercession of the emperor's mother, the life of Plancina should be spared.

The Senate unanimously voted in favor of the consul's proposal. Yet even these laughably mild punishments were considered too severe by Tiberius. Not even Mark Antony's name had been removed from the public record after he made war on the state, said the emperor. So, at Rome, Piso's name would not be erased or his statues removed. Tiberius announced that Marcus Piso would be pardoned, and the half of his father's property confiscated by the state would be granted to him. Thus ended this "mockery of a trial," as Tacitus was to describe it.[21]

So anxious was the emperor to cap public anger and gain closure on the entire Germanicus affair that on Tiberius's orders, bronze tablets would be inscribed by the Senate with details of the Piso trial, the verdict, the sentences, and the commutations, as well as the honors decreed in Germanicus's honor. These tablets would be displayed publicly for thirty days in cities, towns, and legion bases throughout the Roman world, to prove that Tiberius had exacted revenge for the death of Germanicus. Examples of these tablets, known as the Tabula Hebana, the Tabula Siarensis, and the Senatus Consultum de Cn. Pisone Patre, would be unearthed in the twentieth century in Italy and Spain. Other than the private asides about how Piso died and the reference to the mysterious document Piso kept by him, these tablets accord precisely with the record of the trial given by Tacitus in his history, the Annals. One of these tablets, the Senatus Consultum de Cn. Pisone Patre, found in Spain in the 1990s, detailed the punishment meted out to Gnaeus Piso, inclusive of a later decree from Tiberius, subsequent to the trial in the Senate, that Piso's name was to be erased from all public inscriptions where he had served as governor in Spain.

Immediately after the verdicts and punishments had been voted on in the Senate, various senators tried to outdo each other in their sycophancy. One senator proposed that a golden statue of Tiberius be erected in the Temple of Mars the Avenger, another that an altar to Vengeance be dedicated to Tiberius, in celebration of the fact that the emperor had supposedly avenged the death of Germanicus. Tiberius vetoed both these proposals; such monuments were for victories over foreign enemies, he said. Then the elderly senator Valerius Messalinus, who had married into a branch of the Caesar family, proposed that Tiberius, Livia, Agrippina, Drusus the Younger, and Germanicus's mother, Antonia, all be publicly thanked for having avenged Germanicus. The senator Lucius Asprenas then jumped up and admonished his colleague for failing to include Germanicus's brother Claudius in that imperial group. Claudius's name was added to the resolution, and the motion carried. The Senate then adjourned.

Talking animatedly among themselves, the members of the vast crowd outside the Senate House dispersed and went about their business. The news that Piso was dead sated the bloodlust of many of those Romans who had been calling for revenge for Germanicus. But while most Romans would go to their graves convinced that Piso had played a role in the death of the prince, many also continued to believe that Tiberius, and probably his mother also, had plotted the crime and orchestrated it from afar.

Several days after the conclusion of the Piso trial, Tiberius proposed to the Senate that prestigious priesthoods be conferred on the three prosecutors, Vitellius, Veranius, and Servaeus, as a reward for their services, a proposal that, of course, the Senate endorsed without question. Tiberius also told Fulcinius Trio, the senator who had made the time-wasting accusations against Piso, that if he reined in his rancor when he undertook prosecutions he could expect Tiberius's support when seeking promotion. Trio would in fact become a consul with Tiberius's support several years later. Apart from their priesthoods, none of the three prosecutors would receive any further honors or gain promotions during the reign of Tiberius.

"This was the end of avenging the death of Germanicus," Tacitus was to say.[22] But it was not the end of the story of Germanicus's murder. The story had just begun. Spurred by the murder of Germanicus, more murders would follow, and more members of the house of Germanicus and descendants of the Caesar family would perish over the coming years in a concerted effort to destroy all those associated with Germanicus. Four decades and numerous gruesome deaths were to follow before a clearer picture of who murdered Germanicus, and why, would emerge. The persons who took the life of Germanicus were not on the list of suspects in A.D. 20. Yet you have already met them.

# VIII

# DESTROYING THE FAMILY OF GERMANICUS

Tiberius may have feared Germanicus while he was alive, but he now embraced Germanicus's sons. As if to destroy the persistent rumor that he had hated Germanicus and had been behind his death, following the Piso trial Tiberius appointed his own son, Drusus the Younger, to be the guardian of Nero Germanicus, Drusus Germanicus, and Caligula. And shortly after, when the eldest, Nero, came of age at the end of his fifteenth year, Tiberius commended him to the Senate and asked that the same privileges that had been granted to him as a young man also be granted to the son of Germanicus.

When young Nero Germanicus entered the Roman Forum for the first time wearing his gown of manhood at age sixteen, Tiberius had a gratuity distributed to every citizen at Rome in celebration of the occasion. The people rejoiced, said Tacitus, "at seeing the son of Germanicus now grown to manhood."[1] In this same year, with Tiberius's full blessing, sixteen-year-old Nero Germanicus was married to his cousin Julia, daughter of his uncle Drusus the Younger from the latter's first marriage. Nero's engagement to the daughter of Germanicus's friend Creticus Silanus had apparently been terminated by the emperor. The young man's bride, Julia, was barely a teenager—Roman women could legally become engaged at twelve and marry at thirteen—yet she was already a widow. The following year, Tiberius also commended Germanicus's second son, Drusus Germanicus, to the Senate when he came of age. On the face of it, the children of Germanicus were being embraced by the emperor, and this helped soothe the anger of the Roman people over the death of Germanicus.

The children of Germanicus continued to be raised by their mother, Agrippina, at the Palatine palace of Germanicus. She herself was greatly honored and respected by the Roman people, but it was clear that she was not popular with either the emperor or his mother. It was equally clear that despite the fact that the emperor officially continued to honor the memory of Germanicus, any friend of Germanicus now had to watch his step. Even a careless word or two could cost you your life, as, in December A.D. 21, twenty months after the Piso trial, a poet was to discover.

As that year of A.D. 21 was ending, a prosecution was brought in the Senate against the knight Gaius Lutorius Priscus. He was a poet of some renown who, the previous year, had written a poem in praise of Germanicus that was immediately and immensely popular with the public. Like the Germanicus poem written by Pedo, this poem became a best seller. Privately, the last thing Tiberius would have wanted was more hero worship of Germanicus. But publicly, in recognition of the popularity of the poem, the emperor had given Lutorius Priscus a reward in gold. In the fall of A.D. 21, when Tiberius's son and heir, Drusus the Younger, suddenly fell gravely ill, Priscus wrote a poem on the assumption that Drusus would die, eulogizing him, in the hope that in the event of the prince's death this new poem might be published and make another great profit for him and enhance his reputation, just as his poem to Germanicus had done. With Drusus still very much alive, Priscus unwisely read the unpublished poem to a gathering of noble ladies at the house of the senator Publius Petronius. An informer told Sejanus about this poetry reading.

When the poet was arraigned in the Senate on a charge of treason—for having anticipated and sought to profit from the death of the prince—most of the ladies who had been present at the reading were frightened into giving evidence against him. Only the hostess on that occasion, Petronius's mother-in-law, Vitellia, a member of the Vitellius family, close friends of Germanicus, refused to testify against the poet. She claimed that she hadn't heard a single word of the offending poem. Despite this, the unfortunate Lutorius Priscus was found guilty. A consul-elect proposed the death penalty, but Marcus Lepidus, one of the defense advocates in the Piso case, proposed instead that the poet be banished from Italy, with all his property confiscated by the state. Lepidus was supported by just one other former consul, for it became clear to the senators—perhaps via a message from the Praetorian prefect—that the emperor wanted the poet severely dealt with. Sentenced to death, Lutorius Priscus was dragged to the city prison, which sat on the Street of the Banker just around the corner from the Forum, and there he was executed by the Praetorian Guard, that same day.

When Tiberius learned of this sentence and rushed execution, he wrote to the Senate, praising the senators for their loyalty. But, he said, he considered the poet's punishment hasty and extreme, and he praised Lepidus for the milder measure he had proposed. In light of this, the Senate passed a motion that in the future their decrees would be registered at the Roman Treasury and acted on only after nine days had passed, giving the emperor time to veto or reduce any punishment. Yet there had been another lesson learned here as well. The original poem in praise of Germanicus would not have gone down well at the Palatium, and while the public airing of this latest poem about Drusus the Younger had been premature and unwise, the rush by senators to punish the poet would be seen to have more to do with censuring the man's poem about Germanicus than that about Drusus.

As it happened, Drusus the Younger recovered from his illness, but he was not destined to live much longer. Praetorian prefect Sejanus had made Drusus's wife, Germanicus's sister, Livilla, his secret mistress. They conducted their lovemaking sessions with the complicity of Livilla's doctor and friend Eudemus; she would go to the doctor's house on the pretext of a medical examination, and there she would secretly rendezvous with Sejanus. To prove to Livilla that he was serious about her, Sejanus now divorced his wife, Apicata, the mother of his three children. But it appears that he continued to maintain a close if discreet relationship with Apicata, for she would be privy to his subsequent plans and schemes.

Livilla was so besotted with Sejanus, and so determined to make him her husband, that she actively plotted with him to murder her own husband, Drusus the Younger. Even though Drusus was unaware of this affair, he became increasingly jealous of Sejanus, complaining about this "stranger" who was "invited to help govern" while he, the emperor's son, was perfectly capable of fulfilling the same role.[2] Inevitably getting into an argument with the Praetorian commander in public, Drusus punched him in the face. Sejanus could not retaliate with a counterpunch—that, against the prince, would have been construed as a treasonous act. But Sejanus would have his revenge in another way, on another day.

In early A.D. 23, just as Germanicus's second son, Drusus Germanicus, was coming of age and being presented to the Senate by Tiberius, his uncle Drusus the Younger began to feel unwell. It would emerge, years later, that Sejanus bribed Drusus's most trusted freedman, a handsome young eunuch named Lygdus, to poison his master. Drusus had been seriously ill two years earlier, so this gave Sejanus the idea of poisoning him gradually, over a long time, so it would appear to be another natural illness. Over a period of months, then, Lygdus used a poison that left no telltale signs, adding it to his master's wine at dinner.

As the weeks passed, Drusus became increasingly stricken by what appeared to be a mystery illness. Drusus's doctor, Livilla's accomplice Eudemus, was unable to diagnose or treat this illness, and in September A.D. 23 Drusus the Younger, like his adoptive brother, Germanicus, died, murdered by poison. At the time, it was thought that Drusus had died from natural causes. It would be another eight years before the fact that Drusus had been poisoned, and by whom, would come to light. Obviously, the poison used in his case was not belladonna. The poison used to kill Drusus left no trace.

Tiberius seemed strangely unaffected by the death of his biological son and heir, which now brought the sons of Germanicus to the fore: Nero Germanicus, Drusus Germanicus, and Caligula now superseded the infant sons of Drusus in the line of succession, with Nero Germanicus now becoming Tiberius's heir apparent. The emperor went to the Senate shortly after the death of Drusus. The two current consuls removed themselves from the curile chairs to ordinary benches as a mark of respect, and Tiberius addressed the solemn House. He told the gathered senators that while some senators might condemn him for appearing before them when many who mourned could not even bring themselves to emerge from their homes to see the light of day, he sought the consolation of the whole country for his loss. He then requested that the Senate summon the elder children of Germanicus to help console him and the House in their shared grief. So the consuls hurried away to the nearby palace of Germanicus and returned with Nero Germanicus, who was approaching eighteen, and Drusus Germanicus, who had just turned sixteen.

Tiberius took Germanicus's sons by the hand and said, "Senators, when these boys lost their father, I committed them to their uncle and, although he had children of his own, I implored him to love and raise them as his own." He sighed, and cast his eyes around the House. "Drusus is now lost to us, so I turn my prayers to you, Senators, and before heaven and the nation I ask you to accept into your guidance and care the great-grandsons of Augustus, descendants of a noble ancestry. Fulfill your duty, and mine." Then he turned to the two youths. "Nero and Drusus, these senators must now be your fathers. Your blood is such that your prosperity and adversity must both affect that of the state."[3]

In death Drusus the Younger received similar honors to those accorded Germanicus following his death, but in addition he received a state funeral. Tiberius himself delivered a funeral oration to Drusus, from the Rostra in the Forum and before thousands of sad-faced Romans. Yet, says Tacitus, this was mostly an appearance of sorrow by the public—"Inwardly they were overjoyed by the prospect of a brightening future for the family of Germanicus."[4] This resurgence of notoriety for the children of Germanicus, "whose succession to the throne was now certain"[5] with the death of their uncle, gave new hope to their widowed mother, Agrippina, whose driving ambition for her sons to ascend the throne was poorly concealed, according to Tacitus.[6] It also spurred Sejanus to set out to destroy the house of Germanicus and clear the way to the throne for himself.

With Drusus the Younger out of the way, Sejanus set in motion a long-term plan to destroy Agrippina and her sons, Nero Germanicus, Drusus Germanicus, and Caligula. Because there were three boys to be eliminated, and because the staff who surrounded them proved to be incorruptible and totally loyal to the family of Germanicus, Sejanus decided that rather than try to employ poison to destroy their bodies he would poison minds instead.[7] The process would take considerably longer than belladonna or hemlock, but it could be just as effective if Sejanus was prepared to be patient. And as Sejanus was to demonstrate, patience was a quality he had in great abundance. He was aided, unwittingly, by Germanicus's widow, Agrippina.

No one could argue that Agrippina wasn't proud and affected. When she was still a teenager, her grandfather Augustus had written to her, in a letter in which he had praised her intelligence, to caution her: "Please take great care to avoid affectation in writing or talking."[8]

While Germanicus was alive, he had kept Agrippina's pride in check. As Germanicus revealed on his deathbed, he knew that Agrippina possessed a dangerous pride; it lurked just beneath the surface. Now, with Germanicus gone, Agrippina's pride had swollen into what her critics perceived to be an arrogant and "imperious disposition."[9]

Sejanus set out to use that arrogance against her. He began by having his lover, Livilla, Agrippina's sister-in-law, whisper in the ear of Livia, the emperor's mother, to inflame the old woman's longtime hatred of Agrippina. Sejanus's objective was to prompt influential old Livia into warning Tiberius that Agrippina possessed a "dream of empire."[10] Sejanus also used others to whisper accusations about Agrippina to the emperor's mother. At the same time, he encouraged Agrippina's friends to speak openly about her proud spirit. The poisoning of minds had begun.

Germanicus's eldest son, Nero Germanicus, was meanwhile impressing all who came in contact with him. Like his younger brothers, Drusus Germanicus and Caligula, he was a handsome boy; all bore a striking physical resemblance to both their father and their maternal grandfather, Marcus Agrippa. Young Nero was also displaying the modesty and grace worthy of a prince, and when on one occasion Tiberius sent him to the Senate to deliver a speech of thanks on his behalf, the youngster enjoyed the warm regards of the senators. They, said Tacitus, "with memories of Germanicus fresh in their minds, imagined that it was his face they saw and his voice they heard."[11] Sejanus was able to use this projection of the sons of Germanicus by Tiberius against his family when on New Year's Day, A.D. 24, the pontiffs, the chief priests, added prayers for the health of young Nero Germanicus and Drusus Germanicus to those traditionally offered for the emperor on January 1.

No doubt spurred on by Sejanus, Tiberius angrily called the priests to the Palatium to explain why they had done this. Sejanus would have pointed out that January 1 was the day on which the men of the legions throughout the empire traditionally swore an oath of allegiance to the emperor for the year ahead, and connecting the two youths to prayers for the emperor on that day could be considered seditious. Tiberius demanded to know of the priests whether they had added the boys to the prayers at the request of Agrippina, or under threat from her. The priests—some of them Agrippina's relatives; others, friends of Germanicus—flatly denied that Agrippina had anything to

do with it. Tacitus believed that with a wave of pro-Germanicus senti-
ment then permeating Roman life, the priests had done it to flatter
Tiberius, who seemed, outwardly, to be promoting the sons of the dead
hero; but the priests' sycophancy had backfired on them, and on Agrippina and her sons. While Tiberius only mildly rebuked the priests, it is
clear that he did not believe their protestations. This episode would
have been enough to convince him that the rumors he was hearing
from his mother about Agrippina's ambitions for her sons had some
basis in fact.

Sejanus now openly warned Tiberius against Agrippina. He would
have reminded the emperor that Agrippina had long harbored "a mas-
culine desire for power." Back in A.D. 14, when one of Germanicus's
armies had failed to return from Germany on schedule from the latest
incursion across the Rhine, which had involved a complex three-
pronged attack, Agrippina, waiting at the military staging camp at
Vetera, today's Xanten in Holland, had boldly crossed the temporary
bridge of boats that Germanicus had thrown across the Rhine River,
taking just two-year-old Caligula and her female servants with her.

With Germanicus himself deep inside northern Germany at the
head of another army, there, on the far side of the Rhine, his wife had
maintained a vigil at the bridge and waited for the overdue troops to
return. When officers at Xanten had begun to panic, fearing that the
Germans had wiped out the missing army, and issued orders to destroy
the bridge to prevent the Germans from using it, Agrippina had refused to permit the destruction of the bridge. There, on the far bank,
she had remained, certain that the missing Roman army would return,
and determined not to give up on them. As it happened, that army, led
by General Aulus Caecina, one of Germanicus's subordinates, had
been ambushed by Hermann in Germany and was locked in a desperate battle, the Battle of Long Bridges.

Caecina's four legions fought their way out, after several days and
nights of desperate struggle during which Caecina had come close to
losing to Hermann. When General Caecina's army finally returned to
the Rhine bridge, bloodied, battered, hungry, without their baggage
train, and carrying their many wounded on temporary stretchers,
Agrippina, with little Caligula at her side, had proudly welcomed the
troops back. She had praised and thanked the exhausted soldiers as
they passed, and handed out bandages, food, and gifts of money—
acting more like a general than a general's wife.

At the time, Sejanus, who was just settling into the post of sole Praetorian commander, had "inflamed and aggravated" Tiberius's suspicions of Agrippina. Even back then, Tacitus was to say, Sejanus had a "complete understanding of Tiberius's character," and knew how to manipulate him. Says Tacitus, Sejanus played on the then new emperor's prejudices and fears, sowing the seeds of future distrust. Sejanus had declared that this sort of activity at the Rhine bridge was not a woman's work. In Sejanus's opinion, Agrippina had wanted to cement the loyalty of the legions.[12] As indeed she had. Back then, her ambitions had been for her husband. Now, in the wake of the death of Germanicus, her ambitions were for her sons.

"There are those who call themselves 'the party of Agrippina'," Sejanus was quoted as saying in A.D. 24 following the New Year's Day prayers incident. "Unless they are checked, there will be more of this sort of incident."[13] Sejanus suggested that the solution would be to persecute one or two of the more outspoken leaders among Agrippina's backers, and Tiberius gave him a free hand to pursue that course.

The men targeted by Sejanus were all former friends or clients of Germanicus. In Roman society, every wealthy, well-placed man acted as patron to a select group of less wealthy and well-placed men, including their relatives, who were called the patron's "clients." In return for a client's loyalty, support, and inside information, a patron would aim to help the client and his family, providing helpful introductions and recommending them for official appointments, often also giving them financial assistance. Even after the death of Germanicus, many of his former clients continued to maintain the client-patron relationship with his widow, out of respect for her and for the memory of Germanicus. This was the so-called party of Agrippina.

Sejanus, for his demonstration against the party of Agrippina, now carefully chose two victims. One was Gaius Silius, a consul in A.D. 13 who had been an able, brave, and loyal lieutenant general under Germanicus during his swashbuckling German campaigns of A.D. 14–16. Silius had remained on the Rhine until A.D. 21, very successfully commanding the four legions of Rome's Army of the Upper Rhine at Mainz for a total of seven years. General Silius had returned to Rome heaped with honors, including the award of a Triumph by the Senate for putting down a brief revolt in Gaul led by a Gallic noble, Julius Sacrovir. Sejanus knew that if Silius were to be brought down, the dust

from his fall would send all but the most courageous or foolhardy supporters of Agrippina scurrying for cover.

The other victim of Sejanus's intrigue was to be a Roman knight,
Titius Sabinus. The firm friendship of General Silius and Titus Sabinus
with Germanicus would be fatal to both men, Tacitus would say.[14]

There was another reason for targeting General Silius: his wife,
Sosia Galla, was a very close personal friend of Agrippina, and had
been for years. As Sejanus knew, the destruction of both husband and
wife would doubly wound Agrippina, so the campaign against Silius
and his wife was the first to be launched. In the Senate, Silius was
charged by the current consul, Varro, with treason. The accusation
specified that Silius had been complicit in the Sacrovir Revolt, the
rebellion by several Gallic tribes that Silius had actually bloodily put
down with two of his Rhine legions, and for which he had been
awarded his Triumph by a grateful Senate. He was also charged with
embezzling funds from the provincial government in Gaul. At the
same time, Sosia was charged with unseemly conduct.

When Silius's trial began in the Senate, the general refused to either offer a plea or to defend himself. He knew why he was being prosecuted, and knew who was behind it. He had been heard to remark
that had he not kept his legions steadfastly loyal to Tiberius, despite
the scandalous murder of Germanicus, Tiberius would not have kept
his throne, and this was the price he was paying for his loyalty. When
he did speak now, it was to hint at the identity of the person who was
pressing for his destruction: Sejanus. Faced with false witnesses swearing that he had stolen money from the Gallic provincials, and foresee-
ing an inevitable verdict, General Silius went home on the evening
following the first day of his trial, took a knife, opened his veins, and
bled to death overnight.

The next day, on the recommendation of the consul, the Senate
voted to confiscate all Silius's property. Tacitus was to remark that no
one suggested using the general's estate to repay to the provincial
treasury the money he had supposedly embezzled from the Gauls.[15]
And, in fact, not a single Gaul petitioned for the money's return—
because it had never been stolen; this had been a trumped-up charge.
On the motion of Marcus Lepidus, one of Piso's defense counsels in the
Germanicus murder trial, Silius's wife, Sosia, was exiled, losing all
her property, a fourth of which went to those who had prosecuted her,
with the balance going to her children.

The comprehensive destruction of Silius and his wife, previously one of Rome's most respected couples, because of their connections with Germanicus and Agrippina, sent shock waves through the Roman aristocracy. To protect themselves, many friends of Germanicus now broke off contact with his widow—among them Vitellius, Veranius, and Servaeus, the prosecutors at Piso's trial. But the second man secretly marked by Sejanus to be made an example of, Titius Sabinus, continued to defiantly visit Agrippina and her children at their Palatine palace and accompany them when they went out in public. A Roman woman of the upper classes could only venture out in public in the company of a male chaperone, normally her husband. A spinster or a widow had to secure a chaperone to go out her door. Had Sabinus not filled that role for Agrippina, she would have been isolated inside the family home, which would have well suited Sejanus and Tiberius.

Flushed with victory over the destruction of Silius and Sosia, Sejanus turned to his next victim, Sabinus. But this time, Sejanus struck problems. Despite intense inquiries, there was no scandal in Sabinus's background, no crime that Sabinus could be accused of, and his staff proved too loyal to be bribed into inventing charges against him. So Sejanus set his mind to patiently await a chance to one day trap the marked man, and looked for fresh victims in his campaign against the friends of the family of Germanicus. With Tiberius's strong support, Sejanus now went after Germanicus's loyal former quaestor, Publius Suillius Rufus.

Redheaded Suillius was charged in the Senate with having accepted a bribe in a recent case in which he had sat as magistrate. In this instance it proved easy enough to buy false evidence, and witnesses promptly came forward to testify to Suillius's guilt. He was duly convicted, but received a mild sentence—he was to be expelled from Italy—for many in the Senate knew that Suillius was being targeted by the Palatium for his connection with Germanicus and his family, and there was considerable sympathy for him. But Tiberius sent a letter to the Senate containing a strongly worded reference to Suillius and his conviction. Tiberius declared that Suillius must be banished to some remote island in punishment for his crime. Uniquely, the emperor then required all senators to take an oath that they would vote for just such a punishment for Suillius as a state necessity. The Senate so voted, and Suillius was banished.

As the Praetorian commander's power continued to grow, senators realized that the only path to senior appointments, including that of the consulate, was through Sejanus. His own uncle, Junius Blaesus, had been appointed to the lucrative post of governor of Africa, the best-paid of all the governorships of the senatorial provinces, while all other appointments went to men who pleased Sejanus and who served him. Having gained the emperor's total confidence, and urged on by his lover, Livilla, sister of Germanicus and widow of Drusus the Younger, Sejanus decided that he should now join the imperial family. He wrote a letter to Tiberius seeking the emperor's permission to marry Livilla, even though he was not of high rank. Apart from the supposed glory of an alliance between the emperor's niece and himself, Sejanus wrote that such a marriage would secure his own family against the "unjust displeasure" of Agrippina.[16]

Tiberius replied with a letter full of praise for Sejanus. But in tactful language, he declined to give the marriage his approval. As for Agrippina's enmity toward Sejanus, Tiberius suggested that it would blaze even more fiercely if Livilla were to marry Sejanus. Such a marriage would only split the house of the Caesars into two factions, he said. He claimed to have other plans for strengthening the ties between Sejanus and himself, plans he would not disclose, hinting that when the time was right he would propose to the Senate that Sejanus become a consul.[17] The implication was that Tiberius was content to allow Sejanus to do his dirty work for him but was not prepared to allow this man of comparatively low rank to marry into the imperial family. Sejanus could have been expected to have been enraged by this response, but he showed no outward signs of it. Instead, he continued to prepare his own path toward the throne while appearing to be Tiberius's most faithful servant.

That path continued to be over the bodies of the friends and relatives of Germanicus and Agrippina. Sejanus's next target was Agrippina's cousin Claudia Pulchra, who was particularly close to Agrippina. Claudia was charged with adultery and with having attempted to assassinate the emperor using poison and sorcery. This attack on a kinswoman stirred Agrippina into action. Up till now she had borne Germanicus's deathbed instructions in mind and tried not to provoke Tiberius. But in the wake of the banishment of her good friend Sosia, the general's wife, and now this attack on her cousin Claudia, Agrippina could see a new phase in Sejanus's campaign against her opening. Agrippina snapped, and went stomping up the Palatine hill to the Palatium. The emperor's servants were powerless to stop Agrippina as she stormed through the imperial palace looking for Tiberius. She found him making an animal sacrifice in front of a statue of Augustus, who had been deified by the Roman Senate as a god.

"How can the same man who makes sacrifices to the Divine Augustus persecute his memory at the same time?" railed Agrippina. She pointed to the statue of Augustus, declaring that it didn't contain the spirit of Augustus. "Here is the spirit of Augustus!" she declared, patting her own chest. Agrippina, Augustus's last surviving grandchild, did not stop there. She could see that she herself was in danger, she said, for the prosecution against her cousin Claudia was a pretext. "The only reason for her destruction is her friendship with me. In her foolishness she forgot that Sosia was ruined for the same reason!"[18]

A ruffled Tiberius turned on Agrippina with uncharacteristic fervor, lambasting her with a piece of Greek verse: "I have not wronged you, because you are not a queen!"[19]

Chastened by this reminder that she had neither position nor power and had better watch her step, Agrippina returned to her palace, and awaited the outcome of her cousin's trial. Inevitably, Claudia and her lover were found guilty and condemned to death. Soon after this, Agrippina fell ill. Even while she was in the grip of a fever, Tiberius came down from the Palatium to pay her a visit. He found his daughter-in-law on her sickbed. Agrippina, nearing the end of her emotional tether, only had to look at his face to burst into tears, for they both knew that Tiberius, through Sejanus, was progressively and deliberately destroying the security net of friends and relatives that surrounded her. Silently she wept, long and hard. All the while, the emperor sat looking at her with his notoriously inscrutable expression.

Finally, Agrippina found words. "I beg you to relieve my loneliness," she said. "Provide me with a new husband. I am still young enough for marriage. That is the only solace of a virtuous woman. There are plenty of Roman citizens who wouldn't refuse to make the wife and children of Germanicus their own."[20] Tiberius left Agrippina's bedchamber without denying or agreeing to her request to remarry.

Once Agrippina had recovered from her illness, several men came to her to warn her not to eat with the emperor, as poison was being prepared for her. Shortly after, she received a formal invitation to be the emperor's guest at a dinner at the palace. Nervously, she went to the dinner, and took the place allocated to her, reclining on one side of Tiberius while her old enemy the emperor's octogenarian mother, Livia, reclined on the other. Unbeknownst to the emperor, Sejanus had sent the men to Agrippina with the warning to be wary of poisoning, and had then suggested to Tiberius that he invite Agrippina to dinner to show his magnanimity toward her.

There was no poison, but since the poisoning of her husband and the removal of so many close friends and relatives by one means or another, Agrippina was by now so fearful for her own life, a fear exacerbated by the warning she had received just prior to the dinner invitation, that she was in dread of eating anything from the emperor's table. Neither was she a good actress, and the strain soon showed on her face. After a while Tiberius noticed that his daughter-in-law had not relaxed like everyone else at the dinner. He also noted that she had failed to eat or drink a thing all night.

Tiberius began to think that Agrippina suspected him of trying to poison her. So to test her, he praised the apples being placed on the table in front of them as the last of the meal's many courses, then took one from the bowl and handed it to Agrippina, recommending it. He then pretended to become involved in conversation with his mother, but out of the corner of his eye he watched as Agrippina beckoned to one of her female servants. When the girl knelt by her mistress, Agrippina slipped the apple to her, and Tiberius saw her do it. Tiberius didn't say a word about this to Agrippina, but instead leaned closer to his mother and said, so that others could hear, "No one should be surprised if I decide on harsh treatment for those who believe that I would poison them."[21]

Agrippina returned to her palace. She never again received an invitation to dine with the emperor, and became more and more paranoid as a rumor reached her ears that Tiberius was plotting to murder her in some secret way, a way that could not be connected to him. Again, Sejanus was behind the rumor.

Having cleverly managed to firmly cement mutual distrust in the minds of Agrippina and the emperor, Sejanus next convinced Tiberius to spend more time away from Rome. The chosen place of semiretirement was the island of Capri, near Naples. Augustus had originally acquired the island from the city of Naples as an imperial vacation place, and Tiberius subsequently extended the facilities there to twelve

palaces spread around its rocky, mountainous heights. Encouraged by
Sejanus, the increasingly unhealthy Tiberius withdrew there with just
his servants; his German Guard bodyguards under the command of
their prefect, Naevius Sertorius Macro; Sejanus; one senator; one
knight; and a number of Greek freedmen.

With Tiberius now completely out of touch with what was happen-
ing in the outside world, receiving all his news via Sejanus, the Praetorian Guard commander was able to step up his campaign against the
family of Germanicus. He next set in motion a plot to destroy the immediate heir to the throne, Germanicus's son Nero Germanicus. Sejanus began by inserting spies into Nero's entourage, who reported
everything the young man said or did. Even Nero's own teenage wife,
Julia, would pass on pillow talk. And, most diabolically of all, Sejanus
began to win the confidence of Drusus Germanicus, the second son of
Germanicus, who was jealous of the fact that his elder brother, Nero,
was their mother's favorite. To encourage Drusus's betrayal of his own
brother, Sejanus reminded the boy that with Nero out of the way, he,
Drusus Germanicus, would become the new heir apparent and the next
emperor of Rome. Slowly but surely, Sejanus built a wedge between
Drusus and his elder brother, and prepared the stage for Nero's
downfall.

At the same time, Sejanus continued to work against the family of
Germanicus on other fronts. The plan to destroy Agrippina's loyal attendant the knight Titius Sabinus, originally conceived by Sejanus
when the general Silius and his wife, Sosia, had been eliminated, had
been brewing for some time. Once he began something, Sejanus never
relented, and eventually a cunning plan for the ruination of Sabinus
came together. In the summer of A.D. 27, four ex-praetors in Sejanus's
confidence agreed to combine to bring Sabinus down, with one of their
number, Latinius Latiaris, volunteering to act as the bait in the trap.

Latiaris one day drew the victim Sabinus into conversation in the
street, discreetly saying that he admired Sabinus for remaining loyal to
Agrippina, and speaking admiringly of Germanicus. Sabinus burst into
tears. Thinking he had found an ally, Sabinus let his guard down and
spoke his mind, criticizing Sejanus and Tiberius. Over the next few
months Latiaris began to regularly call on Sabinus at his home, where
he would talk about his personal problems and encourage Sabinus to
do the same. Then, meeting Sabinus in the street one December day,
as if by chance, he invited him back to his house.

There, in a particular room of his house, Latiaris talked about the way Sejanus and Tiberius had persecuted the family and friends of Germanicus, and speculated on what future crimes the emperor and his Praetorian Guard commander might commit. Sabinus again unburdened his soul, saying what he really felt about the emperor and Sejanus and their systematic destruction of the house of Germanicus. Sabinus went home later that day not knowing that the three other senators involved in the plot had, prior to his arrival at the house of Latiaris, crawled into the space between ceiling and roof above the room where Latiaris had taken Sabinus for their "secret" chat. There they had lain throughout, taking in every seditious word uttered by Sabinus below.

On January 1, the first session of the Senate for A.D. 28 took place. As was the usual practice, the consul read aloud a letter from the emperor to the House. Following the normal New Year's Day greetings and commendations, Tiberius's letter then announced that he had received written testimony from three senators who swore that they had overheard Sabinus utter seditious comments about the emperor in the house of Latiaris. The letter also claimed that several freedmen on the emperor's staff had testified that Sabinus had attempted to bribe them with a view to assassinating Tiberius. The letter ended with Tiberius calling on the Senate to punish Sabinus to the full extent of the law. The presiding consul then proposed that Sabinus be convicted of treason. The vote of the Senate was a formality. Sabinus was convicted. The House's sentence was death. It was all over in minutes.

Soldiers of the Praetorian Guard immediately marched to Sabinus's home and arrested him. A canvas hood was thrown over his head, his hands were chained behind his back, and a rope halter was placed tightly around his neck. Sabinus was dragged through the streets to the city prison, as people fearfully scattered from the soldiers' path. As he went, Sabinus yelled, "This is how the year is now inaugurated, with victims slain to Sejanus!"[22] The nine-day waiting period was ignored, on Sejanus's assurance that it was the emperor's will. At the prison, Sabinus was immediately strangled with a garrote.

Sabinus's naked body was taken to the nearby top of the Gemonian Stairs, from where it was ceremonially tossed down the steps, the traditional fate of traitors. A huge iron hook was then passed through his corpse, which was hauled through the streets to the bank of the Tiber River before being tossed into the water. This was another traditional

aspect of the fate of a convicted traitor. No one was permitted to rescue the body for burial or cremation. It was even a crime to cry for an
executed traitor. Cassius Dio tells the story that Sabinus's pet dog followed the arrested man to the prison, where it waited loyally outside in
the Street of the Banker. When Sabinus's body was finally thrown into
the river, says Dio, the dog jumped in after it, to share its master's
fate.[23]

Tiberius now sent the Senate a letter in which he thanked the honorable members for so swiftly punishing the traitor Sabinus, "a bitter
enemy of the state." But his life was still an anxious one, Tiberius
added, for he continued to fear the treachery of certain nameless foes.
There could be no question, Tacitus was to write, that this comment
was aimed at Nero Germanicus and his mother, Agrippina.[24]

Still, Agrippina had not yet been totally abandoned. She had a distinguished brother-in-law, Asinius Gallus, a consul in 8 B.C., who had
married Agrippina's half-sister Vipsania. Gallus had no love for Tiberius, and the feeling was mutual—Vipsania had been Tiberius's first
wife; Tiberius had loved her passionately, and possibly still did. Augustus had forced Tiberius to divorce Vipsania in favor of a doomed political marriage to his daughter, Julia, after the death of her first husband,
Agrippina's famous father, Marcus Agrippa. Years later, when Tiberius
had come across Vipsania in the street, he'd burst into tears at the
sight of her. Early in Tiberius's reign, in the Senate, Gallus had proven
a very wily opponent of the new emperor, but since the rise of Sejanus
he had not bothered to attend the House. It took the plight of his sister-in-law Agrippina to bring him back into public affairs. Taking his
seat in the Senate once more following the execution of Sabinus, Gallus made a call for the emperor to disclose his fears about traitors and
treachery so that the Senate could remove those fears for him.

This was a very clever way of calling Sejanus's bluff. Gallus was
saying that Tiberius must either lay specific accusations against Agrippina and her son Nero Germanicus before the House, or cease this
campaign of innuendo against them. Tacitus says that Tiberius was in-
censed by this challenge, and was all for making a rare appearance in
the Senate and engaging in a verbal joust with his old opponent Gallus. But according to Tacitus, Sejanus held the emperor back; Sejanus
knew that he could not yet produce evidence, much less solid witnesses, to prove that the wife and son of the revered Germanicus were
plotting the overthrow of Tiberius. Evidence might be concocted

against others, but with so much residual popular goodwill for the family of Germanicus, it would take an ironclad case to exterminate Agrippina and her son without creating an uprising of the Roman people. Revenge on Gallus, Sejanus now proposed, would keep for a later time. So Gallus's challenge went unanswered, and no charges were laid against Agrippina or her son. Agrippina continued to exist under the weight of Palatium suspicion, yet without the opportunity to defend herself in a public forum.

Shortly after this, Julia, daughter of Augustus, mother of Agrippina, and Tiberius's estranged wife, died in exile in southern Italy. Unusually for the times, she died of natural causes. She had been made an exile by her father, Augustus, twenty years before, for brazenly debauched behavior that had scandalized the emperor. At first kept a prisoner on an island, Julia had later been transferred to the Italian mainland, where she had lived out the rest of her life under guard in a rural backwater, but was made reasonably comfortable through funding provided by, of all people, her stepmother, Livia. Agrippina had not been able to see her mother in all that time, although she may well not have had any desire to do so, for her mother's selfish personality and thoughtless acts had not made her an endearing parent.

To keep up the public impression that he had no quarrel with Agrippina or her children, Tiberius now gave the hand in marriage of Agrippina's thirteen-year-old daughter, Agrippina the Younger, to Gnaeus Domitius Ahenobarbus, a prominent member of a leading family that had supplied Rome with many a general and consul. More importantly, Ahenobarbus had the blood of the Caesars flowing through his veins. Following the example set by Augustus, this marriage, arranged by Tiberius, was another political union of cousins, if somewhat distant cousins. Octavia, sister of the emperor Augustus, had been Ahenobarbus's grandmother, just as she had been Germanicus's grandmother. This was not a match made in heaven. Ahenobarbus was in his thirties and old enough to be young Agrippina's father. He was also a notoriously cruel and vindictive man who was infamous for deliberately running down a child in the street while driving his chariot, and getting away with it. Nine years after the wedding, the marriage of Agrippina the Younger and Domitius Ahenobarbus would produce a son, Lucius, their only child.

One of Agrippina the Elder's most bitter enemies finally departed the scene in A.D. 29, the year following the marriage of her daughter.

Livia, Tiberius's venal eighty-six-year-old mother and a suspect in the murder of Germanicus, died of old age. Tiberius gave his mother a state funeral, and sent sixteen-year-old Caligula, Germanicus's third son, to read the funeral oration. But Tiberius himself failed to attend, and he vetoed many honors proposed for his mother, whom he'd grown to detest. But Agrippina would have little time to celebrate Livia's demise; the tide of fortune was about to turn against her.

A letter from Tiberius was read to the Senate just days after Livia's remains had joined those of Augustus and Germanicus in the Mausoleum of Augustus. Tacitus was to say it was believed that the letter had been written some time before, but had been held back until now at the intercession of Livia,[25] who must have feared it would provoke riots against Tiberius. Now that Livia was dead, the explosive document had been sent to the Senate. In the letter, which was now read to the House by a consul, Tiberius complained of Agrippina's defiant nature and insolent tongue. He didn't dare to invent any false charge against her, but he wasn't so delicate when it came to her eldest son. Meek and mild Nero Germanicus, seen as the mirror of his revered father, Germanicus, by many, was accused of "unnatural" sexual passions. Tacitus records that when this letter was read to the senators, there was panic-stricken silence in the Senate House.[26] Most senators could not believe that Tiberius was at last publicly attacking the wife and son of Germanicus.

Several senators who had been primed for this event by Sejanus now demanded a debate about the contents of the letter, and a former consul made a savage speech against Agrippina and Nero Germanicus. But the other former consuls and magistrates held their tongues. They were perplexed, because Tiberius had failed to make any specific allegations about mother or son. Some senators were prepared to vote for whatever Tiberius wanted, but many others wavered. Junius Rusticus, a favorite of Tiberius who had been given the job of registering Senate debates, and a man who had never before shown any courage, says Tacitus, now attached himself to the waverers.[27] Rusticus came to his feet and warned the current consuls not to enter the debate, suggesting that the emperor might one day rue the fall of the house of Germanicus, if that were to occur. Many a head around the Senate benches nodded.

Meanwhile, word had quickly escaped the chamber that Agrippina and Nero Germanicus were under verbal attack, and, as if to back up

Rusticus, a huge crowd swelled around the Senate House, with thousands of people milling discontentedly. Some protesters carried busts of Agrippina and her eldest boy, and there were shouts from others that the emperor's letter had to be a forgery, that Tiberius could not possibly have authored such a heinous attack on the family of Germanicus. Fearful of creating a riot or a revolution, the Senate adjourned without further debate.

The next day, forged letters in the names of ex-consuls were circulated in the city, all deprecating Sejanus. The general suspicion was that Sejanus was behind this attack on Agrippina and Nero Germanicus in the emperor's name. Sejanus was quick to counter, declaring that in failing to act on the content of Tiberius's letter the previous day the Senate had ignored the emperor's problems with Agrippina and Nero Germanicus. Tiberius swiftly issued an edict in which he repeated his complaints against Agrippina and her eldest son and went on to reprimand the people of Rome for their riotous behavior.

At the same time, Tiberius wrote to the Senate, declaring that the imperial dignity had been damaged by the senators' failure to act. In language more forceful than he had ever used before, Tiberius now declared that he would reserve the right to make the decision about the fate of Agrippina and Nero Germanicus. Suddenly afraid, a majority of senators hastily passed a motion—the House was prepared to exact vengeance on the emperor's behalf, they said, but it found itself constrained on this occasion by the strong hand of the emperor himself.

Agrippina and Nero Germanicus had been thrown to the Palatium dogs.

# THE DOWNFALL OF SEJANUS

Tiberius had finally moved against Germanicus's wife and eldest son. Or Sejanus had, in Tiberius's name. Within days of Tiberius's contretemps with the Senate, and the Senate's backdown, mother and son were arrested by the Praetorian Guard at the palace of Germanicus on the Palatine. In the dead of night, says Suetonius, Agrippina the Elder and Nero Germanicus were hustled out of Rome in closed litters, with their hands and feet chained, before the public knew about it or could do anything to help them.[1]

From Ostia, the port of Rome, the pair was shipped to Campanian prison islands off the western coast of Italy. Agrippina was sent to Pandataria, today's Vendotene. Small, flat, and treeless, it was occupied by a single clifftop villa. The choice of Pandataria was quite deliberate: Agrippina's mother, Julia, Tiberius's former wife, whom he had detested, had been kept on this same island years before. Nero was sent to the nearby island of Pontia, today's Ponza, which was just as rocky and desolate as Pandataria. On orders from Sejanus, each prisoner was to be closely watched by a Praetorian centurion and freedmen jailers. With Tiberius declaring that the detention of mother and son was a matter of state security, the public, hoping that the pair would eventually be released, and probably fired by fear promoted by agents of Sejanus that any public demonstrations might lead to the executions of Agrippina and her boy, remained quiet.

With this momentous act against the widow and the eldest son of Germanicus having been accomplished without the Palatium being stormed by the public, Tiberius and Sejanus now moved against the last remaining supporters of Agrippina. Her brother-in-law Gaius Asinius Gallus, a prime target for their attentions, now surprised many by coming to his feet in the Senate and proposing honors for Sejanus, including a state celebration of his birthday, for having forestalled the so-called threat posed by Agrippina. Gallus then had himself appointed as an envoy of the Senate to Tiberius on Capri, to congratulate him on avoiding this latest "threat" to his reign.

Cassius Dio was to speculate that Gallus did this so he could gain the emperor's ear and warn him about Sejanus. Gallus was duly invited to Capri to meet with the emperor. Whatever passed between Gallus and Tiberius was never revealed, but Dio says the emperor warmly entertained Gallus, and the pair drank to friendship between them.[2] But while Gallus was away from Rome, eating and drinking with Tiberius, a letter from the emperor was read to the Senate accusing Gallus of treason. The Senate promptly condemned Gallus to death.

When Gallus unwittingly stepped foot back onto the mainland the next day after what had seemed a successful visit to Capri, he was arrested by a praetor sent by the Senate from Rome. Tiberius had not asked for Gallus's execution. He required a different punishment for Gallus: he was locked in a single room at the Palatium at Rome, and not permitted to see or talk to anyone, not even his jailers. He was given just one meal a day, with just enough food to keep him alive. The intention was to make Gallus think every day would be his last, and day after day Tiberius delayed giving an order for Gallus's execution. This wicked mental torture was devised as the punishment of the man who had married the woman Tiberius loved. That punishment would stretch out for months, and then for years.

On the arrest of Agrippina and Nero, Germanicus's second son, Drusus Germanicus, would have seen the way open for him to become Tiberius's heir, as Sejanus had promised. Young Drusus had recently been married, on the emperor's orders, to Aemilia Lepida, daughter of Marcus Lepidus. This was the same Lepidus who had been one of the defense advocates at the Piso trial. Drusus Germanicus's wife, Aemilia, now encouraged her new husband to talk about his ambitions for the throne. But Sejanus had seduced Drusus's bride, and behind his back Aemilia noted down Drusus's every word.

Using Aemilia as his informant, Sejanus was able to show Tiberius documentary evidence of Drusus Germanicus's seditious talk. Before the year was out, naive young Drusus was arrested and, on Tiberius's orders, locked in a cellar at the Palatium. The centurion in charge of Drusus Germanicus's imprisonment was also instructed to note down everything that was said to Drusus by his guards, and everything that Drusus said in return. Tiberius, in his gratitude to Sejanus for saving him from yet another supposed Germanicus family plot, now granted the Praetorian commander permission to marry Germanicus's sister, Livilla, as he had previously requested. At the same time, Tiberius appointed Sejanus to serve as consul with him for the next year, A.D. 31, calling him in his official decrees at this time "Sharer of my cares" and "My Sejanus."[3] Now at the height of his powers, a delighted Sejanus prepared for a grand wedding at Rome in the new year, and in the last days of December A.D. 30 he returned to the capital from Capri to take up his long-desired consulship on New Year's Day, with Tiberius assuring him he would follow along after him within a short time.

Before dawn on New Year's Day, A.D. 31, a vast number of senators gathered at Sejanus's city house to pay their respects to the new consul—so many, according to Dio, that a reception room couch collapsed beneath the weight of a number of guests in the crush.[4] Sejanus, his teenage son, and Germanicus's youngest son, Caligula, had all been recently made priests by Tiberius, and after leaving his house, Sejanus went through the crowded predawn streets to the Temple of Jupiter on the Capitoline Hill to personally conduct the sacrifice that preceded the first session of the Senate. The omens were auspicious, and at the subsequent Senate session Sejanus was voted wide powers. It was even moved by one sycophantic senator that in the future the new consuls for the year must emulate Sejanus in their loyal and upright conduct. Sejanus and his supporters began preparations for his wedding, which would take place at Rome in front of the emperor.

But the emperor did not appear. As the days passed, Tiberius sent a succession of messages from Capri to say that he had been delayed. Sometimes he would excuse his nonappearance by saying he was ill. Before long, another message would say that he was better and preparing to travel. Days later, he was reported to be ill again. January slipped by. More months passed. Increasingly, the emperor's messages would contradict the previous ones. Sometimes he would praise Sejanus and propose honors or appointments for his friends. At other times he would scold him, and admonish some of his supporters. No one, least of all Sejanus, could work out what was going on. Was the emperor merely a victim of his famous moodiness? Was he becoming senile? Or was there something more worrying behind the old man's shifting attitudes? Sejanus was having to continually postpone his wedding, but he kept his famous patience. He wrote to the emperor to suggest that he might rejoin Tiberius back on Capri, but the emperor told him not to bother, as he would soon arrive at Rome. But he never came.

As the spring arrived, and then the summer, Tiberius and Sejanus gave up the consulship to suffect (replacement) consuls as was the custom. Sejanus remained at Rome, with Tiberius still on Capri and always about to set off for the capital but never leaving the island. It seems that during this period Sejanus did finally marry Livilla, Germanicus's sister and Drusus the Younger's widow, but the details of where and when the wedding took place are lost. Most certainly, the ceremony took place without Tiberius present. Now, too, out of the blue, Tiberius quashed a prosecution against an enemy of Sejanus. And then a friend of Sejanus who had been a governor in Spain was prosecuted on Tiberius's orders. Association with Sejanus was no longer a guarantee of favor or success.

Sejanus, meanwhile, was beginning to have concerns about Caligula, third son of Germanicus. Since the time when Tiberius had appointed the youth to a priesthood, there had been a rumor that the emperor would soon name him his heir. Dio was to say that Sejanus began to regret that he had not instigated the removal of Caligula and the overthrow of Tiberius while he still had the consular powers. The only reason he had not done so, Dio wrote, was that the general public was extremely pleased by the compliments paid to Caligula because of their "reverence for the memory of his father, Germanicus."[5] The ever-patient Sejanus continued to advance his plan for the gradual eradication of the imperial family and his own assumption of power.

Now news reached Rome that Caligula's elder brother Nero Germanicus had died while a prisoner on the island of Ponza, starved to death. It is unclear on whose orders this starvation occurred—Tiberius's or Sejanus's—but it removed one more heir from Sejanus's path. This now left the imprisoned Drusus Germanicus as Tiberius's heir apparent. Tiberius, in a letter to the Senate announcing the death of Nero Germanicus, merely referred to Sejanus by name, without giving him his customary titles. This suggested to many that Sejanus had fallen even further out of favor with the emperor, and some senators began to pull back from Sejanus. Some actively went out of their way not to be seen with him or even greet him in the street, instead turning and going the other way if they saw him approaching.

Up to this point, as one of Sejanus's friends, Marcus Terentius, had said of Sejanus, "To even be known to his freedmen and hall porters was considered to be something grand."[6] But attitudes were changing, and Sejanus's status was deteriorating. By the fall, Sejanus, seeing his influence and power dissolving little by little, set in motion a plan to murder Tiberius and take the throne for himself before the year was out.

From time to time, the Senate would sit in one temple or another at Rome, depending on the religious significance of the day. On October 17, the Senate was due to sit in the Temple of Apollo, which was attached to the Palatium on the Palatine Hill. That morning, before dawn, Sejanus climbed the path to the temple to take his seat on the front benches as an ex-consul. In the throng outside the temple as he arrived he spotted, to his surprise, Macro, colonel of the German Guard, who was supposed to be on Capri with the emperor. When Macro came over to Sejanus and greeted him warmly, Sejanus asked what he was doing in Rome. Macro told him he had arrived at the capital from Capri the previous evening on a mission for the emperor.

Sejanus was immediately worried because he had failed to hear anything from the emperor about this, but Macro told him not to be concerned, as he had come with a message for the Senate, on the emperor's orders. He indicated a sealed scroll in his left hand. When Sejanus asked what the document contained, Macro took him aside and said in a low voice that the emperor was about to ask the Senate to confer the tribunician powers on Sejanus. In the days of the Republic, the ten civil tribunes, the so-called Tribunes of the Plebs, could veto any vote of the Senate. Once Augustus became emperor he had taken that power of veto for himself, and had also conferred it on Tiberius late in his reign. This meant that if awarded the tribunician power, Sejanus would have the same power of veto over the Senate as the emperor himself, ranking him above all men but the emperor.

Beaming, Sejanus thanked Macro for this great news, and hurried into the temple. There he told his closest senatorial associates that he was about to receive the tribunician power. Macro watched Sejanus disappear indoors; then, in the growing light of the new day, the German Guard prefect called over the tribune of the Praetorian Guard cohort on duty at the temple, who was subordinate to him. Prefect Macro then showed the tribune a letter from the emperor calling on all officers and men of the Roman armed forces to obey Macro's commands. He then ordered the tribune to march his men back to the Praetorian Barracks in the city's 4th Precinct; all Praetorian troops were to be subsequently confined to barracks until they received further orders from Macro.

The tribune looked at Macro in surprise, and hesitated to obey. The German Guard prefect then indicated that he had another letter from the emperor in which Tiberius decreed that every Praetorian soldier was to receive a large cash bonus if they followed Macro's orders to the letter. The tribune now nodded, and ordered his thousand guardsmen to fall in. The Praetorians then marched down the hill and through the heart of the city to their barracks outside the old city walls to the northeast.

As the Praetorians marched away, cohorts of the Night Watch marched up the hill to take their place, and quickly surrounded the Temple of Apollo. The Night Watch was a unit of seven cohorts, each a thousand men strong, created by Augustus to act as police and firemen at Rome in the hours of darkness. Night Watch soldiers were all former slaves, and they didn't have the military training, prestige, or salaries of the Praetorians, but they used similar arms and equipment. The Night Watch commander, the prefect Graecinus Laco, now greeted Macro and took up his position at the head of his troops. This replacement of the Praetorian cohort by the Night Watch had been prearranged between Macro and Prefect Laco the night before.

Macro then entered the Temple of Apollo. Inside, the benches of the senators, the curile chairs, and the Senate water clocks had all been set out in preparation for a full day of Senate debate. The Senate attendants stood around the perimeter, brushing away yawns. The official stenographers were at their desks, readying pots of ink and quills and fitting scrolls of paper into wooden document holders in preparation for their note-taking. The official record of what took place here would be sent to the emperor on Capri for his perusal and then returned to Rome, to be kept in the Tabularium.

In the crowd of chattering senators inside the temple, Macro located the presiding consul, Memmius Regulus, and handed him the emperor's sealed letter. The consul nodded, then made his way to his president's chair. With an anticipatory smile, Sejanus eyed the document in the consul's hand as Macro made his way outside once more. All around Sejanus, fawning senators clapped him on the back and congratulated him for the upcoming award of tribunicial powers, as the word of Sejanus's expectations spread throughout the chamber. With Macro's departure, the session was convened. Outside, leaving Night Watch prefect Laco in charge of the encircling of troops, Macro went down the hill and hurried across town to the Castra Praetoria, to ensure that his orders were followed to the letter and the Praetorian troops did not leave their barracks.

The consul Regulus broke the seal on the emperor's lengthy letter and came to his feet. His fellow senators fell silent. An expectant Sejanus had seated himself in the front row, with other former consuls on either side of him. Regulus began to read aloud. The letter discussed a number of matters. The first section was of minor importance. The next contained a mild censure for Sejanus. The consul read on. There was another side issue, then another matter for which Tiberius criticized Sejanus, more acutely this time. Sensing trouble in the wind, senators sitting around Sejanus began to move away from him.

Yet the man himself seemed oblivious to either censure or the movement around him. Sejanus's attention was glued to the consul, as he waited to hear the news he had been led to believe to expect—that he was to be granted the tribunicial powers, which equaled those of the emperor. Sejanus must have believed that these admonishments being read out by the consul were Tiberius's way of making the award of the power of veto more acceptable to the Senate. These charges seemed minor, and easy to bat away.

Regulus read on. And then he was saying that the emperor required that two senators who were Sejanus's close associates be punished severely. As for Sejanus, said the emperor's letter, he was to be placed under guard. Praetors and civil tribunes moved to stand behind Sejanus, but he seemed not to comprehend what was going on, and remained in his seat. Throughout the chamber, astonished senators were talking animatedly behind hands and in hushed voices.

"Sejanus, come forward," called the consul Regulus. When Sejanus, looking dazed, ignored him, Regulus called to him a second time, but still Sejanus failed to move. Now Regulus pointed to him, and with a raised voice said, "Sejanus, come here!"

"Me?" responded Sejanus, who wasn't accustomed to being addressed like this. "Are you calling me?"[7]

Slowly Sejanus came to his feet, and as he did, the prefect Laco, the Night Watch commander, appeared beside him with one hand on the hilt of the sword sheathed on his left hip. Sejanus, of course, was wearing a toga, and was unarmed, as were all senators. Regulus finished the reading of the emperor's letter, and then hundreds of senators began yelling, shaking their fists, and venting their spleen on Sejanus. Many who had once fawned on him now competed with one another to show how much they hated him, in a frantic bid to disassociate themselves from Sejanus and his looming fate. Others, Sejanus's secret enemies, men who had held their tongues for almost two decades, yelled with venomous joy.

The consul Regulus raised a hand, and slowly the tumult subsided. Now, instead of calling on the entire House to vote, in case Sejanus's friends and relatives stuck by him in sufficient numbers to defeat a vote against him, the consul turned to a single senator, and asked him if he thought that Sejanus should be imprisoned, as the emperor had asked. The unidentified senator said that he did indeed believe that Sejanus should be imprisoned. Regulus ordered Sejanus taken off to jail.

Laco took Sejanus by the arm and marched him, speechless, from the chamber, with all fifteen serving praetors and the other lesser magistrates forming around the pair as a judicial escort. Sejanus would have been expecting to be able to call on the Praetorian troops outside the temple to set him free. But to his utter amazement, when the group emerged from the temple he found that his Praetorians had almost magically been replaced by Laco's Night Watch troops. Only now, as chains were fastened around his wrists, did Sejanus realize that his downfall had been carefully planned and that he was doomed.

Both Suetonius and Cassius Dio would express the belief that Tiberius had planned Sejanus's overthrow when he appointed him his joint consul for A.D. 31, late the previous year.[8] Yet that overthrow did not take place for ten months after Sejanus became a consul, and indeed after he had ceased to be a consul. It seems that in reality the decision to terminate Sejanus's career came only shortly before the act itself, sometime in the first half of October A.D. 31.

The consensus among historians of the period was that Tiberius's decision to destroy Sejanus was sponsored by Tiberius's sister-in-law Antonia, the mother of Germanicus. Antonia had continued to live at her son's Palatine palace, where, after the arrest of Agrippina, she had raised Germanicus's children Caligula, Agrippina the Younger,

Drusilla, and Julia. A strong woman, Antonia "was greatly esteemed by Tiberius in all matters," according to the Jewish historian Josephus.[9] Josephus, who was born five years after the fall of Sejanus, would write that Antonia came to learn of Sejanus's plot to overthrow Tiberius, a plot that involved senators, freedmen, and soldiers.[10] Someone deeply involved with that plot must have gone to Antonia and told her all about it.

Antonia put the details of the plot in a letter, which she dictated to one of her servants, the young freedwoman Caenis—later mistress of the emperor Vespasian. Using a stylus, the Roman penknife, Caenis wrote the letter on wax tablets, from which she would transcribe it to papyrus with pen and ink. These wax tablets were commonly allowed to dry out and kept as a record of outgoing correspondence, but Dio says that to ensure that there was no record of this letter, Antonia ordered Caenis to erase the writing on the wax as soon as the papyrus version was completed and dispatched.[11] Antonia then sent Pallas, her most trusted freedman, hurrying from Rome to the isle of Capri with the letter. At this time Sejanus was living at the Palatium at Rome and so was not on Capri and in a position to intercept Pallas. According to Josephus, Tiberius, because he trusted his sister-in-law, agreed to see Pallas when he arrived at his Capri villa. Pallas was able to then hand over the letter from his mistress.[12]

We do not know the contents of the letter, but the details of Sejanus's plot described by Antonia must have been comprehensive, convincing, and above all terrifying, to motivate the elderly Tiberius to act so swiftly and so decisively against a man he had trusted implicitly and relied on for so many years. It appears that Antonia's warning must have also implicated the two senators named by Tiberius in his letter to the Senate. Once the decision was made to move against Sejanus, Macro was given the task of masterminding the arrest of the Praetorian commander at Rome, in a way that prevented the Praetorian Guard from intervening on his behalf.

Macro had deliberately arrived at Rome in darkness on the night of October 16 so he could prepare for the coup against Sejanus the next day without his presence being known or his movements observed. He first went to Night Watch commander Laco at his quarters, and then to the consul Regulus at his home, bringing them both into the plan for the overthrow of Sejanus the next morning. Regulus was chosen because he was loyal to Tiberius. His fellow consul at this time,

Fulcinius Trio—the same Trio who had frittered away part of the prosecution time at the Germanicus murder trial eleven years earlier—had
long been warm to Sejanus and could be expected to warn him, so Trio
was excluded from the small circle of senior men who needed to know
what was going to occur the next morning.

Meanwhile, back on Capri, Tiberius waited anxiously at the Jovean
Villa for news that the arrest of Sejanus had gone as planned. In case
the arrest went awry and the Praetorian Guard rose up in support of
Sejanus, the warships of the Tyrrhenian Fleet at Misenum near Naples
had been ordered to lay off Capri in readiness to take the emperor to
safety among the legions in the East. In addition, if Tiberius were to be
killed in a pro-Sejanus revolt, says Suetonius, Macro had orders to release Germanicus's son Drusus Germanicus from imprisonment in the
Palatium basement and then take him to the troops and declare him
the new emperor.[13]

Bonfires had been prepared on the Italian mainland opposite Capri.
If the fires were lit in a certain way, it was a warning to Tiberius that
the arrest plan had backfired, that Macro had failed to secure Sejanus,
and that the emperor must flee. If the fires burned in a different pattern, it meant that all had gone to plan, that Sejanus was in custody
and Macro was in control at Rome. Suetonius says that Tiberius stood
on a clifftop at Capri all through October 17 until he saw the bonfire
signal that informed him that the counterrevolution had been a complete success and Sejanus was in custody.[14]

Sejanus was dragged to the City Prison guarded like a runaway
slave, says Dio.[15] On the way there, roughly hauled along by Night
Watch soldiers, Sejanus was so humiliated by his fall from grace that
he attempted to cover his head with his purple-bordered toga so that
the people he passed along the way wouldn't see his face and recognize
him. But his escort quickly uncovered his head so that his shame
would be all the worse. Several soldiers even slapped his face for attempting to hide his identity. All along his route, as ordinary people
saw who it was the soldiers and magistrates had in chains, crowds gathered to throw insults at the man they had come to loathe and fear during his years in office. This was a man universally considered a
monster, who had taken the lives of many good men and women.
When the soldiers told the people that their prisoner had been arrested
for planning to overthrow the emperor, members of the public jeered
him as he passed. Throngs of people rushed to where Sejanus's statues

had been erected around the city. They dragged them down, then kicked and bashed his images as if they were beating the man himself.

That afternoon, the Senate met again, this time in the Temple of Concord, close to the prison where Sejanus languished. This was a traditional meeting place for the Senate after Rome had been saved from one calamity or another. Seeing the general popularity of Sejanus's arrest, and noting that the Praetorian Guard had remained in its barracks and had not attempted to free its commander, a motion was proposed for Sejanus's immediate execution as a traitor, knowing the emperor would not oppose it. The motion was overwhelmingly carried. Instructions were sent to the prison for the execution of Sejanus at once. The Night Watch was ordered to also arrest Sejanus's eldest son and deliver him to the prison to share his father's fate.

Sejanus was garroted before the sun went down on October 17. His naked body was then cast down the Gemonian Stairs, and the public were permitted to do what they pleased to the cadaver for three days, before a hook was passed through his rotting corpse, which was hauled away. The mutilated corpse of Sejanus was tossed into the Tiber. His son was executed in the same manner.

A purge of Sejanus's followers now followed. It would go on for months and years, with accusations interminably cast about the Senate about this one and that one being a secret friend of Sejanus, and with many a conviction following. Sejanus's uncle, the general Junius Blaesus, apparently one of the two senators and close associates of Sejanus condemned in Tiberius's letter, immediately committed suicide. Some blatant friends of Sejanus tried to flee. Others stood their ground and faced the charges in the Senate.

Publius Vitellius, a former close friend of Germanicus and one of the three prosecutors in the Piso trial, had earned promotion to praetor under Sejanus and then appointment as the ex-praetor in charge of the military treasury. It was now alleged that Vitellius had handed the treasury keys to Sejanus to fund his planned rebellion against Tiberius. Vitellius patiently sat through several Senate sessions as colleagues assailed him with accusatory speeches, then calmly borrowed a stylus, Using the penknife, Vitellius, uncle of future emperor Aulus Vitellius, slit his wrists, and died to satisfy the current emperor's lust for revenge.

As scores of senators and knights were accused of and condemned for being satellites of Sejanus, the lust for venegeance knew no bounds. Sejanus's eldest son, a young man, had been executed, but now the

Senate decided it was necessary to also punish his two younger children, a boy and a girl. Both were dragged from the arms of their mother, Apicata, Sejanus's former wife, and taken to the City Prison. Neither was yet a teenager. The boy, says Tacitus, was aware of his impending doom, but the little girl kept asking what she had done wrong. She promised that whatever it was, she would be a good girl in the future, if only she received a spanking. The boy was garroted. But the executioner was reminded that under Roman law a virgin could not be executed. He came up with a gruesome solution, raping the child before strangling her.[16]

The children's mother, Apicata, had waited, in tears, outside the prison, begging for their release. Now she was told to go to the Gemonian Stairs, where she found their little bodies. Prevented from even taking away her dead infants for cremation, she went home and wrote Tiberius a bitter letter. In it, she told the emperor how her ex-husband, Sejanus, and the emperor's niece Livilla, sister of Germanicus, Sejanus's second wife, had planned and carried out the poisoning of Tiberius's son and heir, Drusus the Younger, even naming the doctor Eudemus and Drusus's eunuch Lygdus as chief players in the murder plot. After sealing the letter and sending it to Tiberius, Apicata took her own life.

Shocked by Apicata's letter, Tiberius immediately had Eudemus and Lygdus arrested. Under torture, the pair admitted their part in the murder and gave details implicating Livilla and Sejanus in the poisoning of Drusus. Some later historians would question these confessions. Apicata's accusations had been born out of spite, they would say, while confessions gained through torture could not necessarily be taken at face value, because most prisoners undergoing torture would say and admit to anything just to end their pain. Yet no one could deny that Livilla had been Sejanus's lover for years and had subsequently married him once her first husband, Drusus the Younger, had conveniently died. In light of Sejanus's later progressive and systematic removal of the family of Germanicus, the probability is high that he and Livilla had conspired to murder Drusus in just the way that Apicata, Eudemus, and Lygdus described.

Tiberius certainly believed the confessions. On the strength of the letter from Apicata and the admissions of Eudemus and Lygdus, he ordered the arrest of Livilla. She, like her sister-in-law Agrippina, was now held in seclusion. Tiberius could not bring himself to order

Livilla's execution, because she was the daughter of Antonia. His sister-in-law had, after all, been "the greatest benefactress to Tiberius"[17] through her warning to him about the Sejanus plot. Antonia herself was not as charitable; she also believed the accusations against Livilla, and was disgusted with her daughter. "I have heard," Dio was to write, "that of her own accord Antonia killed her daughter by starving her."[18]

Tiberius rewarded Macro with Sejanus's job as prefect of the Praetorian Guard. The Senate attempted to add rewards of their own—for Macro, the rank of an ex-praetor, and for Night Watch commander Laco, the rank of an ex-quaestor, giving them both entry into the Senate, along with large cash donations and various other privileges. But Macro and Laco were both wise enough to politely decline the sort of Senate honors that a Sejanus would have welcomed, to show the emperor that they had acted only out of loyalty to him, not for rewards.

The persecution of associates of Sejanus continued. Latiaris, leader of the scheme that had trapped Germanicus's friend Sabinus into saying things he shouldn't have while colleagues had listened in the ceiling above, was condemned by the Senate and paid with his life. His three companions in that plot also received various punishments. Another of the Piso prosecutors, Germanicus's friend Quintus Servaeus, paid for his links with Sejanus, discreet as they had been; he was one of a number convicted in the thinning Senate for association with Sejanus. Bodies continued to cascade down the Gemonian Stairs.

Few members of Rome's upper classes were free from the fear of being embroiled in the purge of followers of Sejanus. One of the minority of men who had absolutely nothing to fear was Lucius Anneaus Seneca, son of Seneca, the renowned Spanish teacher of rhetoric, and nephew of Gaius Galerius, the prefect of Egypt. Destined to become famous as one of Rome's greatest philosphers, thirty-four-year-old Seneca arrived at Rome with his aunt Marcia in A.D. 31 shortly after the fall of Sejanus, having spent the past fifteen years in Egypt, well away from the malestrom of Roman politics. For more than a decade after he had met Germanicus in the East, Seneca had continued to live at Alexandria, working in the provincial administration of his uncle and in his spare time demonstrating a vast capacity for learning, among other things studying the geography and ethnology of both Egypt and India. Now, having brought under control the ill health that had sent him to Egypt, and with his uncle no longer governor of the province, Seneca arrived at Rome ambitious to make up for lost years and to make his name as a writer, lawyer, and politician.

While Seneca himself was not tainted by a connection with Sejanus, one of his brothers who lived at Rome did have a link to the disgraced Praetorian prefect. A year or two older than Seneca, the brother's original name had been Lucius Annaeus Novatus, but at Rome he had been adopted by a wealthy patron, Lucius Junius Gallio. Adoption of adult Romans was a common practice when rich men had no male children; otherwise, if they were to die without a son and heir, their estates went to the emperor. When a Roman was adopted in this way, he took the name of his adoptive father. So Seneca's elder brother had become Lucius Junius Gallio Jr. Lucius Junius Gallio Sr. was a known satellite of Sejanus,[19] and was suffering for it. In an attempt to win Tiberius's favor following Sejanus's destruction, Gallio Sr. had proposed in the Senate that the men of the Praetorian Guard receive special privileges in the theater. When he heard this, Tiberius exploded, declaring that Gallio was interfering with military affairs, the exclusive province of the emperor. Gallio found himself banished from the Senate, then from Italy. When he chose to take his exile on the pleasant Greek island of Lesbos, Tiberius ordered him confined in the houses of various leading citizens in Rome instead.

Fortunately for Seneca, he had a well-connected contact of his own, in the family of Germanicus. We are not told precisely how that connection was established, but the indications are that his aunt Marcia was a friend of Antonia, the mother of Germanicus, who was now very much in favor with Tiberius. Since she had exposed Sejanus, Antonia had become Tiberius's most trusted ally, and she had great influence with her brother-in-law. As an example of how great that influence became, Marcus Julius Agrippa, grandson of Herod the Great and the future King Herod Agrippa I of Judea, twice sought and received Antonia's help when he visited Italy and fell afoul of Tiberius. First she gave Agrippa a loan of 300,000 sesterces after Tiberius banned him from his court until his debts in Rome were paid. Then, after Agrippa was overheard by a servant making incautious remarks to Caligula about Tiberius and was arrested on the emperor's orders, Antonia convinced her brother-in-law to turn Agrippa's imprisonment into house arrest. Josephus says that through Antonia's intervention the centurion in charge of Agrippa's guard was even under orders to sit down to dine with him each day.[20]

It seems that Seneca's aunt Marcia took Seneca to the palace of Germanicus for an interview with Antonia, and there he met Antonia's grandson Caligula and her granddaughters, sixteen-year-old Agrippina the Younger, fifteen-year-old Drusilla, and fourteen-year-old Julia. Seneca would have been able to tell the girls how he had been acquainted with their father and mother in the East, and probably spoke of bouncing baby Julia on his knee on a visit to Germanicus and Agrippina the Elder at Daphne. This introduction quickly bore fruit—apparently on the recommendation of Antonia, Seneca was promptly made a quaestor by Tiberius, to serve on the staff of one of the consuls for the new year, A.D. 32. One of those two consuls was Gnaeus Domitius Ahenobarbus, husband of Agrippina the Younger, and it is probable that Seneca joined his staff via the Germanicus family connection.

Seneca's sudden, smooth elevation into a much-sought-after quaestor's position, which would give him automatic entry into the Senate once he had served his short term as quaestor, as well as acceptance into the imperial court, was in stark contrast to the bloody purge of pro-Sejanus freedmen, knights, and senators still taking place around him. As it turned out, Seneca's wilderness years in the East, which seemingly would have been a frustrating barrier to his launching a career at Rome, had insulated him from the mayhem of the Sejanus years and had given his career a launching pad free of the taint of association with the fallen Praetorian commander. Now, with Sejanus no longer around to persecute anyone connected with Agrippina and her children, and with Germanicus's mother in such strong favor with Tiberius, Seneca hitched his fortunes to those of the family of Germanicus. Time would tell whether it was a wise choice, for more members of Germanicus's family were destined to meet gruesome deaths before much more time had passed.

# X

# THE GERMANICUS
# EMPEROR

F or two years following the death of her great enemy Sejanus,
Germanicus's wife, Agrippina the Elder, still a prisoner on the
island of Pandateria, hung on to the hope that Tiberius would
end her banishment and allow her to return to Rome and her children.
Her son Drusus Germanicus was now also dead. For what reason we
don't know, some time after the execution of Sejanus the order had
come to the Palatium from the isle of Capri for the second son of
Germanicus to be starved to death in his basement cell. In his last
eight days of life, young Drusus had resorted to eating the straw from
his mattress. Tiberius even had the daily journal that had recorded
Drusus's life as a prisoner read to a horrified Senate. Senators had to
sit through turgid accounts of Drusus Germanicus's guards tormenting
the young man, and of his last, agonizing days.

In a letter to the Senate excusing his destruction of another of the
sons of Germanicus, Tiberius claimed that Drusus Germanicus had
been intent on "his own family's ruin" through his association with
Sejanus, and had possessed "a spirit that was hostile to the state."[1] Yet,
in his unpublished memoirs, which Suetonius would find at the Tabularium when he was put in charge of the imperial archives seventy
years later, Tiberius would assert that Sejanus had been executed because Tiberius had discovered that he was persecuting the sons of Germanicus. This was nonsense, as Suetonius would point out; with
Drusus Germanicus being killed sometime after Sejanus's removal,
the execution of Drusus Germancius was clearly Tiberius's idea.[2]

On October 17, A.D. 33, exactly two years to the day since the execution of Sejanus, Agrippina the Elder, widow of Germanicus, died on Pandataria. The official cause of her death was starvation, and the story was circulated that Agrippina had starved herself to death. But Tacitus speculated that this may have been a fiction created by Tiberius to free himself from blame for ordering the execution by starvation of the wife of Germanicus.[3] In announcing her death to the Senate in his latest missive, Tiberius claimed that Agrippina had previously had an affair with her brother-in-law Asinius Gallus, the man he had kept imprisoned incommunicado, without contact with a living soul, ever since his attempt to support Agrippina in the Senate. Tiberius had executed Gallus in the wave of executions that followed the downfall of Sejanus. Once Agrippina had learned this, the emperor claimed, she had decided to follow Gallus, and ended her own life.

The death of Agrippina was widely lamented. One senator, a close friend of Tiberius named Cocceius Nerva, became so depressed by the current state of Roman affairs in the wake of her death that he starved himself to death. Even if Tiberius deluded himself into believing that Agrippina had taken her own life and that Nero Germanicus and Drusus Germanicus had perished at the hands of Sejanus, few other people were fooled. Not only was it Romans who knew the truth. Suetonius says that King Artabanus of Parthia now wrote Tiberius a scathing letter in which he accused him of murdering his own immediate family.[4] "Dread of Germanicus," says Tacitus, had previously made Artabanus compliant to Rome, but following the death of Germanicus he had changed his behavior to one of "insolence to us."[5] With no dread of Tiberius, Artabanus had put a Parthian king over Armenia on the death of Artaxias, the king installed by Germanicus. Proving himself no Germanicus, Tiberius had failed to counter the loss of Armenia to the Parthians.

Shortly after Agrippina's death, Plancina, the widow of Gnaeus Piso, who had been accused of complicity in the murder of Germanicus but had escaped punishment after the Piso trial at the intercession of the emperor's mother, was charged with "notorious" behavior. Details of the charges involved were not recorded. Plancina committed suicide before she could be brought to trial. Now just one of the original suspects in the Germanicus murder case, Tiberius, survived.

Likewise, just one son of Germanicus, Caligula, now remained alive. To the minds of many, Caligula was also in great peril, for with the death of his mother, Agrippina, Tiberius summoned the boy to live with him on Capri. Caligula must have gone there expecting to sooner or later share the fate of his mother and elder brothers, so he set out to please Tiberius in any and every way he could, just to stay alive. Whatever the emperor told him to do or say, Caligula did. Suetonius was to say of Caligula and Tiberius during this period, "Never was there a worse slave, or a worse master."[6]

At the same time, Caligula began an affair with Ennia Naevia, the wife of Macro, the new Praetorian commander. Some later Roman authors believed that this affair was actually cultivated by Macro to control the young prince, but the Jewish writer Philo of Alexandria, who was to meet both Caligula and Macro as a member of an Egyptian Jewish delegation to Rome several years later, was convinced that Macro was "ignorant of the dishonor being done to his marriage bed and to his family."[7] According to Suetonius, Caligula even promised Ennia that he would marry her, putting the promise in writing.[8] Encouraged by his scheming wife, Macro spoke in Caligula's favor to Tiberius, even giving a personal guarantee that the young man would be loyal, trustworthy, and obedient. In short, Philo of Alexandria was to write, Macro told Tiberius, on behalf of Caligula, all the sorts of things a person could say on behalf of his brother or his own child.[9]

Tiberius lived on Capri for another four years after the death of Agrippina the Elder, never again setting foot inside Rome, keeping Caligula with him all that time. In March A.D. 37, the now ailing seventy-three-year-old Tiberius left Capri and took up residence nearby on the mainland, at the Marian Villa, built 150 years before by seven-times consul of the Roman Republic Gaius Marius. The villa had later been used by Julius Caesar as his coastal resort. Situated on a promontory near the Misenum naval base, the villa had a commanding view of the Bay of Naples. Tiberius's small court, including twenty-four-year-old Caligula and Praetorian prefect Macro, accompanied him in this relocation.

The health of Tiberius continued to decline, and on March 13, a visiting friend of the emperor, a freedman named Charicles, who also was a doctor, assured Macro that Tiberius would not live for more than two days. Late in the evening of the fifteenth, the Ides of March, Tiberius, in his bed, appeared to stop breathing. Caligua was congratulated by all at the villa for surviving the despot and succeeding him as emperor. But in the early hours of the following day, word came that

Tiberius was sitting up and calling for food. Panic sent men flying in all directions, while a stunned and terrified Caligula was left speechless. Macro, thinking fast, ordered everyone out of the emperor's bedchamber. Then, says Tacitus, he had Tiberius smothered to death with a pile of clothing.[10] Tiberius, second emperor of Rome, the man at the center of so many allegations concerning the murder of his nephew and adopted son Germanicus, had himself been murdered.

Tiberius's will made Caligula and his cousin Tiberius Gemellus his joint heirs. Tiberius Gemellus was one of the twin sons of Germanicus's adoptive brother, Drusus the Younger, and sister, Livilla, born shortly after the death of Germanicus; the other twin had died in infancy. Macro took Tiberius's will to the Senate and had it annulled; Gaius Caesar—or Caligula, as we know him—was declared Tiberius's sole heir and the new emperor of Rome. His mother's ambition, of seeing a son of Germanicus take the throne of Rome, had been achieved, but Agrippina had not lived to see it happen. Caligula ascending the throne, Suetonius was to say, seemed to the Roman people to be like a dream come true. Inspired by "remembrance of Germanicus, and feelings for a family that had been almost wiped out by a succession of murders," citizens and soldiers alike throughout the empire celebrated the accession of Caligula as Rome's third emperor.[11]

Caligula cemented public favor when he took as his name, now that he was emperor, Gaius Caesar Germanicus, a name that honored his father. For the same reason, he changed the name of the month of September to Germanicus, just as the month of Sextillius had previously been renamed July in honor of Julius Caesar. Caligula's popularity knew no bounds. When he presided over Tiberius's funeral, the people crowded around him, calling him names like "baby," "chicken," and "pet."[12] That popularity reached stellar heights when, within days of Tiberius's funeral, Caligula boarded a warship that took him to Pandataria and Ponza. From each island he collected the remains of his mother, Agrippina, and his brother Nero Germanicus. Back at Rome, he ceremonially consigned these remains and those of his other brother, Drusus Germanicus, to the Mausoleum of Augustus, placing their urns alongside that of Germanicus.

Caligula now granted his seventy-three-year-old grandmother Antonia the same honors enjoyed by Tiberius's mother, including the title Augusta; she was to die six weeks after he became emperor. He also granted special honors to his sisters, Agrippina the Younger, Drusilla, and Julia. In the Forum, Caligula publicly burned what he said was all written evidence compiled by Tiberius against members of the family of Germanicus and their supporters. He commenced prosecutions against all who had persecuted his mother and brothers. He cancled all prosecutions that had been pending at the time of Tiberius's death. And he recalled all who had been exiled by Tiberius. Among those to return to Rome as a result of Caligula's mass pardon was Suillius, his father's former quaestor. All these measures were hugely popular with the Roman people.

For seven months, Caligula's reign was marked by reason, reforms, and public rejoicing. He made his overlooked uncle Claudius, brother of Germanicus, his fellow consul for two months, from July 1 that year of A.D. 37. He improved the legal system, extended the Saturnalia to five days, and allowed the publication of banned books. King Artabanus of Parthia even sent overtures of friendship in remembrance of Caligula's father. It was all good. Then, suddenly, Caligula fell seriously and dangerously ill. A vast throng of anxious Romans crowded around his Palatium on the Palatine Hill and waited for news, day and night. Suetonius would write that some people carried placards volunteering to die instead of Caligula, while others vowed to become gladiators if the gods permitted him to live.[13]

Live Caligula did, but the illness had affected him mentally. Once he recovered, he was a changed man. Suetonius was to describe the new Caligula as "the Monster,"[14] and attributed his change in personality to "brain sickness."[15] Caligula now declared himself a god. He squandered vast amounts of money on public spectacles. He personally drove in chariot races; in one race, against several senators, he ran over and crushed the leg of Aulus Vitellius, nephew of the late Publius Vitellius, and future emperor. Caligula had his cousin and potential rival Tiberius Gemellus executed by a Praetorian tribune, without charge or trial. He had the throat of his father-in-law, Marcus Silanus, slit with a razor. He executed his close friend Marcus Lepidus, husband of his sister Drusilla. He invited his cousin Ptolemy, king of Mauretania, to Rome, then executed him. He eliminated Macro, the Praetorian commander who had made his reign possible, and Macro's wife, Ennia. "It is said that the wretched man [Macro] was forced to kill himself," Philo of Alexandria was to note, "and his wife also experienced the same miserable fate."[16]

Caligula seized other men's wives, including a bride on her wedding day, and made them his mistresses. He committed incest with all three of his sisters. Suetonius claimed that his grandmother Antonia caught him in bed with his sister Drusilla, and for this he had her poisoned,[17] but as Antonia died very early in Caligula's reign, when he was going through his "angelic" period, this seems unlikely. A rumor had it that Antonia had actually taken her own life. When Caligula's sister Drusilla died, some said giving birth to Caligula's child, he declared her a goddess. Then, in A.D. 39, he accused his other sisters, Agrippina the Younger and Julia, of immoral acts with Drusilla's late husband Lepidus and others, and banished both sisters to the Pontian Islands—Ponza and Pandataria. In that same year, Caligula married his mistress Caesonia Milonia, a woman considerably older than he who had three children from another marriage. She had wanted to marry him for some time, but he agreed only after she had given birth to his child, a girl, Julia Drusilla.

Caligula fantasized that he was really the son of Augustus and his daughter Julia, not the son of Germanicus and Agrippina, and would fly into a rage if reminded that his grandfather was Marcus Agrippa, a commoner. Any man who was handsome or clever could find himself executed or hauled into an amphitheater to fight for his life, simply because Caligula was jealous of him. An author who displeased him was burned alive on a cross in an arena. In A.D. 39, while attending a session of the Senate during which Lucius Seneca, who was making a name for himself as an orator and lawyer by this time, successfully argued for the acquittal of an accused senator, Caligua was so displeased by Seneca's elegant oratorial skills—he called him a "textbook orator" and "sand without lime"[18]—that he ordered his execution. Seneca was saved only when one or another of Caligula's mistresses convinced the emperor not to go through with the execution on the grounds that one of Seneca's long-term illnesses—said to be tuberculosis—would kill him soon enough anyway.

Deciding to invade Britain, Caligula created two new legions to add to the twenty-five already in existence, and in the summer of A.D. 40 assembled a massive army in Gaul. Lining up the legions on the beach near today's Boulogne, facing the water, he ordered the artillery to bombard the sea, and had the troops collect seashells as war trophies. He awarded himself a Triumph for his so-called victory, and returned to Rome. By January A.D. 41, four months after Caligula's return from Gaul, his behavior was considered more than erratic; it was insane. And it had to be terminated.

Three separate plots to kill Caligula were now in existence. Conceived by leading men of the state, they had been in the works for many months. Two plots had been put together by senators and one of Caligula's most senior staff members, the Palatium freedman Callistus. Another was conceived by officers of Caligula's Praetorian Guard and German Guard. The three plots eventually melded into one, with the tribune Cassius Chaerea of the Praetorian Guard taking the lead. The plotters set down the assassination for January 21, the first day of the four-day Palatine Games in honor of the deified emperor Augustus, and made their preparations.

# XI

# THE MURDER OF
# CALIGULA

T he plotters had agreed that they would murder Caligula on the first day of the Palatine Games. But when the day arrived, most of the conspirators acquired cold feet, and the murder was put off, first to the next day, then to the next. And still the deed was not done. On the night of January 23, with just one festival day remaining, and with Caligula planning to sail soon to Alexandria for an inspection tour of Egypt, the frustrated Praetorian tribune Cassius Chaerea told the other conspirators at a secret meeting that they must act now or lose their opportunity forever. As he would be officer of the day on the twenty-fourth, commanding the Praetorian Guard cohort on Palatine duty, Chaerea volunteered to personally strike the first blow to eliminate the mad young emperor, if everyone else played their part.

A career soldier of about forty-five, Chaerea had served under Caligula's father, Germanicus, during his German campaigns of A.D. 14–16, first as an officer cadet of one of the Rhine legions, and later as a prefect of auxiliaries. Chaerea had made a name for himself early, as a "high-spirited youth"[1] who had drawn his sword to protect the commanding general of the Army of the Lower Rhine, Aulus Caecina, at Cologne, during the army mutiny of A.D. 14. By A.D. 41, the tribune Chaerea had been commanding a one-thousand-man cohort of the Praetorian Guard for some time, and had come to be regularly teased by Caligula, who accused him of being a girl when he was unenthusiastic about torturing innocent victims of Caligula's arbitrary moods. When, as officer of the day, Chaerea had asked for the next day's watchword for the city's guards, Caligula would scornfully give him watchwords such as "Love" or the names of goddesses and female mytholgical figures. For both personal and idealistic motives, Chaerea was determined to cut the cancer that was Caligula from the heart of Roman society.

Before dawn on January 24, tens of thousands of Romans flooded through the single public entrance to the temporary wooden drama theater erected in the Palatium grounds every year for the festival. Twenty-nine-year-old Caligula—tall, slim, pasty, and balding—also arrived, via a second entrance used by the theater's players and musicians. This entrance connected with Caligula's Palatium, a new palace built on the Palatine Hill separate from but connected to Augustus's original palace, which was now called the Old Palatium, and a little above the palace built by Caligula's father, Germanicus. Before the day began, Caligula, accompanied by an entourage of friends and servants, presided over the customary animal sacrifice at an altar. To Caligula's great amusement, the priest conducting the sacrifice of a flamingo managed to spray the bird's blood over the tunic of one of Caligula's companions, the senator Publius Nonius Asprenas, a man in his forties who had been a consul four years before.

With his entourage—including Cassius Chaerea, the on-duty Praetorian tribune—Caligula then took his seat in the imperial box, on the right side of the tiers of wooden seats that were occupied randomly by senators, knights, freedmen, and slaves, a mixture of men, women, and children. In unusually good spirits, Caligula sat through the morning's events, which culminated in a play about the crucifixion of a thief and a pantomime by a Greek troupe describing the assassination of a Greek king, both of which involved copious amounts of fake blood. Toward the middle of the day, as a performance was at its height, one of the emperor's companions, Marcus Cluvius Rufus, a senator who would one day write his memoirs and decribe this day, looked around as a dwarf named Vatinius took a seat in the imperial box. The freedman son of a shoemaker, Vatinius had amused the emperor so much with his quick wit over the past few years that he had been made a rich man.

"Any news?" whispered Cluvius Rufus to Vatinius.

"Only that a game called 'Slaughter of Tyrants' is to be played today," the dwarf replied with a knowing look.[2]

Rufus paled. He was one of the assassination conspirators, and he was suddenly afraid that Vatinius knew all about the murder plot. He tried to make a joke of it, cautioning Vatinius not to say anything to anyone else in case the actors heard they would have competition. As lunchtime arrived, the tribune Chaerea, sitting behind the emperor, came to his feet and left the box. The plan was for Chaerea and several other officers to jump Caligula outside the theater when he left for lunch. Now the senator Annius Minucianus, a particularly nervous party to the plot, who was sitting beside the emperor, began to worry that Chaerea might lose heart and fail to go through with the assassination. Deciding to go out and find Chaerea and ensure that he followed through on his resolution to strike the first blow, Minucianus came to his feet.

As he did, Caligula reached up and grabbed hold of Minucianus's tunic. "Where do you think you're going?" he demanded.[3]

Minucianus gulped and resumed his seat. There he sat, as nervous as a man whose wife was about to give birth, until, after a few minutes, he rose again. This time Caligula, apparently thinking Minucianus must be answering a call of nature, let him go. In the corridors outside the theater, Minucianus found Chaerea and a number of other officers of the Praetorian Guard congregated, and primed to act. As the middle of the day arrived, the assassins waited impatiently for Caligula to leave the theater. But the emperor failed to emerge, and Chaerea the tribune became increasingly agitated.

Inside the theater, fruit was being thrown by slaves to the audience, with the emperor's compliments. As this was going on, the senator Asprenas, who was also in on the plot, leaned toward the emperor and asked whether he himself was ready for lunch. Caligula was feeling queasy after a large formal banquet the previous evening, and he was not yet all that interested in more food. Shaking his head, Caligula continued to watch the play in progress. With the time approaching two o'clock, Asprenas then suggested that the emperor would find his appetite again after a visit to the baths. The exact time is disputed—Josephus[4] put it during the ninth hour, at about 2:00 P.M., while the less reliable Suetonius[5] made it during the seventh hour, between noon and 12:45 P.M.

With a sigh, Caligula agreed to Asprenas's suggestion. Coming to his feet, the emperor moved toward the theater door via which he had made his entrance. The members of his entourage all followed Caligula's lead. As he lingered to chat with the ex-consul Lucius Paulus Arruntius, the others strolled toward the double doors. On the other side of the doors, the tribune Chaerea was about to reenter the theater

with the determination to kill Caligula where he sat, but now word
was passed from inside that the emperor was on his way out. On learning this, Chaerea and several colleagues hurried away down a passageway to prepare an ambush. The theater doors opened onto a large
gallery, which was lined with waiting imperial servants, both freedmen
and slaves, and several centurions of the Praetorian Guard. A narrow
passageway led from the gallery, and off this there were a number of
partitioned areas that served as dressing rooms and storage rooms for
actors and musicians.

Caligula's uncle, the fifty-year-old Claudius, was the first to emerge
through the theater door. He went on ahead, limping as he favored his
clubfoot, accompanied by Marcus Vinicius, husband of Caligula's exiled youngest sister, Julia, and Publius Valerius Asiaticus, an ex-consul
who had been a loyal and valued friend of Caligula's grandmother Antonia. Caligula and Arruntius followed some distance behind, deep in
conversation. As the emperor emerged from the theater with Arruntius, followed by a squad of bearded soldiers of his German Guard
bodyguard, palace staff pressed forward to also follow, but they were
held back by the waiting Praetorian centurions. Claudius and his two
companions were out of sight by the time Caligula and Arruntius left
the gallery and entered the passageway.

Ahead, Claudius, Vinicius, and Asiaticus had been met by the tribune Chaerea and a party of Praetorians. The three of them were hustled away, to a chamber in Caligula's palace called the Hermaeum,
dedicated to the god Hermes—the Greek equivalent of the Roman
god Mercury, the messenger. Here, the three of them were told, the
emperor would meet them. Behind Caligula, the Praetorian centurions
had barred entry to the passageway, keeping out both imperial staff and
the men of the emperor's bodyguard. The German soldiers began to
argue with the centurions, saying in their heavily accented Latin that
they must be allowed to pass so they could catch up with the emperor,
yet being hesitant to push their way by centurions, their superiors, who
pretended not to understand the foreigners.

Caligula and Arruntius turned into a side passage that led to the
palace of Germanicus, where Caligula intended to take his bath. Members of the emperor's household staff, including the bearers of his litter,
could be seen waiting ahead. Beyond them again, in the atrium of the
palace of Germanicus, a boys choir from the province of Achaea in
southern Greece stood practicing a hymn they were scheduled to sing

in the emperor's honor in the theater that afternoon. A voice called to Caligula from behind. Caligula half-turned, to see the tribune Chaerea striding toward him in company with several Praetorian centurions and Cornelius Sabinus, a former gladiator who had replaced Macro as prefect of the German Guard.

As the two parties joined, Chaerea asked Caligula for the watchword for the next day. A new watchword, or password, was distributed to all soldiers on sentry duty at Rome every day, the same way that watchwords were daily distributed in legion camps around the empire. Traditionally, in legion camps, the watchword for the next day was given at sundown by the senior officer present. At Rome it was always given by the emperor or, in his absence, by the consuls. In Caligula's Rome, the formality of waiting until sundown was not observed—the officer of the day had to take whatever opportunity he could to ask the emperor for the next day's watchword.

"Jupiter," said Caligula with a smile.[6] Jupiter was the principal male god of Rome. He was also the god responsible for the weather— storms in particular.

"So be it," said the tribune Chaerea, who was primed to create a storm of his own.[7]

Weeks before, Caligula had received a warning from the Oracle of Fortune at the shrine at Antium in central Italy to beware of a man named Cassius. On the strength of that warning, Caligula had ordered the arrest of the wrong Cassius—the innocent Cassius Longinus, Roman governor of the province of Asia.

As Caligula turned to continue on, Cassius Chaerea quickly drew his sword.

"Take this!" Chaerea yelled before plunging the gleaming, twenty-inch blade into the back of Caligula's neck. The blade passed through the lower part of Caligula's skull, splitting his jawbone, just as he was turning back to Chaerea.[8]

Chaerea removed his bloodied sword. Caligula staggered, but remained on his feet. "I'm not dead!" he said with a gasp, as blood coursed from his mouth. He looked at his assailant in wonder, almost as if to say that he could not be killed.[9]

The German Guard's prefect Sabinus, who had been in on the murder plot with Chaerea from the beginning, now grasped Caligula by the shoulders and forced him down onto his knees "Strike again!" Sabinus called to Chaerea, as he also drew his own sword.[10]

Chaerea did strike again, this time plunging his angled sword into Caligula's back, between the shoulder blades and the neck, aiming for the heart. The blow missed its target, with the tip of Chaerea's sword hitting Caligula's breastbone.[11] Out came the blade again. Yet still the emperor did not die. Yelling almost maniacally, Sabinus and the centurions all plunged their swords into Caligula. According to Suetonius, the emperor received a further thirty wounds, including thrusts to the genitals.[12] As he lay writhing in agony on the floor, the fatal blow, Josephus wrote, was delivered by the centurion Aquila, ending "this virtuous slaughter."[13] So it was that the emperor Gaius Caesar Germanicus, third and last remaining son of Germanicus, was brutally murdered. And as he died, says Dio, Caligula "learned from personal experience that he was not a god."[14]

At the time of the commencement of the attack on Caligula, the emperor's terrified companion Arruntius had run back toward the theater to summon the German Guard. As he came down the passage yelling that there was murder afoot, the waylaid German Guards drew their swords, pushed their way by the centurions in their path, and came dashing to the fallen Caligula. By the time they reached their emperor, they found their own prefect Cornelius Sabinus standing over the bloodied corpse. Chaerea and the centurions with him had meanwhile run into the palace of Germanicus. Sabinus told the Germans that the assassins had gone in the opposite direction. The tempers of the shocked guardsmen flared; Caligula had paid them well, and now they were potentially without a job. All they could think of was vengeance. Led by Sabinus, whom they failed to connect with the assassination, they ran toward Caligula's palace, swords in hand and yelling angrily in their native tongue.

The first person of note encountered by the enraged Germans was the conspirator Publius Asprenas, who had heard the ruckus and was coming from the Hermaeum to find out if the assassination had been successful. Seeing blood on Asprenas's tunic—from the sacrificial ceremony that morning—the Germans assumed that this was the blood of the emperor and that Asprenas had been one of the assassins. German sword blades flashed. Asprenas was cut to pieces. Next, in their fury, the Germans came on the elderly ex-consul Lucius Norbanus Balbus. Despite his age, he had great strength, and when a German Guard took a swipe at him, the senator sidestepped the blow, then grabbed the man's sword arm. As he strugggled with his opponent, the other

Germans plunged their swords into the senator's back, and he fell down dead on the spot.

The Germans' next victim was a young senator, Publius Anteius. He had come hurrying quite deliberately from the theater to see for himself that Caligula was dead, and to gloat, for he hated the young emperor after Caligula had banished and then executed his father, who had served as a general under Germanicus on the Rhine. Unarmed Anteius and several freedmen with him paid with their lives at the hands of the bloodthirsty Germans.

The prefect Sabinus had meanwhile sent a soldier to summon all the men of the German Guard in Rome at that time—up to four of the unit's ten cohorts were always stationed at the Palatium, with the balance rotating around several towns outside Rome. As many as two thousand Germans came at the run, and, on Sabinus's orders, the Germans surrounded the temporary Palatine theater. There, Sabinus assured his men, the emperor's assailants must be hiding. Most of these German troops believed that Caligula was still alive, and so would reward them well if they found those who had attacked him. The majority of the people in the theater, meanwhile, had remained in their seats, not knowing for certain what was going on. Conflicting reports had reached the theater; some said that Caligula was dead, others that he had survived the attempt on his life and was in the hands of a surgeon. As German Guards flooded in through the two doors to the theater with their swords drawn, panic seized the thousands of members of the public inside. Wailing pitiously, men and women begged the Germans to spare their lives.

At the same time, the ex-consul Arruntius, who had been with Caligula when he was cut down, climbed up on the plinth of a pillar so he could be seen and called to the German troops to put up their swords, as the emperor was dead and nothing could be accomplished by indiscriminately killing people. Civil tribunes in the theater followed his example, and the city crier Euaristus boomed out the same message in his loud voice. The German troops finally realized that their emperor and employer was indeed dead. With no one to reward them, the Germans, lost and confused, desisted from harassing the theater audience. In a sudden rush they departed the theater, and swept through the Palatium in disorder. Some Germans paraded the severed heads of Asprenus, Norbanus Balbus, and Anteius around the corridors. Others began to loot the palace. Fighting even broke out in the Germans' own ranks.

Caligula's uncle Claudius, meanwhile, had been deserted in the Hermaeum, and had waited patiently there for Caligula to come. But now, hearing the uproar throughout the palace and realizing that murder was in the air, he looked for somewhere to hide. Seeing a nearby balcony, he drew the curtains in front of it and hid behind them. Soon after, a group of soldiers of the German Guard came into the room. One of them, a common soldier named Gratus,[15] spotted Claudius's feet beneath the curtains. Throwing back the curtains, Gratus revealed the terrified Claudius, who dropped to his knees and clasped the soldier's knees. Sobbing, Claudius begged to be allowed to leave.[16]

Gratus, recognizing Claudius as the brother of Germanicus and uncle of Caligula, turned to his comrades. "This is a Germanicus!" he exclaimed. "Let's make him our new emperor!"[17]

# XII

# THE NEW GERMANICUS EMPEROR

As the bearded comrades of the German Guard soldier Gratus crowded around Claudius, looking down at him with grins on their faces, Claudius, cringing on his bended knees, was convinced that they were planning to kill him, just as he believed that some of these very men had killed Caligula. But when he realized that they were seeking vengeance for the death of his nephew, he begged them to spare his life, swearing that he had no knowledge of who had killed Caligula.

Gratus smiled, and took Claudius by the right hand. "You can stop worrying about saving yourself, my lord," he assured him, helping him to his feet. "You should be elevating your thoughts, and thinking about ruling the empire, which the gods, in their concern for the habitable world, have commited to your virtuous hands by removing Gaius [Caligula]. So come with us and accept your ancestral throne."[1]

A stunned Claudius was escorted from the Palatium by the band of German soldiers who had found him, and placed in a litter. Because all the litter-bearers had run off, some of the soldiers lifted the litter onto their own shoulders, while the others led the way. When the small procession came down into the Forum and reached the Treasury, which occupied the basement of the Temple of Saturn, men of the duty Praetorian cohort flooded around to see who was inside the litter. Gratus and his comrades told the Praetorians that Claudius should be made the new emperor, and these men all agreed, "on account of their fondness for Germanicus, his brother, who had left behind him a vast reputation," Josephus was to say. These soldiers also realized that if they made Claudius emperor, he might reward them financially.[2]

So in a large body many hundreds strong, the few men of the German Guard, surrounded by their Praetorian colleagues, carried Claudius through the city streets toward the Praetorian Barracks. Those streets were crowded with people who were milling about amid both shock and elation at the news of Caligula's assassination. All along the route to the barracks, people looked with pity at the emperor's uncle as he was carried past by the soldiers, feeling sure that he was an innocent man being hurried to his execution by the troops.[3]

It was true that the bloodshed had not yet come to an end, but it was not Claudius who was to die; it was other members of the imperial house who were fated to soon meet their ends. The tribune Chaerea felt that the business of terminating the reign of Caligula could not be considered complete until his wife, Caesonia, and eighteen-month-old daughter, Julia Drusilla, also were dead. Another Praetorian tribune who also was a party to the assassination plot, Julius Lupus, was dispatched by Chaerea to find and kill mother and child. Caesonia wasn't difficult to track down; the tribune Lupus located her beside Caligula's bloodied corpse, which, since the murder, had been removed to a palace bedroom.

After the murder, Gaius's body had been found where it had fallen by his longtime friend the Judean king Agrippa, who was staying at the Palatium on a visit to Rome. Agrippa felt in Caligula's debt, for on the death of Tiberius four years before, Agrippa had been freed from house arrest by Caligula, who had subsequently given Agrippa his grandfather Herod's kingdom of Judea. So Agrippa had lifted up the body and reverently carried it to the bedchamber.

Now the tribune Lupus discovered Caligula's wife, Caesonia, on the bed beside Caligula, berating her dead husband. In the preceding months there had been rumors of an assassination plot, and Caesonia had urged Caligula to act on them and seek out the conspirators, but Caligula had dismissed her concerns. Now the tribune Lupus found Caesonia cursing the dead Caligula for not taking any notice of her.[4]

Looking around, Caesonia saw Lupus the tribune standing across the room with a bloodied sword in his hand and a pained look on his face. Caesonia knew at once why he had come. Quite composed, she climbed down from the bed, sank onto her knees, and projected her neck to receive his blade. When Lupus hesitated to act, she called to him not to stand there gaping but to finish the deed he had been sent to accomplish. With this encouragement, Lupus stepped up and, with a double-handed swipe of his short sword, sliced through her slender neck and took off her head. Lupus then located Caligula's infant daughter and, to finish his gruesome task, grabbed up the child and dashed out her brains against a pillar.[5]

In the early evening, as a measure of calm returned to the city, the consuls Gnaeus Sentius Saturninus and Quintus Pomponius Secondus convened the Senate behind the guarded gates of the Capitoline complex, at the Temple of Jupiter, Rome's largest, oldest, and most sacred temple. They were protected here by the four cohorts of the German Guard, who, apart from the few Germans who had taken Claudius to the Praetorian Barracks, had remained under the control of the prefect Sabinus and the tribune Chaerea and had ended their rampage in the palace. To prevent the national treasury from falling into the hands of looters should civil unrest break out, the German troops also had been ordered to bring to the Capitol the thousands of millions of sesterces in gold and silver coin normally kept in the Treasury of Saturn.

Not every senator turned up for the hastily called Senate sitting; a number were in hiding, fearful of being caught up in the bloodshed that had been initiated by the German Guard immediately after the assassination. As the Senate was coming to order, each senator present was asking his colleagues who had been behind the assassination. Valerius Asiaticus, one of the two senators who, with Claudius, had preceded Caligula from the theater just prior to his murder, proclaimed for all to hear, "I wish that I had been the one who killed him!"[6]

The consul Sentius Saturninus now called for order and gave a passionate speech to the Senate, condemning Julius Caesar for dissolving Roman democracy a century before, and equally condemning his successors the emperors Augustus, Tiberius, and Caligula for continuing the oppression of the Roman people. He advocated a return to the days of the Roman Republic prior to Caesar, when consuls elected annually ruled with the aid of the Senate and there were no emperors. He was not alone. "Some people wanted all memory of the Caesars wiped out," Suetonius was to say, "and their temples destroyed."[7] This was the course advocated by the consul.

The consul Sentius knew that Claudius had been taken to the Praetorian Barracks and that troops there were demanding that

Claudius be made emperor. But in Sentius's opinion, soldiers were meant to obey the Senate, not issue orders to it. As for Claudius, he had always been thought of as an idiotic fool by most senators. The Senate, said Sentius, now had the opportunity to reclaim its power, and should do so. And when it came to Caligula's chief assassin, the tribune Cassius Chaerea, he should, in the consul's opinion, be honored. "For, this one man, with the aid of the gods, has by his actions given us back our liberty," Sentius declared.[8]

Sentius's speech was cheered by his fellow senators, and when the tribune Chaerea, who was present, asked the consuls for a new watchword for the coming day, they gave him "Liberty," to the great approval of the House. Well into the night, after much debate, the Senate decided to send envoys to the Praetorian Barracks to see if Claudius could be convinced to give up all claim to the throne. The chosen envoys, the civil tribunes Veranius and Brocchus, went to the Praetorian Barracks escorted by the tribune Chaerea and a large detachment of German Guard troops.

During the afternoon, Claudius had been visited at the barracks by Aprippa, the Judean king. Claudius knew forty-nine-year-old Agrippa very well—Agrippa had been raised at the Palatium alongside Claudius and Germanicus and their cousin and adoptive brother, Drusus the Younger. Agrippa had in fact been one of Drusus's closest friends. At the barracks, Agrippa had found Claudius in mental turmoil. Claudius had been ready to withdraw from the scene and allow the Senate to take charge, but Agrippa discreetly counseled otherwise. After urging Claudius to claim the throne for himself, Agrippa had returned to his quarters on the Palatine.

The Senate envoys, Veranius and Brocchus, were permitted by the Praetorians to enter their barracks to address Claudius. Finding him surrounded by troops, the envoys said that if Claudius would agree to live quietly out of the way, he would be heaped with honors, but if he attempted to use the Praetorian troops to take the empty throne he would find himself at war with the Senate. When the envoys asked Claudius to come to the Senate and discuss a transition of power, he shrugged helplessly and replied that the soldiers would not let him leave their barracks.

After the tribunes returned to the waiting Senate with this response, the Senate sent for King Agrippa, knowing of his close friendship with Claudius. Unaware that Agrippa had already counseled

Claudius to take the throne, the senators asked his opinion of the state of affairs. Seeing the senators unable to agree on a course of action, Agrippa cunningly claimed that he supported the Senate, but reminded the senators that many more troops backed Claudius than backed the House—13,500 Praetorian Guards and City Guards, against the 2,000 German Guards then in the city. In response to this, the senators told him they had more than enough treasury money to purchase weapons, and they would free all the slaves of the city and arm them. Agrippa scoffed at this, saying that slaves didn't know how to draw a sword, let alone use one. When he volunteered to go to see Claudius as an official ambassador of the Senate, the senators gladly sent him to the barracks with their other envoys.

Now Agrippa met with Claudius a second time and, taking him to one side, informed him that the Senate was in disarray and told him what answer to send back to the senators. So, although he was not confident of the outcome, Claudius gave a stammering speech to the envoys, telling them that if they were to accept him as their new ruler he would be an emperor in name only, for he would share government with the Senate. After Agrippa and the other envoys had left the barracks, Claudius, probably at Agrippa's suggestion, promised every soldier of the Guard a bonus of 150 sesterces if they made him emperor, and more again for their centurions.

The envoys reported back to the Senate with Claudius's response, which the senators found unacceptable. The Senate broke up without agreeing on their next step, and in this atmosphere of stalemate the night passed uneasily. But Claudius rested more comfortably under the protective eyes of the troops at the barracks, relaxing somewhat "now that no immediate danger threatened, but feeling little hope for the future."[9]

Well before dawn the next morning, the Senate met again at the Temple of Jupiter, with the senators determined to break the deadlock. Little more than a hundred senators turned up for this session. The remainder, fearful that the soldiers at the barracks would take matters into their own hands, either hid in the city or hurried away from Rome to their country estates. As those senators who had taken their seats debated the best course of action, the soldiers of the German Guard flooded into the chamber. Disgusted by the lack of decision, the German troops called on the Senate to choose one ruler, any ruler, whom they could throw their support behind. The republican argument held no attraction for the Germans; accustomed to taking orders from a single commander in chief, they weren't interested in government by committee. They could see what chaos that achieved—here was evidence of it.

Some of the senators responded by offering themselves for the job of emperor. Marcus Vinicius was one of those who put up their hand. Vinicius said that as the husband of Julia, youngest daughter of Germanicus, he was eminently qualfied for the throne because of this connection with the family of the Caesars. Josephus says that he even urged the consuls to have the House vote on his appointment, but they refused to put his nomination to a vote.[10]

Word now reached the Capitol that the seven thousand men of the Night Watch had marched to the Praetorian Barracks in support of Claudius, as had gladiators from the city's gladiatorial schools and crewmen from warships downriver at Ostia. On top of that, a large crowd of city residents had surrounded the Praetorian barracks and was calling on Claudius to become their emperor.

The German Guard soldiers in the Senate chamber became increasingly unruly on hearing this news, and when the tribune Chaerea tried to address them, they shouted him down, demanding one ruler without further delay. If the ruler was to be Claudius, they said, so be it. Chaerea angrily told the Germans he would give them Claudius's head before he gave them Claudius as their emperor. But the guardsmen, says Josephus, drew their swords and took up their standards, then departed from the temple. Deserting the senators, they marched to the Praetorian Barracks to offer Claudius their allegiance.[11] It was all over; all the soldiers at Rome now supported Claudius, brother of Germanicus. The Senate could only match the troops' swords with words.

After appointing Rufrius Pollio as his prefect of the Praetorian Guard, Claudius was carried through the city streets to the Palatium in his litter, followed by twenty-two thousand troops and half the population of Rome. At the same time he summoned the Senate to appear before him at the Palatium. Uneasy senators answered the summons. But before he addressed the Senate, Claudius met with his friends, including Agrippa, to discuss what he should do next. They convinced him that he must arrest and execute Caligula's assassins; otherwise he would only send a signal that the murderers of emperors could expect to go unpunished, putting himself in peril in the future.

So, looking ahead, with his own safety in mind, says Dio,[12] Claudius ordered the Praetorian Guard to arrest and behead the tribune Chaerea, the tribune Lupus, and the centurions who also had participated in the assassination. Yet the prefect Cornelius Sabinus, chief of the German Guard, one of the assassination's chief conspirators, and one of those who had used their swords on Caligula, escaped capital punishment. While he did not lose his head, he lost his job, and went back to being a gladiator. Sabinus would commit suicide several years later.

The Senate duly gathered before Claudius at the Palatium and, realizing that with all the troops at Rome behind Claudius they were in no position to oppose him or to restore the Republic, they resignedly voted unanimously to call on him to become their new emperor. And so it was that the brother of Germanicus became Tiberius Claudius Caesar Augustus Germanicus, emperor and high priest of Rome. Until recently, Claudius had been greeted by the public when he went to the theater with cries of "Hail the brother of Germanicus!"[13] Now it was "Hail the emperor!"

# XIII

# THE MURDER OF CLAUDIUS

One of Claudius's first acts as emperor was to recall from exile his two nieces Agrippina the Younger and Julia Livilla, the surviving daughters of his brother Germanicus. Both young women quickly returned to Rome, to the Germanican palace on the Palatine, and to positions of wealth and influence. Agrippina the Younger also was able to reunite with her three-year-old son, Lucius Domitius Ahenobarbus. The boy's father, Gnaeus, having quite recently died, the child had been cared for by his father's sister Domitia Lepida while Agrippina was in exile.

Now that he was emperor, Claudius surrounded himself with staff who had close associations with his family and who had shown him and them great loyalty in the past. As his secretary for finances he appointed Pallas, the most trusted retainer of his mother, Antonia; he was the man who had delivered Tiberius the letter from Antonia that had exposed the Sejanus plot. Callistus, the former member of Caligula's staff who had been a member of the Caligula assassination conspiracy, had long been respectful of and generous toward Claudius, and he was appointed Claudius's secretary for petitions. All Palatium correspondence, petitions for pardons and citizenship, and applications for audiences with the emperor were to pass through his hands, giving him considerable power of recommendation.

Men who had been close to Claudius's brother, Germanicus, and who had survived Sejanus, Tiberius, and Caligula also were favored by the new emperor. Publius Suillius Rufus, Germanicus's quaestor, who had been exiled by Tiberius, became a trusted confidante of Claudius. He was to gain notoriety and achieve popular dislike for leading prosecutions against men and women who offended the new Palatium. Another favorite of Claudius was Vibius Marsus, who had been in Syria with Germanicus. Marsus had narrowly escaped a death sentence from Caligula during that emperor's four-year reign. Now, with some irony, Marsus was sent back to Antioch by Claudius, as his appointee to the post of governor of Syria. Quintus Veranius, the lone survivor among the trio of friends of Germanicus who had prosecuted Piso, was made a consul by Claudius, while Aulus Vitellius, nephew of the late Publius Vitellius, one of Veranius's fellow Piso prosecutors, also received a consulship under Claudius.

In the same way, young Agrippina and Julia both surrounded themselves with men they felt they could trust, men with strong connections to the family of Germanicus who had remained faithful through difficult times. Agrippina had learned the hard way, having seen her father, mother, and brothers persecuted by their enemies and dying horrible deaths, that her continued survival depended on the people she associated with. Her brutal and disliked husband, Ahenobarbus, had died from natural causes while she was in exile, so she now welcomed overtures of marriage. She very quickly wed the wealthy senator Gaius Passienus Crispus. Considerably older than Agrippina and twice a consul, he was famed for his oratorical skills.

Agrippina the Younger's sister, twenty-five-year-old Julia, depended more on her good looks and her close relationship with her uncle the emperor to guarantee her future security. "Extremely beautiful,"[1] and haughty like her mother, the late Agrippina the Elder, Julia soon incurred the jealousy of Claudius's willful third wife, Messalina Valeria. Everyone in the imperial court bowed to the empress Messalina and went out of their way to flatter her—everyone, that is, except young Julia. What was worse, Julia often spent time alone with her uncle, which gave her a sense of invincibility. But heaven help a woman who steps between another woman and her husband, especially when that husband is the emperor of Rome. The jealous Messalina became determined to be rid of her husband's attractive niece.

Since their return from exile, Julia and Agrippina had been receiving former clients. Among these clients of the family of Germanicus was Lucius Seneca, who by now had won a reputation as one of Rome's leading speakers and lawyers. The witty, charming Seneca was spending a lot of time in Julia's company, and before A.D. 41 was out, Messalina was to accuse Julia and Seneca of having an affair. Not only was Julia married at the time, but Seneca was also married by now and had a son. The name of this, his first wife, is unknown, but the wedding had taken place by A.D. 33.

Claudius was completely under the sway of his manipulative wife, Messalina, and even though he was very fond of Julia, he gave in to Messalina. Julia was sent back to the Pontian Islands as an imperial prisoner, convicted of adultery. At the same time and for the same crime, Seneca was exiled to the island of Corsica. Shortly after this, Julia was executed at her place of exile, again at the behest of her jealous aunt Messalina. Of Germanicus's nine children, only Agrippina the Younger now remained alive.

In Claudius's eyes, Messalina could do no wrong. He was blind to her countless affairs, to her trumped-up charges that removed influential men and women from around the emperor, and to her corruption of senior Palatium officials, including the secretaries Pallas and Callistus, which made her, and them, fabulously rich. It became common knowledge that if you wanted a favor from the emperor Claudius, ranging from an official appointment to Roman citizenship, you paid Messalina, via the Palatium freedmen, and she put in a good word with Claudius. This practice became so commonplace that a joke did the rounds at Rome that a noncitizen could acquire citizenship simply by giving Messalina a handful of colored glass.

Jokes like this never reached the emperor's ears. He was totally ignorant of the fact that his wife was playing him for a dupe. For seven years word of Messalina's bad habits was kept from the emperor, until her success made her overconfident. Even though she was married to Claudius, in A.D. 48, while the emperor was away from Rome, Messalina went through a marriage ceremony with her latest lover—the handsome Gaius Silius, son of Silius, the general of Germanicus and his wife, Sosia, who had both been destroyed by Sejanus.

It was Narcissus, Claudius's Greek chief secretary, a role that made him in effect his prime minister, who tipped off the emperor. Narcissus had great influence with Claudius. On his recommendation, for example, General Vespasian, a future emperor, had been put in command of the 2nd Augusta Legion just prior to that unit's participation in the invasion of Britain, during which Vespasian made his name as a brilliant soldier. Via his influence, too, finance secretary Pallas's brother

Felix would later be appointed prefect of Judea. Narcissus had the emperor's ear and his confidence, so Claudius listened when Narcissus warned him that Messalina intended murdering him and setting young Silius up as the next ruler of Rome. Horrified, Claudius hurried back to Rome and, at Narcissus's urging, went straight to the Praetorian Barracks to cement the loyalty of the Praetorian Guard, the force that had put him on the throne in the first place.

As young Silius and scores of those who had been in Messalina's sex-dominated circle were arrested, Messalina herself fled to the Gardens of Lucullus, which she had owned ever since dispossessing the previous owner with one of her trumped-up charges. One after the other, Silius and various knights and senators were beheaded by Praetorian Guard death squads. Even the current commander of the Night Watch perished in this swift and bloody purge—he, too, had come under Messalina's corrupt influence. But when Claudius wavered about authorizing Messalina's execution, Narcissus, the chief secretary, personally gave the order. As the Praetorian tribune sent to kill Messalina forced his way into the Gardens of Lucullus, Messalina tried to kill herself with a dagger. But when she didn't have the courage to push the dagger into her chest, the tribune impatiently gave her a helping hand, thrusting the blade into her heart.

As soon as Messalina was dead, Claudius's advisers pushed the emperor to marry again, for the sake of the state. Each of his three senior freedmen—Narcissus, Callistus, and Pallas—proposed a different candidate. Pallas urged Claudius to marry his thirty-three-year-old niece, Agrippina the Younger. She had recently become available for marriage by becoming a widow for the second time—her husband, Gaius Passienus Crispus, had died prior to A.D. 48; there was a suggestion in some quarters that he had been poisoned. His great wealth had been inherited by Agrippina's young son, Lucius.

Agrippina the Younger had grown into an attractive woman, with her mother's looks and her father's presence. Pallas stressed that also in Agrippina's favor was the fact that a marriage between Claudius and Agrippina would unite the descendants of the Claudian family. And, importantly, "she would bring with her the grandson of Germanicus," ten-year-old Lucius, who, he said, was entirely worthy of imperial rank because the blood of the Caesars ran through his veins from both his mother's and father's sides.[2] Claudius cherished fond memories of his late brother, Germanicus; once he became emperor he even entered a play written by Germanicus in the leading playwriting contest of the day. And he knew that Agrippina's boy, Lucius, was a popular sensation whenever he appeared in public, because of the Roman people's "fond remembrance of Germanicus."[3]

The prospect of marrying the daughter of the brother he had adored, and of becoming father to Germanicus's grandson, overshadowed all the qualifications of the other marriage candidates. Pallas's advice prevailed, reinforced, as it was, Tacitus was to say, by pretty Agrippina's intimate charms.[4] Claudius, dominated by his freedmen as he had been dominated by Messalina, agreed to make Agrippina the Younger his fourth wife. But there was a legal problem to overcome before Claudius could take Agrippina as his bride: under Roman law, an uncle could not marry his niece. So Aulus Vitellius, whose family had always supported the house of Germanicus, went into the Senate and pushed through a vote changing the law to permit an uncle to marry his niece. Claudius and Agrippina the Younger were wed soon after, in early A.D. 49. According to Suetonius, only two other uncles, one a freedman, the other a former first-rank centurion with the Praetorian Guard, took advantage of the new law and married their nieces.[5]

Claudius was born to be dominated by others. Immediately after Agrippina moved into the Palatium with Claudius, says Dio, she "gained complete control over him."[6] She quickly convinced the emperor to end the exile of Lucius Seneca. During the eight years that Seneca had been banished from Rome for his adulterous relationship with Agrippina's younger sister Julia, both his wife and his son had died. During the same period, with plenty of time on his hands, he had written some of his best philosophical work. When Seneca returned from Corsica, Agrippina immediately appointed him tutor to her son, Lucius. What was more, Claudius made both Seneca and his elder brother Gallio praetors that same year, A.D. 49. Suetonius would recount a tale told in his day that the night after Seneca was appointed to the post of tutor to Agrippina's son, he dreamed that his pupil was actually the dead Caligula. This alleged dream was, wrote Suetonius, a portent of things to come.[7]

Two years later, through the influence of his brother Seneca, Gallio also would be appointed senatorial governor of the province of Achaea, in the southern part of Greece. There, that same year, Gallio would dismiss charges brought by local Jewish leaders against the

Christian apostle Paulus of Tarsus, the later St. Paul. The younger brother of Seneca, Lucius Anneaus Mela, also would benefit from his brother's influence, flourishing at Rome during this period.

In A.D. 50, within a year of marrying Claudius, Agrippina convinced the emperor to adopt her boy, Lucius, as his own son, just as Tiberius had adopted Germanicus. This made the boy Claudius's heir apparent, ahead of his own ten-year-old son from his marriage with Messalina, Britannicus. Lucius's name was changed to reflect the adoption, to Nero Claudius Caesar Drusus Germanicus. From this point on, history would know him as Nero. To further cement Nero's position in the imperial hierarchy, he was betrothed to his cousin Octavia, the daughter of Claudius and Messalina.

Agrippina now worked hard to sideline or eliminate rivals to both herself and Nero. Females who had previously been touted as potential brides for Claudius soon became victims of plots to remove them; their fate, exile or enforced suicide. Then there was Claudius's son, Britannicus (who had initially been named Tiberius Claudius Germanicus), a potential rival to Nero's claim to the throne. Josephus was to say that Agrippina feared that once Britannicus reached manhood and his father died he would take the throne for himself and avenge the death of his mother, Messalina, by destroying Agrippina and Nero.[8] To begin with, Agrippina progressively diminished Britannicus's status at the imperial court. Next, she had his tutors and servants removed, and some even executed, branding them bad influences. She subsequently surrounded the boy with staff of her choosing. At the same time, she had Praetorian tribunes and centurions who had been sympathetic to Britannicus's mother, Messalina, promoted and transferred to distant legion postings, on the frontiers of the empire and well away from Rome.

Agrippina also believed that the joint commanders of the Praetorian Guard, Lucius Geta and Rufius Crispinus, were too fond of the memory of Messalina and too fond of Messalina's son, Britannicus. So supposedly to prevent factionalism within the Guard, Agrippina convinced Claudius to replace both Geta and Rufius with a single consolidating Praetorian prefect, recommending Sextus Afranius Burrus for the job. A provincial Equestrian knight from the province of Narbonne Gaul in southwestern France, Burrus was an astute and physically powerful man who had made a name for himself with the legions as a tough officer and fierce fighter despite a withered left hand.

Precisely where in the empire Burrus had acquired his "brilliant"[9] military reputation we are not told, but it is likely he served with one of the four legions that invaded Britain for Claudius in A.D. 43. The unit that saw the most action and won the most praise during this campaign was General Titus Vespasian's 2nd Augusta Legion, and it is quite possible that Burrus had served as military tribune and second-in-command with that unit, or possibly with the 14th Gemina Martia Victrix or the 20th Valeria Victrix, legions that also were in the thick of the fighting against the British tribesmen. Once again, Claudius took Agrippina's advice: Geta and Rufius were removed from their posts, to be replaced by Burrus, who, says Tacitus, knew all too well to whom he owed his promotion: Agrippina.[10]

The teenage Nero married Claudius's daughter Octavia in A.D. 53, even though, says Tacitus, Nero loathed her.[11] Claudius, meanwhile, had no affection for his adopted son, and was increasingly unhappy with his domineering wife and her constant pushing of Nero. "Nothing seemed to satisfy Agrippina," Dio observed.[12] She had destroyed anyone who opposed her, and took Claudius's powerful secretary Pallas into her bed, to control both him and Claudius. Nor did she hesitate to act to save her favorites from precarious situations. She stepped in to overturn prosecutions by her senatorial enemies against Pallas and against Praetorian commander Burrus, using Seneca as her eloquent agent in the Senate to win their acquittals.[13] On another occasion she secured an acquittal for Aulus Vitellius. At the same time, like her predecessor Messalina, Agrippina became increasingly rich through the largesse of grateful clients. And just like Messalina, Agrippina thought she had succeeded in deceiving Claudius.

Now she was terrified to learn that Claudius, when drunk at a banquet, had been overheard to say, "It is my destiny to have to suffer my wives' infamy only to finally punish it!"[14] Conscious of the fate of her predecessor, Agrippina thought increasingly about self-preservation. When, in the summer of A.D. 54, sixty-two-year-old Claudius became seriously ill, Agrippina hoped he would not recover; his death would make Nero emperor. When Claudius did unexpectedly regain his health, Agrippina set in motion a plot to murder him.

But it would not be an easy thing to accomplish. Having spent his first fifty years surrounded by family intrigues, executions, and the threat of an unnatural death, and having seen his predecessor die by the sword, Claudius had always been extremely security-conscious.

Since he had become emperor, everyone who came into his presence, female as well as male, was searched by his German Guard bodyguards for weapons before they were permitted near him. Prior to Claudius's reign, the emperors Augustus, Tiberius, and Caligula had not bothered with guards at their banquets, but Claudius began the habit of stationing men of the German Guard in his dining room to stand guard while he and his guests dined, a habit that would be continued by future emperors for hundreds of years to come.

With death by the sword effectively ruled out by these security measures, Agrippina settled on poison as the best means of eliminating her husband. But even that would prove difficult, as Claudius used a slave named Halotus, a eunuch, to taste all the emperor's food before it reached Claudius's mouth. Halotus would be the key to the crime. Agrippina decided to use a rare, slow-acting poison, one that first addled the brain of victims before killing them. Knowing that there was a woman named Locusta in the City Prison who had recently been convicted of poisoning, Agrippina bribed Locusta's guards to convince the woman to arrange the required poison, on condition that her life be prolonged. Word came back that Locusta agreed to the bargain.

By the fall, Agrippina was in possession of the poison. She then brought food taster Halotus into the plot, apparently by bribing him. "Writers of the time," Tacitus was to say, "have declared that the poison was infused into some mushrooms," which were a favorite delicacy of Claudius's.[15] In the first half of October A.D. 54, when Claudius's powerful but gout-ridden chief secretary, Narcissus, left Rome to take the healing waters of a Campanian spa to provide some relief from his painful complaint, Agrippina set the murder plot in motion. "Had he [Narcissus] been present," Dio was to say, "she would never have accomplished it."[16]

Dio says that Agrippina was at Claudius's side when he dined on the evening of October 12.[17] Claudius had never been able to hold his drink, and as was often the case he became drunk this night, making it easier for Halotus to deliver the poisoned mushroom platter to his master. Agrippina herself ate one of the mushrooms on the plate, recommending the largest to Claudius, who downed it. But, being drunk, he later in the evening vomited up his meal, and with it, much of the poison. Agrippina was personally nursing Claudius, and she sent for Xenophon, the emperor's physician, with the excuse that he was to treat Claudius's "sickness." Xenophon also was party to the murder plot. According to Tacitus, in the privacy of Claudius's bedchamber and under the pretext of helping Claudius vomit, the doctor put a feather down his throat; the feather had been smeared with another, fast-acting poison.[18] In the early morning hours of October 13, Claudius succumbed to the poison and breathed his last tortured breath.

Agrippina wanted to keep Claudius's death a secret for the time being. Many years before, astrologers had told her that her son would enjoy a long reign if he became emperor in the afternoon. She gave orders for the German Guard to seal off the Palatium. The palace gates, which always stood open, were swung shut and bolted. Agrippina also kept Claudius's son, Britannicus, and daughters, Octavia and Antonia, close by her; they had been told that their father was unwell, but none of them knew that he was already dead. The Senate was convened. Informed via missives from the palace that the emperor was dangerously ill but that his condition was improving, the consuls offered prayers for his recovery.

Then, at noon, the palace gates were flung open and Praetorian commander Burrus emerged with seventeen-year-old Nero at his side to announce that Claudius was dead. The tribune of the Praetorian Guard cohort on duty that day then called on his men to hail Nero as their new emperor. There were joyful shouts from the troops, for this was the grandson of Germanicus and, as Edward Gibbon, eighteenth-century author of *The Decline and Fall of the Roman Empire*, observed, "the Romans still revered, in the person of Nero, the grandson of Germanicus."[19] Many among these soldiers believed that young Nero was destined to fulfill the destiny that had been deprived of his grandfather by cruel murder.

As Nero was loaded into a litter, says Tacitus, some soldiers looked around, wondering where Claudius's son, Britannicus, was, but he was being kept back at the Palatium by his stepmother, Agrippina.[20] Nero was carried to the Praetorian Barracks, where he was quickly surrounded by thousands of men of the Praetorian Guard and City Guard, who enthusiastically hailed him as their new emperor. A stunned young Nero smiled and acknowledged their salutes and good wishes.

Even though he was only seventeen, Nero was already an accomplished public speaker. Well tutored by Seneca, he had even served as a defense attorney in court cases on special occasions on the authority of the Senate. Now, with the Praetorian prefect Burrus at his side, he addressed the troops, delivering a speech written for him by his tutor

Seneca that morning. His speech, in which Nero promised to pay every soldier of the Guard a bonus once his ascension to the throne was confirmed by the Senate, was warmly welcomed by the troops. Burrus then had Nero carried to the Senate House, where the Senate quickly decreed in his favor. Claudius, brother of Germanicus, was dead. Nero, teenage grandson of Germanicus, was emperor of Rome. The emperor was dead. Long live the emperor!

# XIV

# THE MURDER OF
# BRITANNICUS

Agrippina the Younger quickly took charge at the Palatium now that her son was emperor, and formed a cabinet of her own choosing. At her instigation, her lover Pallas was retained as secretary of finances by Nero. Uniquely, Pallas was now serving in his third imperial administration, having previously held his post under both Caligula and Claudius. Nero also confirmed Burrus as his prefect of the Praetorian Guard. And, at Agrippina's bidding, Nero's tutor Seneca was appointed to potentially the most powerful post of all at the Palatium, that of chief secretary to the emperor. The man who had occupied that post under Claudius, the able but ailing freedman Narcissus, now slipped away into what he hoped would be a quiet but comfortable retirement.

Seneca, who had known Nero's grandparents Germanicus and Agrippina the Elder, and who for years had been close to Nero's mother, Agrippina the Younger, and the emperor's aunt Julia Livilla, was now fifty-seven, and happily married to his second wife, the considerably younger Pompeia Paulina. Physically, Seneca was no longer dashing or handsome. Middle age had seen him lose hair and gain weight. Bald and fat he may now be, but Seneca was a recognized authority on subjects ranging from geology to meteorology, and he was still a skillful author and a sparkling public speaker. He had transferred much of his learning and some of his oratorical skills to Nero, training him well and writing speeches for him that would swiftly bring Nero acclaim as a young emperor of exceptional learning and sensibility, and win him a reputation as a youth possessed of mature wisdom.

Seneca had probably formed a working relationship with the new Praetorian prefect Burrus long before Claudius's death. Burrus was a man Seneca would have known for a number of years, and it is likely that Burrus's initial appointment some time back had come through Seneca's influence with Agrippina the Younger. With Seneca taking charge of the civil government, and with the able but austere Burrus serving as, in effect, Nero's military chief of staff and defense secretary, the new emperor was served by a formidable duo, a management team unequaled in Roman history.

Agrippina, with her son, Nero, on the throne and her men Seneca, Burrus, and Pallas in control at the Palatium, was riding on such a wave of confidence that she even attended sessions of the Senate, a previously unheard-of thing for a woman to do. Almost immediately, too, on her own authority and without Nero's knowledge, she had men arrested and executed. Junius Silanus, governor of Asia, was killed by a Praetorian death squad on her command simply because Agrippina had previously engineered the death of his brother and she now feared his retribution.

Then there was the freedman Narcissus, Claudius's recently retired chief secretary. He had increasingly opposed Agrippina while Claudius was alive, and now Agrippina wanted Narcissus dead. Not only had she never forgiven him for standing up to her, she also wanted to get her hands on his immense fortune, which reputedly ran to 400 million sesterces. Nero had not long been on the throne before his mother forced Narcissus to commit suicide rather than face arrest and execution on invented corruption charges. Friends of Narcissus such as the famous general Titus Vespasian quickly retired to country estates and maintained a low profile, hoping not to attract Agrippina's attention. Tacitus was to say that Agrippina would have committed further murders had not Seneca and Burrus combined to thwart her "domineering attitude."[1]

Soundly advised by Seneca and Burrus, Nero appointed the tough old warhorse Domitius Corbulo to head a task force in the East designed to recover Armenia from the resurgent Parthians, who had taken over the country that Germanicus had so deftly brought into the Roman sphere so many years before. Taking his time to build up and train an invasion force in the East, General Corbulo would eventually throw the Parthians out of Armenia. At the same time, Seneca's trusted friend Ummidius Quadratus was appointed to the important post of governor of Syria, replacing Claudius's appointee Marsus in what was one of the top-paying and most powerful of all the provincial governorships.

At home, under the influence of Seneca and Burrus, Nero introduced a wave of new measures and reforms covering taxation and the law, and showed such restraint and clemency against wrongdoers that Romans would declare the first five years of Nero's reign a new golden age. At the same time, the young emperor fell in love with a freedwoman at the Palatium, a beautiful former slave from the province of Asia. Her name was Acte, and, according to Christian tradition, she was a follower of Christ. She bore a striking resemblance to Agrippina the Younger, and, Dio was to say, Nero would joke to his closest friends that in bedding her he was having intercourse with his mother.[2]

Seneca humored Nero, and for a long time helped hide the romance with Acte from his mother by having a good-natured relative of his, Annaeus Serenus, pretend to be in love with the girl, and to likewise pretend that Serenus was the giver of the lavish gifts sent to Acte by Nero. Agrippina was livid when she eventually did find out about Nero's freedwoman mistress, and "raved" that she would not have a slave girl for a daughter-in-law.[3] Her opposition did not subside even when Nero had Acte adopted into a leading Roman family—the family of Attalus—in an attempt to give her respectability.[4]

Seeing that her criticism frequently only hardened Nero's determination to have his own way, in the autumn of A.D. 55 Agrippina changed her tactics, inviting Nero to use her Palatium bedchamber for his affairs. At the same time she gave him a large part of her wealth and ceased attempting to put restrictions on him. Nero's friends immediately suspected that Agrippina was up to something and warned him to be on his guard. In December, when Agrippina was heard to make disparaging remarks to Pallas about her son's lack of generosity toward her, Nero was furious, and dismissed Pallas from the Palatium staff—to punish his mother. Agrippina reacted petulantly, declaring to Nero that Claudius's biological son, Britannicus, had a stronger claim to the throne than did Nero. She added that if Nero did not watch out she would take Britannicus to the Praetorian Barracks once he came of age. There, she said, the soldiers of the Guard would see "the daughter of Germanicus" on one side, supporting Britannicus, and the "cripple Burrus and the [former] exile Seneca on the other," supporting Nero.[5]

Nero was dumbfounded by this outburst. Suddenly terrified that his mother would go through with her threat, especially as Britannicus would come of age in February, barely eight weeks away, Nero secretly consulted the Praetorian tribune Julius Pollio, who had custody at the City Prison of the infamous poisoner Locusta. Nero instructed Pollio to have Locusta prepare a fast-acting poison in return for her freedom, apparently unaware that his mother had previously used the same woman to poison Claudius and clear the way for him to become emperor.

A first attempt by Britannicus's tutors to poison him as part of this murder plot of Nero's failed because the dose was not strong enough. Britannicus recovered, so Nero tried a second time. This time it was to be at a family dinner at the Palatium, one winter's night in the last days of December. Because Britannicus used a food taster, an ingenious scheme was conceived—by Nero himself, it would seem. Britannicus was reclining with the younger diners at separate sets of tables from that occupied by Nero, his mother, and other older guests. Hot wine was typically served in winter by the Romans, and a cup of heated wine was passed to Britannicus's taster by a servant who was part of the murder plot. The taster drank a little, then passed the wine to Britannicus. But finding it too hot, Britannicus asked for it to be cooled. The Romans habitually drank their wine diluted with water, and now a little cold water was added to the cup, and the cup returned directly to Britannicus. The cold water contained the poison, possibly poison hemlock. Britannicus drank, and within moments was paralyzed, losing his voice. Then he was gasping for breath. Finally, he went into convulsions.

As those dining with Britannicus scattered and servants rushed to his aid, Nero, at the head table, nonchalantly remarked that this was likely to be a return of the epilepsy from which Britannicus had suffered when he was younger. Britannicus was carried from the dining room on a stretcher while the others continued to dine. He died within hours. His body was cremated that same night. Possessed of a strange sense of honor, Nero duly gave Locusta, the provider of the poison that had killed Britannicus, her freedom, and she walked out of the City Prison a free woman.

Now that Nero had committed his first murder, a second, more horrendous murder would be less difficult to commit, as his mother

realized. Agrippina was gripped with terror and confusion at Britannicus's death, says Tacitus.[6] That terror was compounded when Nero
shortly after removed the bodyguards assigned to his mother. Those
bodyguards had comprised a squad of Praetorian Guards, and, as a special honor to Agrippina, a squad of German Guards. Nero, in his paranoid dread of what his mother might do in reply to his murder of
Britannicus, even considered removing Burrus from command of the
Praetorian Guard because he worried that he was too close to Agrippina. But Seneca talked him out of it, assuring him that Burrus's
only loyalty was to the young emperor.

Meanwhile, Nero's mother, feeling totally insecure now, and fearing that she would be her son's next murder victim, slipped out of the
city and shuttled between her country estates. She owned one estate
inland at Tusculum, today's Frascati, in the hills fifteen miles southeast
of Rome, and also used an imperial villa at the seaside, at Antium, today's Anzio, a port city on the western coast of Italy. Only occasionally
returning to Rome, Agrippina maintained a low profile, and while she
continued to employ spies to keep her up to date with what was going
on at the Palatium, she refrained from meddling in her son's affairs
through fear of reprisal. With mother and son now in terror of each
other, it was inevitable that one or the other of them must go.

# XV

# THE CLAIMS OF
# GERMANICUS'S
# QUAESTOR

B y A.D. 58, in the East, General Corbulo was leading elements from three Roman legions in a surprise attack against the Armenians and the Parthians. Sweeping into Armenia, he overran Armenian fortresses and pushed back Armenian and Parthian troops. He was well on his way to subjugating with his large military force the country once conquered by Germanicus's force of personality.

At the same time, at Rome, a vendetta against Germanicus's quaestor Publius Suillius Rufus was under way. Recalled from exile by Claudius, Suillius had become one of that emperor's favorites, offering him counsel, enjoying his confidence, and profiting from the lucrative appointment as governor of the province of Asia. While Messalina was alive, Suillius had made himself very wealthy and very unpopular by taking fees to prosecute a number of knights and senators who displeased her, and this had not been forgotten by the many friends and relatives of people who had died or been banished as a result of Suillius's prosecutions. They were determined to seek revenge, and now that both Messalina and Claudius had left the scene, Suillius was without friends in the highest places. The chief secretary Seneca gave his support to this campaign against Suillius and may even have instigated it, apparently because he believed that Suillius had been behind Seneca's conviction for adultery with Germanicus's daughter Julia and his subsequent eight years in exile.

So that Suillius could be convicted of a crime, the Senate now re-
vived an ancient law that made it illegal to seek payment for conducting prosecutions. Now in his early seventies, his red hair turned white
by the passing years, Suillius was brought to trial in the Senate. Notably, Seneca didn't take his seat in the House while the Suillius trial
was being conducted. The charges against Suillius were numerous, and
the list of men and women who had suffered as a result of prosecutions
brought by him extensive. Two noble ladies and four leading senators,
including Valerius Asiaticus, a man who had once contemplated seeking the throne for himself following the assassination of Caligula, had
perished at Suillius's hands, as well as a large number of knights.

Suillius patiently held his temper as he sat through the list of accusations; then, with the consul's approval, he rose to his own defense.
Unlike others who meekly took their own lives when the Palatium instigated prosecutions against them, the stubborn Suillius was going to
doggedly fight the charges. With studied indignation, he railed against
the reintroduction of the old law against taking money for conducting
prosecutions, which, he declared, had been revised merely to attack
him. And he taunted the absent Seneca, the man whom Suillius fervently believed was behind his prosecution, saying that he was on trial
only because the chief secretary displayed a savage enmity toward anyone who had been a friend of Claudius while Seneca had languished in
exile. Put simply, said Suillius, his defense was that he had carried out
the prosecutions on the orders of the emperor Claudius.

At the Palatium, Seneca was following the trial closely, with messengers continually bringing him updates on the proceedings. Hearing
this claim—that Suillius had only been following orders—Seneca
promptly sent a letter to the House, ostensibly from Nero, in which he
countered Suillius's defense. The letter, read to the House by the presiding consul, claimed that Nero knew, from a study of Claudius's unpublished memoirs, which he had with him at the palace, that
Claudius had never compelled the prosecution of a single person while
he was emperor.

Once the consul had read out the young emperor's letter, effectively foiling Suillius's defense argument, Suillius was forced to
change his tack. Now he claimed that he had in fact been operating
on orders of the empress Messalina. That had certainly been the case
in his prosecution of Valerius Asiaticus. Messalina had envied Asiaticus's sumptuous gardens, the famous Gardens of Lucullus, created

by one of Rome's most famous and richest first-century B.C. generals, and she had Suillius prosecute Asiaticus so she could get her hands on the gardens, which she did. There was considerable irony in the fact that it was in those very gardens that Messalina perished just several years later, with a dagger to the heart.

This was not a defense that would hold much sway in this House. Messalina had previously been disgraced by her faithlessness, her treasonous acts, and her ignominious end. While she lived she had terrorized this very Senate through the agency of Suillius and others. One senator wanted to know why Suillius had agreed to employ his tongue "in the service of that savage harlot."[1] Another stated that the Senate must punish men who blamed others for their wicked deeds. Witnesses accused Suillius of embezzlement while he was governor of Asia. But it was Suillius's prosecutions of leading Romans that occupied the most attention and drew the most condemnation, from one speaker after another. Some charges even went back as far as the reign of Tiberius, when, it was claimed, Suillius had participated in the destruction of Germanicus's sister, Livilla, after it was revealed she had been involved with Sejanus in the murder of her husband, Drusus the Younger.

The outcome of this trial was foregone, as Suillius must have realized. Seneca wanted him dead, and that was that. But Suillius was determined that if he was to be brought down, then Seneca would pay the price of his secret prosecution, that Seneca's reputation would suffer as much as his own. For Suillius, a trusted member of the retinues of the family of Germanicus, knew more about what had gone on behind closed imperial family doors than most men over past decades. For years he had kept secrets. But when it came to Seneca, his lips were sealed no more.

"That man was only familiar with profitless studies and the ignorance of a boy," said Suillius, referring to Seneca's years as Nero's tutor. "He envied those of us who used their lively and genuine eloquence in the defense of their fellow citizens." He put his hand to his heart. "I was Germanicus's quaestor, while Seneca was a lover in his house." The Senate was stunned into silence. Suillius continued, "Should it be considered a worse offense to obtain a just reward for honest service, with the litigant's consent, than to pollute the bedchambers of the imperial ladies?"[2]

Seneca had denied that he'd had the affair with Germanicus's daughter Julia, the crime for which he had been convicted of adultery and exiled, but most Romans, in his own time and after, did not accept his denial. Tacitus would describe Seneca's banishment to Corsica for his affair with the beautiful Julia as "a most righteously deserved exile."[3] Seneca would gain a reputation in Roman times and down through the ages, especially in the eighteenth and nineteenth centuries, as one of history's great philosophers. Yet Seneca's conduct was frequently "diametrically opposed to his philosophical teachings," Cassius Dio was to say. "It hadn't been enough for him to commit adultery with Julia," Dio went on. "His banishment hadn't made him any wiser, for he had to have improper relations with Agrippina" as well, "irrespective of the sort of woman she was."[4]

It is indisputable that during her lifetime Agrippina the Younger had affairs with many men who could get her what she wanted. This counted in favor of Suillius's accusation, along with the certainty that Seneca had slept with her equally promiscuous sister. And no one, least of all Seneca, had been able to explain why Agrippina had chosen him, of all people, to be recalled from exile to become her son's tutor and live under her roof. She had gone to considerable trouble to have Seneca returned from Corsica to take up the post; yet, while he was certainly a learned and well-written man, tutors of the children of the nobility were most often Greek freedmen. Two of Nero's previous tutors had both been freedmen; one had been an ex-barber, another a charioteer. For a senator, and a praetor and senior judge, as Seneca also had become immediately after his return to Rome from exile, to serve as a boy's tutor was rare indeed. But to be in the Germanican palace as the boy's adviser was a very strategic placement that had benefited both Seneca and Agrippina, quite apart from any sexual relationship they might have enjoyed. It put him close to the emperor and gave Agrippina a strong ally on her own doorstep. According to Dio, Seneca's relationship with Agrippina was much talked about at the time, and Dio was convinced that Seneca had been her lover.[5]

Now, as Suillius conducted his defense in the Senate, he kept up his attack on Seneca by turning to the chief secretary's sudden wealth. "By what kind of wisdom, or philosophical maxims, has Seneca, during four years as an emperor's favorite, amassed 300 million sesterces? At Rome, he has made fortunes from the wills of the childless, while Italy and the provinces have been drained by his extortionate rates of interest."[6]

Suillius was met by silence from the benches opposite. His fellow senators knew all about Seneca's swift elevation from penniless exile to one of Rome's richest men. His loans to the provinces were equally well known, as was the high level of interest he charged; his loans to tribes in southern Britain, amounting to some 40 million sesterces, would be considered one of the causes of rebellion in that province within two years, after Seneca summarily called in those loans and threatened to send in the Roman military if the money was not forthcoming. Only the emperor owned more property at Rome than Seneca, and some believed that Seneca's gardens outdid the imperial gardens in their splendor. And Seneca's expensive lifestyle was legendary. Dio was to note that while Seneca found fault with the rich, he himself owned five hundred dining tables made from citrus wood and equipped with ivory legs, on which he served massive banquets.[7]

"On the other hand, my own money," Suillius told the Senate, "is not excessive, and has been acquired from industriousness. I would rather suffer prosecutions and perils, in fact anything, rather than make the position in society that I have earned and long held take second place to a newly rich upstart."[8] He sank back onto his seat with a look of disgust on his face.

No further attempts to refute Suillius's charges or to discredit Suillius himself came from the palace in the hands of panting messengers. It was left to the senators to silence him with their votes. Not unexpectedly, despite his claims and accusations, the Senate found Suillius guilty as charged. Half his property was confiscated by the state, with the other half going to his son Marcus Nerullinus Suillius and his granddaughter. Suillius was then banished to Spain's Balearic Islands. He took his punishment without a semblance of fear or a plea for mercy. He was duly shipped away to the Balearics, where he reportedly lived out the rest of his days in comparative comfort,[9] supported from Rome by his family.

Even as Suillius was being led away, charges were immediately also brought against his son Marcus, who had been a consul eight years earlier. But a note soon arrived from the Palatium: the emperor wished no action taken against Suillius's son. Tacitus believed that this imperial intercession implied that the twenty-year-old emperor felt enough vengeance had been wrought on the family of Suillius.[10] There would have been another reason for letting Marcus Suillius off the hook. The note from the Palatium would have been written by Seneca; and Seneca wanted to bury the whole Suillius affair, rather than let any more damaging accusations surface about his relationship with members of the family of Germanicus.

# XVI

# THE MURDER OF NERO'S MOTHER

Nero had a new love. He continued to keep the loyal Acte as his mistress, but now he was thinking seriously about taking another wife. Her name was Poppaea Sabina. She was the beautiful wife of his best friend, Marcus Salvius Otho, who was a similar age to Nero and had shared his youthful days of wine, women, and song prior to the death of Claudius. Plutarch says that to keep Sabina for himself, in A.D. 58, at Seneca's suggestion Nero sent Otho to become governor of the province of Lusitania, which covered much of present-day Portugal, and kept Sabina at Rome to warm his bed.[1]

Although Sabina's father had been executed in the reign of Tiberius for being an enthusiastic supporter of Sejanus, and her mother had been punished as an adulteress, Sabina came from a noble bloodline; Triumphs had been awarded to generals who had been her forebears. The ambitious Sabina was anxious for Nero to divorce Claudius's daughter Octavia and then make her his second wife. If Nero was not prepared to marry her, she said, then he should send her back to Otho.[2] But Nero knew that his mother would violently oppose any divorce. Agrippina was determined that the political marriage between Nero and Octavia, which bound the imperial Julian and Claudian families together, should last.

Through her spies, Agrippina came to hear about her son's passionate affair with his best friend's wife. Girding her courage and determination, Agrippina returned to Rome and tried to convince Nero that he did not need to marry Sabina. Various stories would be told about the methods Agrippina used to sway her son away from Sabina. Tacitus says that all the historians of the day but one wrote that Agrippina several times went to Nero's dining room in the middle of the day, when he was enjoying lunch and was "flushed with wine," and attempted to seduce him, lavishing "wanton kisses and caresses on him" to bring him back under her control.[3]

Nero at first resisted his mother's attentions, but then seemed to be weakening. Seneca, warned of this, prepared to counter his former lover's attempt to hijack Nero's affections. The next time Agrippina made an appearance when Nero was lunching, Seneca hurried Acte into the room. Bravely and publicly, Acte warned Nero against incest, assuring him that the soldiers of Rome would not tolerate an emperor who stooped to such behavior. This succeeded in scaring Nero, and after this episode he would not permit his mother to be alone with him. Tacitus was to say that the general belief was that Agrippina certainly would have gone through with such an act had Nero succumbed to her charms. With her background, from bedding her brother-in-law to making her uncle her husband, Tacitus and many others believed, having sex with her own son would have been totally in character.[4]

Foiled for now, Agrippina again withdrew to her country estates. Despite this, Nero despaired that no matter where she lived, with her "overwatchful, overcritical eye,"[5] she would be a formidable adversary who would oppose him no matter what he wanted to do. He began to think about how he could remove her from the scene, encouraged, according to Dio, by Seneca—as "many trustworthy men have stated."[6] Murder seemed the only option.

The murder of Britannicus had served as Nero's apprenticeship in homicide. That, too, had been driven by Nero's fear of his mother. Now, driven to distraction by Agrippina, he would perfect the art of the assassin with matricide. He first considered poison, but then realized that of all people, his mother would have learned to take the most stringent precautions against poison over the years—her servants were incredibly loyal, and it was said that she regularly took antidotes against various poisons.[7]

According to Dio, in early A.D. 59 Nero was attending a public spectacle in the crowded amphitheater, when he had an idea. Before his eyes, a ship automatically split open, disgorged animals that were to be hunted down, then closed again.[8] Back at the Palatium, Nero sent for the commander of the Roman battle fleet based at Misenum, southwest of Rome. The admiral, a freedman named Anicetus, had served as Nero's tutor immediately prior to Seneca's appointment to that position. Seamanship or naval experience were not always qualities required of commanders of Rome's battle fleets; their appointments were often merely rewards for service.

Nero told Anicetus about the collapsible ship he had seen. Then he asked if Anicetus could build a ship that would sail like any other but that could be made to fall apart at sea in an instant. When the admiral replied that it should be entirely possible, and asked what it was to be used for, Nero confided that he wished to be rid of his mother. Anicetus understood immediately, as Nero knew he would—for Anicetus had never forgiven Agrippina for removing him from the prestigious post of Nero's tutor and replacing him with Seneca.

"No place is more prone to accidents than the sea," said Anicetus. "And who would suggest that an offense committed by wind and waves was a crime?"[9]

Nero now had his murder accomplice. Promised significant rewards by the emperor and sworn to total secrecy, Anicetus hurried back to Misenum to have a collapsible ship constructed. Nero told him he wanted the vessel ready by March 19, when he would be celebrating the five-day Festival of Minerva at Baiae in Campania, on the western coast of Italy. In the meantime, Nero pretended to make up with his mother, sending her notes in which he said that children should be more tolerant of the irritability of their parents, and then inviting her to join him at Baiae to celebrate the Festival of Minerva between March 19 and 23. At first suspicious of Nero's motives, Agrippina, anxious to regain her influence over her son and hoping he was sincere, finally, after ignoring several letters from him, agreed to come to Baiae for the Festival of Minerva.

In the third week of March, Nero went down to Baiae, which was on the Bay of Naples. He took up residence at a charming seaside villa there owned by the senator Gaius Calpurnius Piso, a relative of the Piso condemned for the murder of Nero's grandfather Germanicus. At the same time, Nero's mother came up from Anzio aboard a trireme of the Tyrrhenian Fleet. Mastered by a *navarchus* (naval captain) named Herculeius, this particular warship with three banks of oars was the usual mode of transport of Agrippina, the "queen mother," when she took to the water. The trireme, a light, fast warship that would equate with a destroyer today, employed some 170 barefoot freedmen oarsmen and 15 deckhands. Its crew also included 40 soldiers of Rome's marine corps. Accompanying Agrippina on the journey to Baiae aboard the trireme were her lady-in-waiting, Acerronia Pola; her friend and chaperone, Crepereius Gallus; her freedmen, Agerinus and Mnester; and a number of personal slaves.

On the morning of March 19, when the trireme carrying Agrippina tied up at one of the stone jetties of Baiae, where many villas of wealthy Romans extended into the sea, Nero was there, waiting to greet his mother. Behind him spread his entourage, which included the chief secretary Seneca, the Praetorian prefect Burrus, and the prefect of the fleet Anicetus—who had come from nearby Misenum—as well as numerous freedmen and slaves, and officers and men of the Praetorian Guard and German Guard.

When forty-three-year-old Agrippina stepped ashore, twenty-one-year-old Nero came forward, beaming, extending his arms. Mother and son embraced. Nero then conducted Agrippina to waiting litters. With his mother in one litter and himself in another, and surrounded by servants and guards, the emperor led the way around the cove. Midway between Baiae and Cape Misenum there was an estate called Bauli, which originally had been owned by Quintus Hortensius, a consul in 69 B.C. Behind high walls, the expansive Bauli villa spread beside the water like a modern-day holiday resort.

Here, Agrippina and her party were to spend the five days of the festival. Here, too, drawn up on the sands of the beach, was a handsome little ship, commanded by Volusius Proculus, an officer from the Roman Navy's Tyrrhenian Fleet.[10] Richly decorated with gold and jewels, the brand-new ship had a cabin in the stern draped with silk and fitted with a luxurious couch. This beautiful vessel, said Nero, was his gift to his mother. Before Nero parted from Agrippina, he invited her to join him for dinner at his villa at Baiae that night, and she accepted. Nero was then conveyed back to Baiae.

During the afternoon, while she was making herself comfortable at the Bauli villa, word reached Agrippina via her staff that there was a plot against her life, involving a ship. Looking out the open windows of her quarters to the sparkling waters of the Bay of Naples, she could see the ship that Nero had presented to her being readied to take her back around the bay to Baiae for her dinner engagement. Although she was in doubt whether she should believe the rumor, to be on the safe side she gave credence to the warning and issued instructions for her litter to be prepared for the hour-long trek to Baiae.

Late in the afternoon, leaving her freedmen Agerinus and Mnester in charge at Bauli, Agrippina was carried around the cove in her litter, arriving at the emperor's Baiae villa accompanied by her lady-in-waiting, Acerronia Pola, and her chaperone, Crepereius Gallus. Nero graciously received his mother, using soothing words to allay any fears she had. Once she had removed her footwear and had her feet washed by slaves, as was the Roman custom prior to dining, she was conveyed across the dining room in slippers by her son and placed in the place of honor on the dining couch beside him.

It was the first time in a year or more that Agrippina had eaten with her son, and the festive occasion was enjoyed by all present at the dinner table, which included Seneca, Burrus, Anicetus, and Agrippina's two companions. Nero prolonged the banquet, first with lively conversation, and then with more serious remarks. It was not until the water clock denoted the seventh hour, signifying that midnight had arrived, that Agrippina rose to leave. Nero took her hand and escorted her down to the Baiae jetty. In the light of blazing torches, the little ship, Nero's gift to his mother, sat waiting there, having followed her around the bay that afternoon. Nero urged her to use the ship for a swift return to Bauli.

Agrippina, thrilled that her relationship with Nero seemed to once again be on a stable footing, had drunk quite a lot of wine, and her guard was down. Her earlier fears and suspicions having by this time dissipated, she told her companions to board the ship. Nero now emotionally bade his mother farewell, clinging to her for a time, then kissing her on the eyes and on the breasts. "Strength and good health to you, Mother," he said. "For you I live, and because of you I rule."[11]

Tacitus was to suggest that either this show of affection was an act or Nero was genuinely emotional because he anticipated that this would be the last sight he would have of his mother while she still lived and breathed.[12] Agrippina now turned, and climbed the gangway to the ship. The crewmen scuttled about, the gangway was hauled in, lines were cast off, and the ship slid out into the night, its oars rising and falling rhythmically. Nero stood waving until the ship pulled away and disappeared into the darkness, then traipsed back to his villa. Even though it was now into the early hours of the morning and his companions went to their beds, Nero sat up in his quarters, alone, waiting.

It was a stunningly beautiful night. The heavens glittered with starlight, and the sea was tranquil. As the ship slid across the water, following the shoreline around the bay, Agrippina lounged on the couch in the little stern cabin on the main deck. She was in high spirits. Recalling the wonderful dinner with her boy, she was awash with delight at Nero's "repentance" and at the prospect of once more exercising control over him, and the empire.[13] Her lady-in-waiting, Acerronia, lolled at her feet, hiding yawns, while her friend and chaperone, Gallus, stood alertly at the entrance to the cabin. None of them seemed to suspect a thing. The ship's captain, Volusius, now gave a signal to several of his crew who were in on the Anicetus plot.

Without warning, the ceiling of the ship's cabin, which had been deliberately loaded with lead, collapsed on the occupants. Agrippina's chaperone, Gallus, was killed instantly. Agrippina herself managed to duck just in time. The arms of her couch saved both her and lady-in-waiting Acerronia from the same fate as Gallus. For a moment there was silence. And then Acerronia came crawling out from under the debris. "Help the mother of the emperor!" she wailed.[14]

Crewmen who had been brought into the plot by their skipper, hearing the woman's cries in the darkness, took Acerronia to be the emperor's mother and set about her with oars and anything else they could lay their hands on. Mercilessly, they battered Acerronia to death. In the middle of this murderous mayhem, the lever that was supposed to make the ship fall apart failed to work when the captain, Volusius, pulled it. So members of the conspiracy all rushed to one side of the ship in an attempt to capsize it. Other crewmen, the majority of whom were not party to the plot, rushed to the other side to counter them and save the ship. In this chaos, Agrippina dragged herself from the wreckage of the cabin. A crewman spotted her and swung at her with an oar, striking her a painful blow to the shoulder. But in the confusion and the darkness, the emperor's mother was able to slip over the side and into the water, undetected.

Most Romans could not swim, but Agrippina was an exception. Despite her limited swimming skills and her injured shoulder, she made her way toward land. As she swam through the night, she came on six-oared fishing boats standing offshore. Fishermen hauled her from the water and into one of the boats, then rowed her to the beach. As she was staggering through the doorway of the Bauli villa and falling into the arms of astonished servants, the fishermen were running through the district calling out to all the residents that the emperor's mother had just been saved from a terrible boating accident.

Once Agrippina had composed herself, she pondered hard on what to do next. The collapse of the stern section of the ship that Nero had just presented to her was beyond coincidence. Yet it seems she could not bring herself to publicly accuse her son of engineering an attempt on her life. She instructed her freedman Agerinus to hurry to the emperor at Baiae and inform him that by the grace of heaven she had survived a terrible disaster. But, she said, Agerinus was to tell the emperor that he should not trouble himself to come to her, but instead let her rest. As her man mounted a horse and rode away on his mission to Nero, Agrippina quietly lamented the death of her friend Acerronia, and ordered her now wide-awake servants to search for Acerronia's last will and testament. At the same time, uncertain about her own future, she had her own will sealed. As she applied ointment to her wounded shoulder and drank a bracing medicine, she pretended that all was well in her world.

At the villa at Baiae, Nero had been spending a sleepless night sitting in his bedchamber, waiting for news from the bay. Finally, in the last hours of darkness, a hall porter came to him to say that Agrippina's freedman Agerinus had just arrived at the villa and was requesting an urgent audience with the emperor. Nero's heart must have been beating fast as he demanded to know what news Agerinus had brought of his mother. There had been a tragic boating accident, Agerinus had told the emperor's servant, an accident that had killed two friends of the emperor's mother. But Agrippina herself had survived with just a minor injury. Nero looked at the servant with widening eyes. He was temporarily paralyzed by fear, says Tacitus. Once he overcome his shock, he sent for Seneca, Burrus, and the admiral Anicetus. The admiral was, of course, a party to the murder plot, and Tacitus was to suspect that both Seneca and Burrus were already also "part of the secret."[15]

In a panic, Nero told the three bleary-eyed officials what had happened. Then he shrieked, "My mother will show herself here any moment! Eager for vengeance! She'll either arm the slaves or stir up the soldiers. Or she'll rush to the Senate and the people. She'll charge me with the wreck of the ship, with wounding her, with the murder of her friends! What should I do?" Wide-eyed, young Nero looked at his chief secretary, who was several paces in advance of Burrus, who in turn was in front of a shuddering Anicetus. "Seneca? Burrus? Think of something," Nero pleaded.[16]

Neither Seneca nor Burrus replied. After a long pause, Seneca turned to Burrus, raising his eyebrows. The Praetorian colonel knew what was in Seneca's mind, and shook his head—his soldiers would not finish what Nero had begun by drawing their swords against Agrippina. "The Praetorians are attached to the entire Caesar family," he said. "Remembering Germanicus, they wouldn't dare touch his child. It's up to Anicetus to keep his promise."[17]

With narrowing eyes, Nero looked at Anicetus. The admiral gulped and then, knowing that he had failed the emperor, quickly volunteered to put things right. "I will finish it, Caesar."

Beaming, Nero hurried across the room to his former tutor and embraced him, clapping him on the back. "This day will give me my empire, and a freedman will be the creator of this mighty achievement. Go, with all speed. And take those men with you who are the most willing to carry out your orders."[18]

Anicetus then hurried away to complete his mission, intent on making it appear as if Agrippina had committed suicide. Nero was left looking at Seneca and Burrus. There was still the problem of his mother's freedman Agerinus, who was waiting in another part of the villa to see the emperor and deliver the message from his mistress. Too many people knew that Agerinus had come to Baiae, and why. Whether what followed was Nero's idea we are not told. It is quite likely that Seneca or Burrus came up with the plan. As a result of the suggestion of one or the other, Burrus strode to one of the German Guards standing at the door, slid the surprised man's sword from its sheath, then handed the sword to Nero. The emperor then sent for his mother's servant.

Freedman Agerinus was ushered into the emperor's presence. He found Nero standing at the end of the room with his hands behind his back. The German Guard's sword was in Nero's left hand, trailing down his leg, out of Agerinus's sight. After bowing deeply, Agerinus hurried forward and proceeded to gush his message. He was halfway through it when Nero suddenly produced the sword. He held it out. Agerinus looked at the sword in sudden fear. Nero let the sword drop. It clanged onto the tiled floor in front of Agerinus and lay there. The freedman had stopped in midsentence. Totally puzzled now, he looked at the sword, then at Nero.

"Guards!" Nero called. "This man has been caught in the middle of a criminal act. Put him in irons!"[19]

The German Guards at the door strode forward and grabbed hold of the astonished Agerinus. They dragged him, protesting his innocence, from the room. Charged with making an attempt on the emperor's life, his fate would be immediate execution. Nero's intent was to claim to the Senate and the world that his mother had sent her man to murder him and that after Agerinus had been caught red-handed, Agrippina had taken her own life. As Seneca was to write in one of his plays, "The best way to get away with a crime is with another crime."[20] Just one last thing was required for the fiction to be complete: the murder of Agrippina.

When Anicetus left the imperial villa after vowing to Nero that he would finish off Agrippina, he went directly to the Baiae jetty where the trireme that had brought her up from Anzio was tied up. The warship's captain, Herculeius, was a freedman, as were all the marines serving on the ship. Freedmen, being former slaves, were not Roman citizens, and did not feel the same attachment to the family of the Caesars that the citizen soldiers of the Praetorian Guard and the legions did. Marines were actually on the lowest rung of the Roman military. They were even paid less and served a year longer, with twenty-six-year enlistments, than did noncitizen foreigners of the Roman Army's auxiliary infantry and cavalry. With promises of rich rewards, Anicetus quickly convinced the navarchus Herculeius and the centurion Obaritus, commander of the ship's contingent of marines, to join him in ending the life of the emperor's mother.

The trireme's forty marines marched with the three officers from Baiae around the cove to Bauli Villa. On their way, they passed hundreds of anxious civilians, many of them on the beach milling about uncertainly with burning torches after having heard that the emperor's mother had been involved in a boating accident on the bay. A number of people outside the walls of the sprawling Bauli Villa, anxiously awaiting news of Agrippina, quickly dispersed as the marines marched up to the complex. The outer gates had been closed and locked, but the marines soon forced them open.

As marines came through the shattered gates with flaming torches in hand, a large number of Agrippina's slaves stood bunched in their path, unarmed but determined not to let the troops pass. They were quickly dragged away, as riot police might drag away passive protesters today. Anicetus, Herculeius, and the centurion Obaritus forced their way into the house, with chosen marines close on their heels. Several of Agrippina's staff members, including her freedman Mnester, stood with folded arms in front of a particular door, signifying that their mistress lay beyond it. Mnester and his companions were roughly pushed aside. The door was flung open. Inside the room, a *triclinium* (dining room), a single oil lamp flickered, revealing Agrippina reclining on a dining couch facing the window, with a view of the beach and bay beyond. A servant girl sat on the couch beside her mistress. As Anicetus, Herculeius, and Obaritus came through the doorway, the girl suddenly looked fearful and came to her feet.

Agrippina reached out to the girl. "Are you too going to desert me?" Then Agrippina turned, to see the three sour-faced officers. "If you have come to visit me," she said to them, "take back word that I have recovered." Then she noticed that Herculeius the trireme captain had a wooden baton in his hand, the kind used on ships for repelling boarders. "But if you're here to commit a crime, I refuse to believe that my son has anything to do with it. He could not have ordered the murder of his own mother."[21]

As the three men closed around her couch without a word, the servant girl fled from the room. Behind Agrippina, Herculeius raised his club, and crashed it down on her skull. But it was not a killer blow. Dazed but still conscious, Agrippina glared defiantly at her assassins. The centurion Obaritus deliberately drew his *gladius* from the sheath on his left hip.

Agrippina ripped open her dress, exposing her midriff. "Strike here, strike my womb!" she cried, daring the centurion to strike the womb from which his emperor had come.[22]

Obaritus had no compunction about what he had come to do. He accepted Agrippina's invitation and plunged his sword into the emperor's mother. According to Seneca, who should have been in possession of all the gory details, she died a slow death.[23] Tacitus writes that the centurion had to put his sword into her not once, but time and time again.[24] Once this killing frenzy was at an end, Seneca was to write, Agrippina's body had been mutilated by the numerous sword thrusts.[25] Agrippina the Younger, daughter of the legendary Germanicus Caesar, the same Agrippina the Younger whose earliest memories may have included riding through the streets of Rome in a golden chariot on her father's glorious Triumph day, died a bloody, seedy death there on the couch at the Bauli villa.

Tacitus was to relate a story that many years earlier, when Nero was quite young, Agrippina had consulted astrologers about her son's future. This was the occasion on which these same astrologers had told her that Nero must not claim the throne until after midday. The astrologers had warned Agrippina that her son would indeed become emperor, but he also would kill his mother. "Let him kill me," she had allegedly responded, "as long as he becomes emperor."[26]

A messenger hurried around the bay from Anicetus to Baiae Villa, to inform the emperor that his mother was dead. Tacitus says that once he received this news, Nero spent the remaining hours of the night in stupefied silence, waiting, terrified and almost in disbelief, for the dawn. Already he was racked with guilt. And he was in terror of what the Roman people would think when they heard about the bloody death of his mother, the daughter and last surviving child of Germanicus, and what they might do about it.

Some classical authors would write that Nero actually looked at his mother's dead body and praised her beauty. Two hundred years later, Dio would repeat that story in his account of Nero's rule, adding that Nero remarked, "I didn't know that I had such a beautiful mother."[27] Suetonius, writing seventy years after the event, gave a similar account.[28] But the histories of both Dio and Suetonius were fervently biased against Nero, and both authors could on occasion take the most sensational routes with their writings. As for the more sober and reliable Tacitus, he reports that some authors of the day related that same story, "while others deny it."[29]

With Tacitus relating that it took many sword thrusts to complete the murder, and as Seneca, who must be considered the most authoritative source of all, describes Agrippina's body being mutilated by the centurion's sword, there can have been no beautiful body to admire, destroying the credibility of the stories of Suetonius and Dio. Besides, it seems highly unlikely that Nero would so closely associate himself with the murder by viewing his mother's body—that would have meant having the corpse brought to him at Baiae, or, alternatively, he would have gone to the beachside villa at Bauli, scene of the murder. Both acts would have been provocative in the highly charged climate of public concern for the welfare of Agrippina in the district following the boating "accident." Tellingly, no author, not even Dio or Suetonius, talks of the body being brought to Baiae nor of Nero going to Bauli to view it, which seems to effectively scotch that story.

That same night, Mnester, Agrippina's surviving freedman, had his mistress's body carried, on the dining couch on which she had died, up to the promontory of Cape Misenum. She was cremated on the couch, at a spot close to the Marian Villa where Julius Caesar had spent time and where Tiberius had died, and a sepulchre was later built on the spot. Tacitus says that the mournful sounds of a funeral trumpet were heard wafting down from the heights in the early hours of the morning. Once Mnester's mistress had been consumed by the flames, the faithful servant fell on a sword and killed himself.

As the sun began to rise on the morning of March 20, all the tribunes and centurions at the Baiae villa came to Nero, at the prompting of their prefect Burrus, and, shaking his hand, congratulated him on escaping "his mother's daring crime."[30] Nero's friends Seneca, Burrus, and others went to the nearby temples to offer thanks for the young emperor's deliverance, and as the news spread, people throughout surrounding Campania did the same. But Nero was in shock. Suetonius would say that Nero was unable, then or later, to free his conscience of the guilt of his mother's murder.[31] All through the morning of March 20, he wept uncontrollably. He seemed, says Tacitus, almost angry[32]—whether angry with himself, with his mother's killers, with his mother, or with the gods, we can only guess. Pulling himself together in the afternoon, he departed the scene, removing himself and his court to Neopolis, today's city of Naples.

At Naples, the cunning and composed Seneca wrote a long letter to the Senate, which would go to Rome in Nero's name, to explain away the murder of the emperor's revered mother. Agerinus, so Seneca's letter to the Senate claimed, had been sent by Agrippina to murder the emperor, and when the assassination attempt failed, she had paid the ultimate penalty for her folly. Seneca went into great detail, raking up Agrippina's old crimes and misdemeanors stretching back to the reign of Claudius, describing the men and women destroyed by Agrippina when she was Claudius's empress, and attributing all the imperial oppression of that period to her. In a statement designed to cause the disaffection of the military in particular, she had even, said the letter, opposed the cash bequests—the "donatives," as they were called—that Claudius had left to all soldiers and every Roman citizen in his will.

Seneca's letter was hurried to Rome, to be read to the Senate in the emperor's name to disguise the crime and excuse his part in it. Many senators suspected the truth of what had happened at Bauli. Who would be so stupid, Tacitus would ask in his *Annals*, as to believe that Agrippina's ship had caved in by accident, or that she had sent a lone assassin to Nero's villa in the belief that he could possibly get by the emperor's numerous guards?[33] But knowing that the Praetorian Guard was firmly behind Nero, not a single senator had the courage to speak out against him. The person they did feel safe enough to criticize, says Tacitus, was Seneca, for applying his literary talent to the creation of such a lying document to cover up such a heinous crime.[34]

Despite their suspicions about the true cause of Agrippina's death, the senators fell over themselves in their haste to fawn on the emperor. They decreed thanksgivings to the gods for their having allowed Nero to survive the fictional assassination attempt. They voted the creation of statues to celebrate the event. And they heaped ignominy on Agrippina's memory—destroying her statues and all record of her achievements, even declaring that her birthday should be included on the official list of days considered inauspicious.

Such was the fate of the daughter of Germanicus who, only days before, had been much loved by the ordinary people and considered by Romans to be above reproach and beyond punishment. By the time that the assassination of Agrippina's name had also been completed, the only thing she was permitted to share with her father was a murderous end. With one exception: in her case, the identity of her murderers was clear.

# XVII

# DEATH FOR BURRUS
# AND OCTAVIA

**W**hile Romans in general swiftly overcame the death of Agrippina the Younger, Nero never did come to terms with what he had done. According to Suetonius, Nero often confessed that he was hounded by the ghost of his mother.[1] As he tried to find solace and escape his guilt, Nero increasingly took an interest in various Eastern religious cults based on a virgin goddess, a common theme in religions of the East. According to Christian tradition, encouraged by his mistress Acte and his cupbearer, who were both reputedly Christians, Nero even spoke to the apostle Paul about the tenets of the Christian faith. This was supposed to have taken place when Paul was brought to Rome in A.D. 60 to have his legal appeal against charges laid against him by Jewish leaders in Judea heard by the emperor, as was his right as a Roman citizen.

With Seneca and Burrus still exerting a powerful influence over Nero, the empire was seemingly still in good hands. They continued to keep firm hands on the wheel of the ship of state and to steer Nero away from dangerous courses. At one point, says Dio, Nero suddenly became particularly paranoid and decided that he must kill all potential rivals for his throne among Rome's senators, but Seneca talked him out of it, saying, sagely, "No matter how many you kill, you cannot kill your successor."[2]

While Seneca had prevented wholesale slaughter of senators and knights, he made no attempt to dissuade Nero from entertaining his passion for music. At least no one died when Nero appeared onstage dressed as a lyre player and sang in public contests. Seneca and Burrus actually stood onstage with Nero when he made an appearance at Rome in A.D. 59 and sang two pieces of his own composition called "Attis" and "The Bacchantes." Meanwhile, says Dio, on Nero's instructions Seneca's brother Gallio introduced the emperor to the audience under his own original name, Lucius Domitius Ahenobarbus, not the name he had taken as emperor, Nero Claudius Caesar Augustus Germanicus.[3]

At the same time, around the empire, the military commanders whose appointments had been made on the recommendation of Seneca and Burrus did Rome proud. In the East, the dour old general Corbulo drove the Parthians from Armenia and put a king who vowed allegiance to Nero and to Rome on the Armenian throne. In Britain, the Roman governor, Suetonius Paulinus, staged a remarkable comeback after much of southern Britain had been overrun by British rebels led by the rebel queen Boudicca. With just the 5,000 legionaries of the 14th Gemina Martia Victrix Legion, 2,000 men of the Evocati militia who had recently retired from the 20th Valeria Victrix Legion, 2,000 Batavian auxiliaries, and 1,000 auxiliary cavalry—a total of 10,000 men—Paulinus defeated Boudicca's 230,000 warriors in a bloody A.D. 60 battle northwest of London, then regained the province and hounded the Britons using harsh punitive measures over the next twelve months.

With his advisers, governors, and generals handling the various crises, Nero also began to spend time driving chariots, a passion of his since childhood. In the hope of keeping this hobby out of the public eye, Seneca and Burrus enclosed a large area in the Vatican Valley, leading up to the rise where St. Peter's Cathedral stands today. There, Nero trained his teams of chariot horses. But in time, to the frustration of his advisers, he also competed in public at the Circus Maximus. Nero also increasingly appeared on the public stage at Rome and elsewhere, playing the lyre and singing.

By A.D. 62, Praetorian prefect Burrus was suffering from a fast-developing throat cancer that had advanced to the point where his neck bulged significantly. Before the year was out, his throat was almost entirely blocked and the insidious disease had him on his deathbed. Several classical writers were to suggest that Nero finished Burrus off with poison so the emperor would be free to do as he wished once the powerful Burrus-Seneca alliance was broken. Tacitus says that many people of the time asserted that Nero had indeed ordered

Burrus's attendants to smear his cancerous throat with poison on the pretext of providing a remedy, but Burrus saw through the scheme and refused to accept the ointment. When Nero visited him shortly after, Burrus recoiled from the emperor's greeting kiss on the cheek. Then, when Nero asked if he was well, Burrus croaked in reply, "I am very well." According to Tacitus, the tumor closed up Burrus's throat shortly after, killing him.[4]

In replacing Burrus, Nero reverted to the practice instituted by Augustus, appointing two prefects of the Praetorian Guard at the same time. One of the new appointees was Faenius Rufus, the superintendent of the corn supply, who had received that appointment through the favor of Agrippina the Younger when she was at the height of her power. Rufus had shown himself to be an honest man, and was popular with the public and the Praetorian soldiery. But he was weak-kneed and had no military experience to speak of. His coprefect, Ofonius (also written Sofonius and Sophonius) Tigellinus had a very different persona and background. Hugely ambitious despite a lowly upbringing, he had proven to be a man without scruples as he built his career. Tigellinus had been banished by Caligula in A.D. 39 for having an affair with Agrippina the Younger. Allowed to return to Rome by Claudius, Tigellinus had become prefect of the Night Watch under Nero. Now he was joint Praetorian commander. His loyalty to Nero up to this point was "well proven,"[5] for, when Night Watch commander, he had been the emperor's companion and colleague during Nero's whoring in the streets of Rome at night.

The chief secretary, Seneca, now found himself exposed, for the first time in the fourteen years that he had been associated with Nero; the death of Burrus had robbed him of his partner in power. Seneca was not on good terms with either of the new Praetorian prefects, Rufus or Tigellinus, and soon found his influence with Nero waning now that he could not rely on a Praetorian commander to back him up. Seneca's enemies in the Senate also realized that his position had been weakened and began to level various charges at him in the House. Most of those charges did not amount to grounds for a criminal trial, but they chipped away at his credibility. He was accused of courting celebrity with the public. He had, it also was claimed, grown too rich in the emperor's service, to the point that his gardens and country estates exceeded those of the emperor in their size and grandeur. His detractors said that he thought himself the most eloquent of all Romans, implying that this should be considered a crime. More worrying for him, there was a whispered accusation that Seneca had criticized the emperor behind his back for his chariot-racing and had ridiculed Nero's singing voice.

The young senator Fabius Romanus went further. He charged Seneca in the Senate with covertly plotting against the emperor. Romanus had apparently forgotten what a formidable debater Seneca was. To mount his defense, Seneca took his seat in the House. Employing his customary oratorical brilliance, Seneca was able to skillfully turn the charges around so that Romanus was the one who stood accused, of fabricating his accusations, and the charges against Seneca fell in ruins. Still, this was a warning to Seneca that he must now be constantly on his guard.

Burrus had been firmly against Nero marrying his mistress Poppaea Sabina. But now that Burrus was dead, and with Sabina announcing that she was pregnant with Nero's child, she was able to convince the emperor to divorce his blameless but barren twenty-year-old wife, Claudia Octavia, daughter of his late uncle and stepfather Claudius. To facilitate the divorce, Octavia was charged with adultery with a flute-playing Egyptian slave named Eucaerus. And to obtain evidence of this adultery, Octavia's female slaves were tortured by Praetorian prefect Tigellinus. Some of the slaves bravely refused to implicate Octavia. One, a woman named Pythias, even spat in Tigellinus's face as she lay stretched naked on the rack. When he suggested the sort of sexual activities that Pythias should confess to having witnessed between Octavia and Eucaerus, Pythias had reputedly declared, "My mistress's privy parts are cleaner than your mouth, Tigellinus!"[6]

Despite the lack of cooperation from Pythias and others, under torture several servants told Tigellinus what he wanted to hear, and the grounds for divorce were established. The formalities were rushed through, and as soon as the divorce was finalized, Nero had Octavia moved out of the Palatium. With obvious irony, and as if thumbing his nose at the late prefect Burrus, who had been against Nero divorcing Octavia, the emperor sent Octavia to live in Burrus's former city house. But Octavia was very popular, and the people of Rome loudly objected to the divorce, protesting in the streets. This appeared to unnerve Nero, who, eleven days after divorcing Octavia, brought her back to the palace, seemingly restoring her as his wife. But, as it turned out, he planned to secretly marry Sabina the very next day.

In response to Octavia's apparent restoration, the joyful public, who had never believed the story of Octavia's infidelity with a slave, flocked to the Capitol in their thousands to give thanks to the gods. They then pulled down the statues of Sabina, and set up statues and busts of Octavia in the Forum and the temples. Surging around the Palatium, the mob even cheered Nero for restoring Octavia. But this unruly crowd was a threatening sight to the occupants of the Palatium, and it brought the soldiers of the German Guard out to defend the palace colonnades. The duty cohort of the Praetorian Guard then suddenly appeared. Acting the role of riot police, the Praetorian troops drove into the crowd with wooden batons waving, to disperse them, killing a handful of protesters in the process.

According to the Senecan play *Octavia*, Seneca now attempted to talk Nero out of marrying Sabina the next day. Tacitus, in his *Annals* chronology, has Seneca retiring just before this event. Even if that chronology is correct—and Tacitus sometimes moved events around within the annual time frame he used in the *Annals*—it is not impossible that Seneca, as Nero was to urge him to do, came in from retirement to speak to the emperor on this matter. Dio says that it was Burrus who spoke against the marriage to Sabina at this time, but Burrus was dead by then. In *Octavia*, Seneca told Nero that the public would not accept the marriage to Sabina. He said that Octavia was young, innocent, and a well-liked member of the Claudian family, an imperial lady by birth. Meanwhile, he said, Sabina was the ambitious daughter of a noble adulteress, with only her good looks and her pregnancy to recommend her.[7]

"Let me do, just for once," Nero said to Seneca in response, "one thing that is condemned by Seneca."[8]

Not only did Sabina want to make Nero her husband, she also wanted Octavia out of the way. The mobs in the street calling Octavia's name showed how popular she and her bloodline were, and while she lived, Sabina would always feel insecure. Sabina transmitted that insecurity to Nero. Tacitus says that, pleading with him to deal with Octavia, Sabina warned, "If the people give up on the idea of Octavia being your wife, they will quickly find her another husband."[9] This suggestion, that Octavia might marry another man who would then have the credentials to win popular support for the taking of Nero's throne, terrified Nero, in the same way that his mother's threat to replace him with Britannicus had terrified him.[10] In *Octavia*, Praetorian prefect Tigellinus now arrived to report to Nero. The prefect advised that the pro-Octavia riots had been put down, with several ringleaders killed.

"Put down?" Nero retorted. "Is that to be my only satisfaction?" He called for much more severe punishment.[11]

"Who do you wish to punish?" said Tigellinus. He rested his right hand on the hilt of his sheathed sword. "My hand is ready."

"Take her [Octavia's] life, and give me her detestable head."

A horrified look came over the prefect's face. "I'm stunned. Struck dumb with horror, and fear."

"You hesitate?"

"You doubt my loyalty?"

"Yes, if you spare my enemy."

"A woman is your enemy?"

"If she is charged with a crime."

"On what evidence has she been convicted?"

"By the revolt of the mob."[12]

Yet Tigellinus neither arrested nor executed Octavia. Nero and Poppaea Sabina were married the next day.

Both Tigellinus and Seneca would have pointed out that a substantial charge would be necessary if Octavia were to be convicted of a major crime. Urged on by Sabina now that she was Nero's empress, Nero racked his mind for an appropriate charge, one that could not be challenged. Then he had an idea. Nero sent for Anicetus, admiral of the Tyrrhenian Fleet at Misenum, the man who had engineered the death of his mother. Nero informed Anicetus that he expected him to now confess to having had an affair with Octavia. If he agreed, Nero promised him a large, though secret, financial reward, and a magnificent estate where he could retreat and spend the rest of his days. If Anicetus refused, his reward would be execution.

Nero's former tutor not only agreed, he also proved particularly creative with the confession of adultery with Octavia that he made before friends of the emperor. Nero kept his part of the bargain: Anicetus was exiled to the pleasant island of Sardinia, where he would live out the rest of his days in comfort on a palatial estate, to die a natural death. To add a little more spice to the equation, Nero also accused Octavia of having fallen pregnant to one of her lovers and of then having an abortion. He had forgotten that one of the reasons he'd originally given for divorcing Octavia was that she had been barren and so unable to become pregnant and give him an heir.

On the strength of Anicetus's invented claims, young Octavia was now arrested at the Palatium. Praetorian centurions and soldiers flooded around her, her wrists were secured with chains, and she was placed in a closed litter and hustled away to a waiting ship. According to the play *Octavia*, she was taken from the Italian mainland to the prison island of Pandataria in the very same trireme that had previously brought Nero's mother to Baiae.[13] This accords with Nero's previous actions. He'd sent Octavia to live at Burrus's house; now she was sent to the same prison island where his adulteress mother, Agrippina the Younger, grandmother Agrippina the Elder, and great-grandmother Julia had been incarcerated, aboard the same ship that had brought his mother to her death.

Within days of the former empress landing on Pandataria, an order arrived from Rome for Octavia to be put to death. Her guards acted at once. As she was tightly bound by the centurions and soldiers, she appealed to them to spare her—she was the daughter of Claudius, the niece of Germanicus, she reminded them. She had been the obedient stepdaughter of Agrippina, Germanicus's daughter. She had committed no crime. But the unsympathetic Praetorians coldly ignored her pleas. Every vein on her arms and legs was slit open. There she lay, surrounded by the soldiers, as her heart pumped out her lifeblood. But the day was cold; her blood congealed; she would not die.

Impatient to end the business, the centurion in charge had Octavia carried to the island's bathhouse. A ferociously hot bath was prepared. When its steam filled the room, Octavia was plunged into the scalding hot water. There she died. Once her body had been retrieved, the centurion sliced off the twenty-year-old's head. This was sent to Rome to prove that the execution order had been carried out. Sabina, the new empress, asked to see the severed head of her predecessor, and when it was brought to her, viewed it with morbid satisfaction. This latter act was, in the view of Tacitus, who detailed Octavia's death, the most appalling part of the entire episode.[14]

Seneca had failed to prevent either the execution of Octavia or Nero's marriage to Sabina. With his influence waning, and with Nero increasingly avoiding him, Seneca, who was now sixty-five, decided that he should retire while he could. Seeking and receiving a private audience with Nero, he thanked the emperor for having made him wealthy and powerful and for ranking him among the most famous men of Rome. That he had been honored with such wealth and power was all the more significant, he said, because he came from a provincial family that, before him, had never advanced beyond the Equestrian Order. Craftily, he offered to allow his properties to be managed by the emperor's agents and to be included in Nero's estate, while he himself went into quiet retirement. "I can no longer bear the burden of my riches, and need help."[15]

Nero graciously replied, praising his former tutor and faithful chief secretary, and thanking him for all he had done for him over the years. He hid his delight at being freed from Seneca's disapproving presence at the Palatium and permitted him to retire, even making a show of urging him to come to him at any time if he felt he should offer advice on any matter. And so Seneca surrendered the ornamental dagger he wore as his badge of office as chief secretary, then withdrew from the palace and from public life. Previously he had been surrounded by a multitude of clients and traveled with a vast train of servants and dependents. Now he kept a low profile and a small entourage, moving quietly from one of his country estates to another, writing plays and long philosophical letters and rarely visiting Rome.

With Seneca out of the way, Praetorian prefect Tigellinus now planted seeds of doubt in Nero's mind about his coprefect, Rufus. Tigellinus's principal accusation was that Rufus had been too close to Agrippina, who had engineered his early promotion. Ironically, no one had been closer to Agrippina than Tigellinus, who had been convicted of adultery with her. But he was able to persuade Nero not to confide in Rufus. While Rufus found himself losing Nero's favor, Tigellinus was given more and more responsibility by the emperor. Increasingly, Tigellinus became a new Sejanus, brutally terrorizing every class of Roman society. In Nero's name he destroyed on false charges any rich man whose wealth approached that of the emperor, including the immensely rich Pallas, who, when he had retired as secretary for finances prior to Seneca's withdrawal from the Palatium, had amassed a fortune even greater than Seneca's.

Meanwhile, at Anzio in A.D. 63, Sabina, the new empress, bore Nero a baby girl, Claudia Augusta. The child would die of ill health before reaching her second birthday. Her death would be a harbinger of a tragic future for Nero. His death, and the unraveling of the mystery involving the murder of his grandfather Germanicus, were not far off.

# XVIII

# THE PLOT TO MURDER NERO

ouse fires were common in Rome. With the city's closely packed high-rise tenement buildings and mostly narrow, winding streets, once a fire took hold, it quickly spread. Not infrequently, landlords would deliberately start fires that burned down their own buildings. There were no insurance companies in Roman times, but it still paid landlords to burn down old properties so they could eject tenants, build bigger and better properties, and charge higher rents.

Once every ten years or so, a major fire would ravage whole city blocks. But in July A.D. 64, Rome was afflicted by a devastating blaze that came to be called the Great Fire of Rome. Nero was out of town at the time. Now that he had become obsessed with competing in theatrical contests, he had gone down Italy's western coast to Anzio, where a prestigious annual contest for singers and lyre players was held each year. Anzio was a town favored by the imperial family, and Nero had developed a new port there in A.D. 59. While at Anzio for the contest, Nero stayed at the imperial villa built by Caligula as a vacation place and used as the seaside resort of Nero's mother, Agrippina the Younger, for many years; it had been from there that Agrippina had sailed to her death five years earlier. There, too, Sabina had given birth to Nero's daughter.

On July 19, while Nero was playing his lyre and singing onstage at the Anzio singing contest, a fire broke out in shops in an arcade beneath Rome's massive Circus Maximus, a complex that could seat more than two hundred thousand people. This occurrence was the source of the story that Nero "fiddled" while Rome burned. The fire quickly engulfed the timbers of the huge circus's stands, the largest wooden structure ever built, then spread through the neighboring part of the city northwest of the Palatine Hill.

The next day, when news of the fire reached Anzio, and Nero learned that the conflagration was raging out of control through the city and approaching his Palatium, he hurried back to the capital. There was nothing the firemen of the City Guard or Night Watch or the troops of the Praetorian Guard could do to stop the advance of the wall of flames. Nero had recently extended the Palatium of Augustus, building a connecting structure called the Domus Transitoria, which linked the Palatine palaces to the Gardens of Maecenas on the Esquiline Hill. All of this new construction was engulfed before the flames crept up the Palatine and ravaged the palaces on the slope, including Augustus's original Old Palatium. Nero was one of the hundreds of thousands of Romans made homeless by the destruction.

As the fire continued to eat its way through one city precinct after another, Nero opened up the Field of Mars and the imperial gardens to the city's refugees, and had temporary shelters thrown up for the homeless. He also sent for food supplies from Ostia and other nearby towns to feed the population. But while these measures won initial public praise for the emperor, opinions of Nero changed when the rumor spread that when he had been onstage at Anzio he had sung about the fall of Troy, almost as if he had wished for the destruction of Rome.

The fire raged for five days before being brought under control at the foot of the Esquiline Hill. But just as everyone was breathing a sigh of relief, the conflagration sprang up anew, in property owned by Praetorian commander Tigellinus. For another several days the flames flew, destroying temples and the homes of the rich. When finally the fire died, every building in three of Rome's fourteen precincts had been totally destroyed. In another seven precincts only a few half-burned buildings remained. Just four precincts had been left completely untouched by the flames. The loss of life was surprisingly low—the very young and the very old, those unable to flee the flames, had mostly figured among the casualties.

The references in some classical texts including Tacitus's Annals to Christians subsequently being rounded up and burned alive by Nero as scapegoats for the fire are considered by many scholars to be inventions of later Christian copyists who inserted this paragraph into the copies of the *Annals* they made, the only copies that have come down to the present day. The general belief at the time was that the original fire, which began in the circus shops, was accidental, but that the second blaze, five days later, was set by Tigellinus, either on Nero's orders so he could rebuild Rome to his own design or because Tigellinus wanted to profit by building grander rental properties on his land.

The rebuilding of Rome would take many years. While the restored city would be one of striking splendor, according to Tacitus, there would be old men alive in his day who would remember the historical monuments and buildings, including the palace of the early Roman king Numa, and priceless Greek works of art that could not be replaced.[1] As the rubble was cleared and shipped down the Tiber to fill in the marshes at Ostia, and as the provinces vied with each other to provide money and craftsmen for the task of restoring the capital, reconstruction planning gave Nero the opportunity to redesign the city with regular, wider streets and greater access to running water, at the same time implementing building regulations designed to restrict the spread of house fires, with limits on building heights and building densities. It also permitted the creation of more public open space.

More important to Nero, the vast devastation allowed him to pander to his dream of a palace unlike anything ever before built. From the ashes of the Great Fire rose the new Palatium, Nero's Golden House. His Domus Aurea would occupy two hundred acres in the heart of Rome, spreading well beyond the Palatine Hill to the surrounding Caelian and Opian Hills, encompassing numerous buildings, gardens, and lakes. One of those lakes would be drained a decade later to create the site for the Flavian Amphitheater, or Colosseum. A 120-foot-tall marble statue of Nero, known as the "Colossus," which he installed in the Golden House's entry vestibule, would by A.D. 80 be relocated to stand outside the Colosseum, giving the famous amphitheater the nickname that has come down to the present day (the Colosseum's official name was actually the Hunting Theater). Only the massive head of the Neronian statue and one of its huge marble hands would survive through the ages.

While Nero had allowed Seneca to depart Palatium service two years earlier and retire to write what some later authorities would consider to be his best works, Seneca was not yet out of the emperor's life. Seneca was hated by the new empress, Sabina, because he had opposed her marriage to Nero and had opposed the execution of Octavia. And despite Nero's invitation to Seneca to come out of retirement at any time to correct him if he felt he was following a wrong course, in truth Nero was not prepared to be lectured by anyone anymore. Seneca now came to learn through his freedman Cleonicus that poison had been prepared on Nero's command and that Cleonicus had been approached to use it on his master. After this, Seneca existed on a diet of wild fruits and stream water, to avoid being poisoned.

Nero's ongoing attempts to destroy the lives of leading Romans such as Seneca, combined with the vast amounts of money poured by Nero into the Golden House, and his obsessions with chariots and the stage, together with the brutal activities of his Praetorian commander Tigellinus, made Nero so loathed by Rome's nobility that several plots to kill him were fomenting by the spring of A.D. 65, just seven months after the Great Fire. One of those plots centered around the distinguished senator Gaius Calpurnius Piso, the same Piso who regularly loaned his Baiae villa to Nero, the villa from which Nero had carried out the murder of his mother.

At the heart of a second plot was a Praetorian Guard tribune, Subrius Flavus, and a Praetorian centurion, Sulpicius Asper. These two men brought several other Praetorian officers into their murder conspiracy. At the same time, and independent of the Praetorian plot, a number of senators and knights conspired with Piso, planning to make him emperor once Nero had been done away with. Tacitus, citing Pliny the Younger as his source, was to write that Piso planned to divorce his wife and marry Claudia Antonia, the emperor Claudius's last surviving daughter and Germanicus's niece, to give him a credible claim to the throne.[2] To bring the Praetorian Guard over to the assassins, the Piso plotters approached Praetorian cocommander Faenius Rufus, who, they hoped and believed, would happily destroy Nero and Tigellinus now that Tigellinus had caused the emperor to virtually sideline Rufus. The senators knew that without the popular Guard commander, and without the Guard, their plot would fail. Rufus agreed to join the plotters, and through him the conspiratorial Praetorian officers Flavus and Asper also were brought into the Piso plot. The two assassination schemes now melded into one.

It was suggested by some conspirators that the assassination should take place when Nero paid one of his visits to Piso's Baiae villa, but Piso said he had no desire to pollute the place with the tyrant's blood.

Another of the assassination plans being considered involved murdering Nero at sea. With this scenario in mind, Epicharis, a wealthy freedwoman who was part of the general conspiracy, sounded out the naval captain Volusius Proculus, who had been a participant in the murder of Agrippina the Younger. Proculus had privately complained to Epicharis that he felt he had not been well enough recompensed for his role in the murder of the emperor's mother. But after Epicharis discussed killing Nero while the emperor was aboard a warship on a planned imperial visit to Egypt, Proculus went straight to Nero to inform on her. The freedwoman was arrested and tortured, but she confessed to nothing. With no other witnesses to support Proculus's claim, the matter was allowed to drop.

The arrest of Epicharis spurred the other conspirators to hurry forward their plot. Now the plan was for Nero to be assassinated while attending April's Games of Ceres at the Circus Maximus. Nero had lately become very reclusive, and chariot races were the only events that could be guaranteed to bring him out in public. But when April arrived, the revised Piso plot was discovered by the Palatium just days before it was due to be carried out. Its undoing came when one of the conspirators, Flavius Scaevinus, acted so suspiciously that his freedman went to the Palatium to inform on him. The freedman's suspicions had been raised when Scaevinus instructed him to sharpen a rusty dagger he'd recently had blessed at a temple. Knowing that Scaevinus would be sitting with the emperor at the circus during the Games of Ceres several days later, the freedman had put two and two together. So, too, did Nero.

When Scaevinus was interrogated, he denied everything. But when his freedman was questioned further, he named two men who had recently been in fervent and secret conversations with his master. Both these men were brought in by the Praetorian Guard. Neither of them was the courageous type: threatened with torture, they spilled out all they knew about the plot, naming many more conspirators. One of the first men they implicated was Lucius Annaeus Seneca, Nero's famous former tutor and retired chief secretary. For the moment, Nero seemed not to believe that Seneca was involved, even when Seneca's nephew Marcus Annaeus Lucanus (known to later generations as the poet Lucan), son of Seneca's younger brother Lucius Annaeus Mela, confessed to being party to the plot. Lucan had once been a favorite of Nero's, winning the poetry prize at the Neronian Games of A.D. 60, but had since fallen so much out of imperial favor that he had been banned by Nero from performing his works in public—out of jealousy of his talent, it would seem. Not only did Lucan confess to being involved in the assassination plot, he even implicated his own mother, Atilla. Praetorian Guard troops, augmented by men of the German Guard to ensure that the Praetorians did their duty without fear or favor, ranged throughout the city looking for various named conspirators. For the moment, Seneca was not one of those on the wanted list.

Prisoners by the score were dragged to the Servilian Gardens, where Nero, surrounded by a reinforced bodyguard, with a giant German Guard named Cassius standing at his shoulder, personally questioned each suspect together with the prefect Tigellinus. Among the soldiers gathered around Nero was the Praetorian prefect Faenius Rufus. He was, of course, also a conspirator, but his complicity had yet to be discovered, as no one had so far named him. Rufus, for his part, acted tough with the prisoners as they were brought before the emperor. Beside him stood the Praetorian centurion Subrius Flavus, who also was a member of the conspiracy.

Tacitus tells of how, as Nero and Tigellinus questioned suspects, the centurion Flavus whispered to the prefect Rufus beside him that he only had to give him a sign and he would draw his sword and plunge it into Nero. Rufus looked around at the centurion, who now put his hand on the hilt of his sword. But Rufus's courage had failed him; shaking his head, he made the centurion remove his hand from his weapon. It would prove to be a fatal mistake—within days, both Rufus and Flavus would be named by other conspirators during the continuing interrogations and confessions, and both would ultimately lose their heads.[3] Two of the Praetorian Guard's ten tribunes also would be accused and would pay with their lives. Three other Praetorian tribunes whose loyalty was suspect would be removed from their posts by Tigellinus.

Following Flavus's arrest, Nero asked him why he had plotted against him, in contravention to his sacred oath of allegiance. Flavus's excuse was that he had grown to hate Nero. Tacitus says the centurion declared: "No soldier was more loyal to you than I was, while you deserved to be loved. I started to hate you when you murdered your mother, and your wife, and when you became a charioteer, an actor, and an arsonist."[4]

While a number of plotters met the executioner's sword, some conspirators had time to commit suicide by opening their veins, among

them Piso, central figure of the plot, along with the consul-elect At-
ticus Vestinus, and Seneca's nephew Lucan, who recited his latest
unpublished poem, about a dying soldier, to friends as his life ebbed
away. As for Seneca himself, Nero wanted him dead, but he was not
entirely sure how to proceed with him. Seneca had been named by
only a single conspirator, and even then the accusation was not entirely damning. So Nero sent a Praetorian tribune, Gavius Silvanus, to
question Seneca, accompanied by a detachment of Praetorian troops.
The tribune found the former chief secretary at the house of one of
Seneca's friends, Novius Priscus, four miles outside Rome. Seneca was
staying overnight at the villa of Priscus after having only that day arrived from his own country estate in Campania.

In the early evening, the tribune Silvanus surrounded the house
with Praetorian soldiers, then went inside and confronted Seneca just
as he was commencing dinner. With Seneca were two close friends
and his second wife, Pompeia Paulina. She was, while much younger
than Seneca, devoted to her husband. Independently wealthy, Paulina
came from a leading family. She was the daughter of an ex-consul
who had been an energetic governor of Lower Germany and was now
one of the three commissioners of Rome's public revenues appointed
by Nero. He would have received that appointment on Seneca's
recommendation.

One of the two friends with the childless couple this night was
Seneca's doctor, Statius Annaeus, who was probably a former slave
freed by Seneca. Doctors in Roman times were almost exclusively
Greek slaves or freedmen. When a slave was freed, he generally took
part of his former master's name; Statius may well have been a slave
who took the Annaeus family name on receiving manumission. Seneca's other friend and dinner companion would have been the house's
owner, Novius Priscus. Seneca himself, now sixty-eight, had grown
thin and scrawny as a result of his frugal diet over the past few years.
He had also recently suffered from an illness that had weakened him
for a time. But he had since regained much of his strength, and his
bearing was as regal as it always had been.

A little embarrassed, the tribune formally informed Seneca that
Antonius Natalis, an admitted conspirator and one of the two friends
of Scaevinus who had been the first to confess to involvement in the
plot, had given Seneca's name to Nero. Under questioning, Natalis
had claimed he had been sent to Seneca by conspiracy ringleader Piso

to discuss Seneca's support for Nero's assassination. In his confession, Natalis had told the emperor that he had admonished Seneca for refusing to see Piso personally, and in response Seneca had said that it would not be to the benefit of either Seneca or Piso if they were known to be meeting regularly; with Seneca deliberately leading a secluded life, such meetings would have been likely to raise suspicions at the Palatium. Natalis's implication that Seneca knew all about the plot was further supported by a comment that Natalis alleged Seneca had made to him. According to Natalis, Seneca had said, "My own life depends on Piso's continued safety."[5] This could be taken to suggest that Seneca was counting on Piso to eliminate Nero.

When the tribune Silvanus repeated these accusations to Seneca and asked what he had to say about them, Seneca denied any involvement in or knowledge of the plot. He said he had refused to see Piso when he wished to call on him simply because he had been determined to lead the life of a private person, not for any furtive or clandestine reason. Silvanus returned to the Palatium, leaving his troops in position around the Priscus villa.

At the palace, the tribune gave Seneca's answer to Nero in the presence of the empress Sabina and the Praetorian prefect Tigellinus. Nero asked whether Seneca had seemed ready to commit suicide. Silvanus replied that Seneca had appeared quite calm and composed, and certainly showed neither fear nor regret. In short, he was not acting like a guilty man. Despite this, urged by his wife and chief adviser, Nero sent the tribune back to announce that the emperor was convinced that Seneca had either been involved in or had been aware of the murder plot, and he therefore sentenced Seneca to die.

Later, as the Praetorian Guard officers involved in the plot were exposed one by one and testified to what they knew, Nero was to receive confirmation that Seneca, while not an active participant in the plot to kill him, had certainly known all about it. More than that, Seneca also had stood to gain by it, for it emerged that the centurion Flavus had told other centurions of the Guard that the intent of the Praetorian officers was that once Nero had been murdered by Piso's associates, the officers would then kill Piso, whom they considered effeminate and weak, and would then make Seneca, a man they respected, their new emperor. This aspect of the plan—making Seneca emperor—was, Flavus had told his comrades, known to Seneca in advance.[6]

Silvanus did not return directly to Priscus's villa after he left Nero's Golden House. Silvanus, it turns out, also was involved in the plot and apparently had communicated with Seneca about it prior to the whole affair unraveling, acting as the middleman between the conspiratorial officers and Seneca. And this was how the tribune had known exactly where to find Seneca—who, as he would have planned with the officers, had come up from Campania a few days prior to the Games of Ceres, to stay with his friend just outside Rome and wait for the news that Nero was dead before he entered Rome to be acclaimed emperor by the troops at the Praetorian barracks. Instead of going straight back to Seneca with the death sentence from Nero, a troubled tribune Silvanus went to his commander, Rufus. The fact that the Praetorian prefect, like the tribune, was one of the conspirators had not to that point become known to the Palatium.

Silvanus told Rufus that he had been ordered by Nero to deliver a sentence of death to Seneca, and asked him what he should do. Seneca's fate was now in the hands of Rufus. But Rufus, seeing the assassination conspiracy crumbling around him, was by this time only thinking about his own neck. Gripped by fear, and holding on to an unrealistic hope that he would escape being named by the other conspirators, Rufus, says Tacitus, angrily told the tribune to carry out the emperor's orders. So with a heavy heart, Silvanus returned to the villa of Priscus, arriving late in the evening.[7]

Unable to look Seneca in the eye, and terrified of the prospect of Seneca dragging him down with him, Silvanus sent one of his centurions into the house to pass on the emperor's sentence. Seneca calmly received this news and, resolved to his fate, asked the centurion if he could have some wax writing tablets so he could write a revised last will and testament. When the dour centurion refused the request, Seneca, with a sigh, turned to his wife and friends and said, "As I'm forbidden to reward you, I bequeath you the only, but the noblest, possession that is still mine—the pattern of my life. If you keep that safe in your memory, you will earn a reputation for moral goodness and unshakable friendship."[8]

Seneca's friends and his wife, Paulina, all burst into tears, but he rebuked them for it. And he rebuked himself. "Where, Seneca," he now asked himself, "are your philosophical maxims? Why weren't you prepared for this evil day by years of study? Who of us was unaware of how cruel Nero could be? After murdering his mother and his brother [Britannicus], all that now remains for him to do is destroy his guardian and tutor."[9] He then embraced his wife, whom he had loved dearly since their marriage some fifteen years before. "I beg you, and implore you, spare yourself from a future of endless grief. Console yourself with my loss by remembering that yours has been a life that has been virtuously spent."[10]

With tears running down her cheeks, Paulina declared, "I will die with you." She turned to the waiting centurion. "You must also execute me."

Proudly, Seneca beheld his wife. "I have taught you well. You have chosen a glorious death." To his mind, such an end would be far preferable to the life of insults Paulina could expect as the widow of the condemned traitor Lucius Annaeus Seneca. "I will not prevent you from setting such a noble example. We will both face the end with courage, but yours will be a more famous death than mine."[11]

Knowing that the centurion would permit them to commit suicide as long as they wasted no time about it, Seneca had his wife lie beside him on the dining couch. With both of them holding a dagger, they slit the arteries of their arms in one motion. When Seneca's blood merely dripped from the wound, he also severed the veins of his spindly legs and knees. The centurion was satisfied by this and withdrew. Outside, the centurion reported to his tribune, Silvanus, who ordered him to go to Rome to inform the emperor that both Seneca and his wife had chosen to take their own lives and had slit their veins. The centurion mounted his horse and headed for the Palatium.

Back inside the villa, Seneca was becoming distressed by the sight of his wife bleeding to death beside him. He worried, too, that, seeing his distress, she might not go through with their pact to both die in this way, and would instead have her wound bound up. So he convinced her to go into another room to die. His chief freedman, Cleonicus, had Seneca's slaves carry her away. Seneca himself was still remarkably mentally strong, so he called in his freedman secretaries, and, while his blood flowed before their eyes, he dictated several documents for posterity. One, we learn from Tacitus, was a testament to his innocence in the plot to murder Nero—an untruthful testament, as it turned out—and a description of what he considered was the noble way in which both he and his wife were ending their lives.[12]

Dio would say that in his last hours Seneca actually revised a book on which he had been working.[13] Perhaps this was an autobiography, and the reference to his end and Paulina's end comprised the revision referred to by Dio. Suetonius would make reference to a nonfiction work of history by Seneca that may have been an autobiography, which he himself was able to read thirty years later.[14] According to Dio, Seneca then gave this book and other books from his pen to friends, to prevent them from falling into Nero's hands and being destroyed.[15] It is probable that most of these other books contained Seneca's philosophical treatises and plays.

While Seneca was dictating, the Praetorian centurion arrived at Nero's Golden House in Rome and reported what was going on at the Priscus house. The emperor was pleased enough to hear that Seneca was taking the honorable way out, but he had no quarrel with Seneca's wife. Living by a sometimes baffling code of honor, Nero ordered that Paulina's life be preserved. The centurion galloped back to the Priscus villa and Paulina's servants were ordered to bind up her wound, which they did. Tacitus indicates that she was unconscious by that point, for she did not resist as the bandages were wound around her arm.[16] She would in fact recover, and live for several more years, although looking very pale.

It is unclear whether Seneca, in a separate room, knew that his wife's life had been spared. He certainly would not have been happy had he been aware of it, so intent had he been on Paulina making a statement with her courageous suicide. Impatient for his own life to end now, and with the bloodletting taking far too long, he asked his friend Statius the physician to do him a favor. Tacitus says that Seneca asked the doctor to produce a poison for him "which he [Seneca] had some time previously provided for himself." This poison, says Tacitus, was "the same drug used to end the lives of those who were condemned to death in the public courts of Athens"—probably either hemlock or belladonna.[17]

Statius, like all Roman physicians, traveled with a medicine chest whose contents included various poisons, which doctors of the time used in small doses as purgatives in the treatment of various ailments. Statius left the dining room and went to the guest room where he was staying, where he unlocked his medicine chest. The doctor soon returned with the poison, mixed in a cup with water. Without hesitating, Seneca drank this draft straight down. Seneca quickly felt his arms and legs become chilled and without sensation, but still he did not die. For safety's sake, the physician traveled with only a small quantity of the poison, and it turned out that the dose was simply not strong enough to kill.

Seneca knew that if he was not dead soon the centurion would return and finish him off by lopping off his head. To do this, the centurion would use his *gladius* short sword. The blade would be sharp, but it was less than two feet long, and, unless wielded with substantial weight behind it, decapitation using a *gladius* sometimes required two or three blows—or "one and a half" blows, as a Praetorian officer executing one of the Piso conspirators reported to Nero after completing his assignment. This sustained hacking at the neck could entail a painful death for the victim.

Anxious to avoid that possibility, Seneca had himself carried by his servants to the villa's bathhouse. Roman bathhouses contained three baths—one cold, one warm, one hot. A warm bath was known to make the blood flow freely, just as an icy bath could stop blood from hemorrhaging. Seneca slipped into the water of the warm bath. Splashing water on the servants lining the edge of the bath, Seneca, only a mildly religious man—he was a loose adherent to the Stoic philosophy, which accepted that our fates are predetermined—made a joke of it, saying he was offering the water as a libation to the principal Roman god, Jupiter, in his incarnation as the Deliverer.

But when the warm water seemed to be having no effect, Seneca had himself carried to the hot bath. With steam rising all around him, he was lowered into the hot water. And there Seneca died, suffocating in the dense steam. In a codicil of his old will, he had required that his corpse be burned immediately after his death, without any funeral rites. Once the Praetorian officers who'd been waiting outside the villa had come into the bathhouse and satisfied themselves that he truly was dead, Seneca's body was removed from the bath and cremated on the villa grounds that same night, as he had wished.

# XIX

# THE END OF NERO

The accusations, roundups, and interrogations that followed the discovery of the Piso plot against the life of Nero caused fear and consternation in Rome and beyond for several weeks. Yet for all the fuss, only forty-one men and women were actually implicated in the plot, and of them, just eighteen died—either losing their heads to the sword of a Praetorian tribune or centurion or, like Seneca, committing suicide. Others were banished.

Seneca's younger brother Mela, a very wealthy knight who had never bothered to seek entry into the Senatorial Order, followed the example of his son Lucan and also slit his veins. Although Lucan had implicated his own mother, Mela's wife, Atilla, Nero never proceeded against her. Nero did take action against Seneca's friend Novius Priscus, owner of the house where Seneca died, no doubt assuming that Priscus was aware of Seneca's intent to become emperor once the Piso plot succeeded. Priscus also was one of those who forfeited their lives. While charges were brought in the Senate against Seneca's elder brother Junius Gallio, the majority of senators expressed the belief that enough was enough, and the charges against Gallio were dropped.

This same year, as Rome was coming to grips with this drama and its aftermath, Nero suffered a personal tragedy. His wife, Poppaea Sabina, whom he truly loved and who was again pregnant, died suddenly. She was probably taken by illness or a miscarriage, although some classical authors were to write that Nero flew into a rage when she was ill and kicked her to death. He quickly remarried, taking Statilia Messalina for his new bride. Her previous husband, a consul, had been one of those to perish during the purge following the Piso plot.

The following year, Nero began preparations for two major military campaigns, perhaps believing that military conquests would improve his popularity with the public, which was at an all-time low. One plan provided for an expeditionary army pushing south into Africa from Egypt. The other plan called for an invasion of the homeland of the old enemy Parthia. Preparations for these operations were well under way by the summer of A.D. 66, with a new legion created, and existing legions, auxiliaries, and militia units assembling in the East. Nero himself transferred to Greece, to be closer to the scenes of action, taking his staff with him. Once there he seemed more interested in theatrical performances and athletic contests than military conquest.

The Jews of Judea now chose this time to rise in revolt against their Roman overlords. After massacring the Roman legionary garrisons at Jerusalem, Masada, and Cypros, the Jewish rebels overran most of Judea, Idumaea, and Galilee. A Roman army led down into Judea from Antioch by Cessenius Gallus, the current governor of Syria, was repulsed by the Jews, with heavy losses to the Romans, and Nero was forced to put his ambitious military plans on hold while the Jewish problem was dealt with. The general he chose for the new counteroffensive was Titus Flavius Vespasianus—Vespasian, as we know him. The most successful Roman general during Claudius's A.D. 43 invasion of Britain, Vespasian had been accompanying Nero on his Greek tour, and was sent south by the emperor to assemble and lead the new Roman army, which advanced into Galilee and Judea from Syria in the spring of A.D. 67. This campaign would last four years and result in the bloody termination of the revolt and the total destruction of Jerusalem by Vespasian's army.

Judea was not the only seat of rebellion in A.D. 67. Although Gaul had been conquered for Rome by Julius Caesar in 58–51 B.C. and divided into Roman provinces, every once in a while revolt flickered among the Gauls. In A.D. 67, no doubt inspired by the Jewish Revolt on the other side of the Roman world, which was sure to attract Rome's attention and resources, Gaius Julius Vindex, Roman governor of the Gallic province of Lugdunensis in France, and himself a native of Gaul, led a Gallic uprising against Nero. By the end of the year, Rome's Army of the Upper Rhine had marched down into Gaul and defeated Vindex's rebel army, which, apart from a cohort from Rome's City Guard stationed at Vindex's capital, Lyon, was made up of untrained locals. With his army routed, Vindex committed suicide.

But the spirit of revolution was by now in the air. In the spring of A.D. 68, Sulpicius Galba, seventy-year-old governor of Nearer Spain, rebelled against Nero's rule. Having given moral and physical support to Vindex, Galba had little choice, for Nero was now sure to send a Praetorian execution squad to Spain looking for him. Galba was quickly joined by the governor of neighboring Lusitania, Nero's one-time best friend and Sabina's former husband, Otho. By the end of May, Galba's troops had hailed him Rome's emperor, in competition with Nero, and he was marching on Rome with a modest army made up essentially of a new legion, Galba's 7th, which he had raised in the Spanish recruiting grounds of the existing 7th Claudia Legion.

An army sent by Nero to counter Galba deserted to him, and by early June Praetorian Guard commander Tigellinus also deserted Nero and, as Galba's force daily drew closer to Rome, the men of the Praetorian Guard swore loyalty to Galba. When the Senate, in fear of the Praetorians, then declared Nero an enemy of the state and put a price on his head, the German Guard also refused to serve or protect Nero. All of a sudden, with head-spinning swiftness, the emperor found himself without support, without power, and without protection. He ordered fast ships readied to enable him to flee to Egypt or North Africa, but on June 9 a decree of the Senate calling for his execution forced him to flee his Golden House, as word spread that Praetorian troops were on the way to arrest him.

What took place next is open to conjecture. The biographer Suetonius, who was prone to sensationalizing his accounts of the emperors' lives and deaths, gives a questionable account of the death of Nero, an account repeated two centuries later by Cassius Dio. According to Suetonius, Nero's freedman Phaon offered the emperor the use of his villa four miles outside Rome while he himself remained at the capital to gain intelligence for his master. After nightfall, Nero rode out of town disguised in a plain hat and cloak, and accompanied by four servants, including his secretary Epaphroditus and the eunuch Sporus. At one point along the route a soldier of the Praetorian Guard recognized the emperor and gave him a loyal salute. Midway between the Salarian and Nomentan ways the party dismounted and slithered through undergrowth to the rear of Phaon's villa, and gained entry.

A little later, a runner arrived at the villa from Phaon in the city, warning Nero that the Senate intended flogging him to death if he were taken alive. A troop of Praetorian Guard cavalry was then seen approaching the villa; they had perhaps followed the runner from the city. Nero had brought two daggers with him, but couldn't pluck up the courage to use them on himself. In tears, he begged Sporus to kill himself first, to prove his devotion to his emperor, but the eunuch refused. Then Nero pulled himself together, and, with the help of Epaphroditus, pushed a dagger into his throat. His last words were said to be, "So great an artist dies."[1]

According to Suetonius, the centurion in charge of the cavalry troop that soon after arrived at the villa dashed inside and tried to use his cloak to stanch the blood flowing from Nero's throat, but he was too late. There, in the centurion's arms, says Suetonius, died thirty-year-old Nero, fifth emperor of Rome, grandson and last surviving descendant of Germanicus. According to Suetonius, Nero's ever-faithful mistress Acte and his childhood nurses Alexandria and Ecloge carried Nero's body to the Pincian Hill outside Rome, where he was cremated. His remains, according to Suetonius, were placed in a white porphyry casket and deposited in the tomb of his father's Domitius family. According to Suetonius, too, this casket supposedly containing Nero's remains was to be seen in the Domitius family tomb in his day, during the early first century, when people were still putting spring and summer flowers on the tomb in fond remembrance of Nero.[2]

Whether Nero did die in the manner described by Suetonius, and at the time stated by Suetonius, is open to question. Tacitus was to say that there were various rumors in existence about his death, and with no confirmation of how or where Nero died, many people believed that he was still alive.[3] Suetonius gave credence to this belief; for years after Nero disappeared, he says, many people were convinced that he was still alive. For some time after, edicts continued to be circulated at Rome in Nero's name, and there was an expectation among a large number of people that he would one day return, reclaim his throne, and punish his enemies.[4]

One of Nero's freedmen escaped to North Africa by ship, and there would be a number of cases of men claiming to be Nero appearing in the East over the coming years. By the spring of A.D. 69, less than a year after his disappearance, news spread through the provinces of Achaia and Asia that Nero had been seen there. A man looking very much like Nero and declaring himself to be the emperor arrived at the Greek island of Cythnus, today's Kythnos, in a ship containing a band of military deserters who supported him. To back his claim, apart from his striking Nero-like appearance, the man possessed the skills of a singer and lyre player. There was considerable disaffection in the region; the new emperor, Galba, had been assassinated at Rome on January 15, and his replacement as emperor, Nero's former friend Otho, was fighting a civil war in Italy against Aulus Vitellius, commander of the Army of the Lower Rhine, whose legionaries had proclaimed him emperor in opposition to Otho. In this uncertain and unstable atmosphere, the people of Kythnos flocked to the Nero figure.

A detachment of legionaries sailing from the East to Italy in support of Otho landed on Kythnos, and this Nero figure ordered them to join him. Some refused, and he had them executed. The commander of the detachment, a centurion named Sisenna, had custody of the symbol of the clasped hands, traditionally a symbol of friendship, which the legions in the East under the general Vespasian and Mucianus, governor of Syria, were sending to the Praetorian Guard to show their support for the Guard and for Otho. Sisenna had his doubts about this imperial pretender. Escaping the island, he spread the word that there was a fake Nero on Kythnos.

On hearing of this, Calpurnius Asprenas, the governor of Galatia and Pamphylia in southern Turkey, set sail with two triremes of the Tyrrhenian Fleet and quickly reached the island. There the governor found the pretender's ship, which his marines boarded and secured. The pretender was arrested. He begged the trireme captains to take him to Syria or Egypt, but they ignored his pleas. The Nero of Cythnus was beheaded. The severed head was sent to Rome, where people marveled at the dead man's likeness to Nero. Tacitus would say the general belief was that this pretender had been either a freedman from Italy or an escaped slave from Pontus.[5]

Suetonius was to write that toward the end of the first century, when he was a young man, a mysterious individual appeared in Parthia claiming to be Nero. The Parthians believed he truly was Nero, and supported him, until Rome demanded that he be turned over, which they reluctantly did.[6] This Nero was apparently quickly executed once he came into Roman hands.

Despite the fact that Nero's rule, so full of early promise, became erratic and despotic, his death was lamented by many Romans for many years. The emperor Otho restored Nero's statues. The emperor Vitellius, who defeated Otho and ruled for seven months in A.D. 69, came from a family with strong connections to Germanicus and his family. Once he took the throne, Vitellius celebrated funeral rites for Nero, punished men who had betrayed Nero in his last days, and renamed his own infant son Germanicus.

Perhaps Nero did escape to the East. Perhaps he was one of the pretenders executed over the years. Perhaps he died years later in obscurity. But the fact that Nero ceased to be emperor of Rome in June A.D. 68 is beyond dispute. A year in which Rome saw four emperors followed his disappearance. Whether he died sooner or later, the demise of Nero, grandson of Germanicus, the last male survivor of the Caesar family, ended Germanicus's line. It also ended the hopes of the Roman people that a descendant of Germanicus would give them the golden age they had expected from the great hero himself.

With the end of Nero, the end of the family of the Caesars that had been sparked by the murder of Germanicus was complete.

# XX

# UNMASKING GERMANICUS'S MURDERERS

H ad Germanicus not died in A.D. 19, and had he succeeded Tiberius as emperor, it is highly improbable that Caligula, Claudius, or Nero would have become emperor. Germanicus would have been fifty-one when Tiberius died in A.D. 37. If, as emperor, Germanicus had lived into his eighties—Augustus and Tiberius, both of whom endured poor health throughout their lives, survived into their late seventies—he would have reigned for thirty years, and his able son Nero Germanicus, or possibly a son of Nero Germanicus, would have succeeded him. His youngest son, Caligula, would never have become emperor. On the death of Nero Germanicus, the son of Nero Germanicus would have succeeded him, as the rule of succession provided, and his son would have succeded him. If Nero Germanicus had died without a son, his brother Drusus Germanicus would succeeded him, followed by Drusus's sons. Every time his brothers fathered sons, Caligula would have slipped farther and farther down the line of succession, and into historical oblivion.

We would never have seen the emperors Galba, Otho, Vitellius, Vespasian, Titus, Domitian, Nerva, etc., in the event of this Germanican succession, and history would have not necessarily have been the poorer for it.

Tacitus was to say that the Roman people had originally been hopeful that Germanicus's father, Drusus the Elder, would succeed

Augustus, end the monarchy, and restore the Roman Republic. On Drusus's death, he says, Romans transferred that hope to his much-loved son Germanicus.[1] Yet Germanicus was aware that in its last eighty years the Republic had been rent by vicious power struggles and bloody civil wars, while under the first emperor, Augustus, Rome had experienced a golden age for almost half a century, with internal peace, expanding borders, and great prosperity. It is probable that the astute Germanicus would have wanted to follow in Augustus's footsteps, providing strong and enlightened leadership without being an oppressive ruler in the Tiberian mold.

It is not difficult to imagine that the reign of Germanicus Caesar would have been another golden age for the arts and for commerce. The empire would have been enlarged under his generalship. In all probability, Germanicus would have led an invasion of Germany, to finish what he had begun in A.D. 14–16. He had firmly believed that he could spread the Roman Empire's border into Germany as far as the Elbe River, had Tiberius given him one more year in Germany. And he would almost certainly have expanded into Britain, as Tiberius and Caligula contemplated and as Claudius actually did. Perhaps, as some were projecting prior to his death, Germanicus would have become an Alexander the Great and spread the Roman Empire, absorbing Parthia and pushing into India. Perhaps he would have expanded down into Africa, and even as far east as China, doubling or even trebling the size of the empire. And maybe today there would be the ruins of Roman temples in Cape Town, and the indigenous people of China would be speaking Latin.

A pessimist would say that Roman history would not have been all that different over the long term even if Germanicus and his successors were strong, enlightened, benevolent rulers. As we saw with Caligula and Nero, it took only one generation for youth, temptation, and un-limited power to combine to make deeply flawed rulers of German-icus's descendants. On the other hand, if we are to accept the glowing character references given to Germanicus Caesar by Tacitus and the other Roman writers who unanimously sang Germanicus's praises, then Germanicus would have made an incomparable emperor. His reign would have been an exciting, optimistic time unlike any that the Roman people knew before him or after him.

So who deprived Rome, and history, of this great man and poten-tially great emperor, a man who would have ranked with Alexander,

Pompey the Great, Caesar, and Constantine as one of the great figures of antiquity, if not the greatest? A study of the lives of Germanicus and his descendants through the texts of Tacitus and other classical authors can only lead to the conclusion that the five people considered murder suspects in Roman times were not actually directly involved with the death of Germanicus. There can be no denying that three of the five benefited from his murder, and perhaps two of them, Piso and Plancina, expected to benefit from his death, but this is not evidence enough to condemn any of them.

That Germanicus was poisoned seems beyond doubt. Previously as healthy as a bull, Germanicus was floored and then slain by an illness that displayed all the symptoms of a poisoning, the second and last bout of which lasted only days. That no one else around him fell sick suggests that he was not claimed by a contagious virus or an epidemic, or even was felled by accidental food poisoning. He appears to have been the lone, targeted victim of a deliberate and ultimately successful attempt on his life. Tacitus was skeptical about there being physical signs of poisoning, probably because he could not believe that anyone using poison on a prince as famous as Germanicus would want to leave any clue to suggest that his death had been anything but natural. There were, after all, numerous poisons available that left no obvious trace. Such a poison would have been used in the murder of Germanicus's adoptive brother Drusus the Younger.

So why would anyone be unwise enough to leave his or her calling card by using belladonna to kill Germanicus, knowing that belladonna would result in cyanosis, which would shout "murder" to the world? One answer would be that perhaps the murderer was a novice with poisons and was unaware of the telltale aftereffects. This would make all five existing suspects unlikely culprits. Knowing what the public reaction to Germanicus's death would be, all would have diligently covered their tracks. The alternative is that the use of belladonna was intentional, that the murderer wanted poison to be suspected and murder to be trumpeted.

The prosecutors at the Piso trial proposed that Piso and Plancina had employed the known poisonmaker Martina to provide them with the poison. Martina, as an expert, would have known about the cyanosis effect and would have warned Piso and Plancina against using belladonna. This aspect alone would tend to preclude Piso and Plancina from involvement in the crime. The other possibility, as already pointed out, is that the murderer, or murderers, knew that the poison they used would leave signs of its use, and used it quite deliberately for that reason—they wanted it to be obvious that Germanicus had been poisoned. Why would they do that? The answer will point to the identity of the murderer. Not one of the five classical suspects would have deliberately wanted poison to have been suspected, and that is one of the reasons why they can all be discarded as suspects.

There are a variety of other reasons why those five classical suspects can be cleared of the murder of Germanicus, and, commencing with Piso and Plancina, they are these. Piso and his wife were obvious chief suspects. No one could deny that Piso had gone out of his way to make life difficult for Germanicus in the East. And the fact that he and Plancina were delighted when Germanicus died was common knowledge. Piso also foolishly attempted to regain control of Syria by force following Germanicus's death. There was nothing subtle about any of this. It was deliberate provocation. Yet none of it was evidence that Piso or his wife murdered Germanicus. Arrogant he may have been, but Piso, whom the very astute Augustus had considered worthy of occupying the Roman throne, was bright enough to have made himself less of a murder suspect if he planned to kill Germanicus from the outset and then methodically carried out the murder. What did Piso have to gain from murdering Germanicus? Did he do it to please Tiberius? That is highly doubtful—he despised Tiberius. Did he do it out of spite? And in doing so make himself an obvious murder suspect? Also doubtful. It should be remembered that to his dying day, Piso stated that he was innocent of any involvement in the murder of Germanicus and that the charges against him were false. Not even in his supposed suicide note did he confess to involvement in the death of the prince.

What then of Plancina? It was said that she involved herself in sorcery. It also was claimed that she was associated with Martina the notorious Syrian sorceress and poisonmaker. But Martina died before she could implicate Plancina or Piso in the murder. Conveniently for some, she also died before she could clear Piso and Plancina. At no point did Martina confess to having produced a poison for them, but her death gave that insinuation strength. That Plancina was a close friend of Livia, the emperor's mother, is undeniable. So close a friend, in fact, that the emperor's mother interceded on her behalf late in the trial and had her pardoned. But that is not proof that Plancina murdered Germanicus. It merely is proof that Livia protected a friend and possibly herself.

In defense of both Plancina and Piso, the second bout of illness, the one that killed Germanicus, took place some time after Piso and Plancina left Syria and were sailing back to Italy. Certainly they could have employed servants on Germanicus's staff at Daphne to poison him. But following the first bout of illness, after which Germanicus himself was convinced that someone had tried to poison him, security precautions taken around Germanicus, in particular involving food and drink, would have been extremely tight. There also was the fact that his staff were intensely loyal, and at the time there was no suggestion that any of them were involved in his death. Only someone close to Germanicus could have slipped poison to him, especially on that second and ultimately fatal occasion. That someone had to be very close, in his inner circle, someone Germanicus trusted implicitly.

Taking all things into account, the logical conclusion must be that Piso and Plancina were innocent of Germanicus's murder. There is no denying that they were arrogant and mean. But those are not crimes. They were such obvious scapegoats that it becomes increasingly obvious that someone else, the true murderer or murderers, very successfully set them up and, in casting the blame their way, accomplished the perfect crime. As for Piso's death and supposed suicide note, many at the time were not convinced that Piso took his own life in the middle of his trial. His totally unexpected and unheralded death, when the trial seemed to be going his way, very conveniently wrapped up the affair for Tiberius and his mother, Livia. With Piso dead, blame for the murder could be set squarely on his shoulders, and the case could be put to rest.

The weight of evidence strongly suggests that Tiberius also can be crossed off the list of Germanicus's murder suspects. Tiberius certainly had the most to gain from the death of Germanicus, and he would have breathed a sigh of relief once the man he considered his chief rival for the throne was out of the way, and once the furor following his death faded away without a revolution resulting. There is no doubt that Tiberius was a very insecure man. The precarious path he trod to the throne, during which many other contenders had died, had obviously made him paranoid. Yet Tiberius would have been so insecure, so afraid of the revolt that he must have dreaded would be unleashed by the death of Germanicus as a result of foul play, or even the suspicion of foul play, that he would not have chanced his throne by ordering the death of his hugely popular adopted son. It was enough to have Germanicus secluded in the East, as commander in chief there, well away from Rome and the troops loyal to him in the West, while Tiberius cemented his grip on power at the capital. Tiberius may have encouraged Piso to make sure that the legions in the East did not develop a strong loyalty to Germanicus. And there is no doubt that Tiberius was grateful to the murderers of Germanicus, but it is almost certain that he had no idea who those murderers were.

This being the case, was Livia, Tiberius's mother, guilty of Germanicus's murder? There can be no doubt that she had acted shamefully as far as Germanicus and Agrippina were concerned. Almost certainly the letter that Piso clutched during his trial was a vindictive missive from the emperor's mother to Plancina, urging her, and her husband, to make life as difficult as possible for Germanicus and Agrippina in the East, and to ensure that the legions of the region did not form as strong an attachment to Germanicus as had those of Rome's Rhine armies. This letter probably also contained Livia's assurance that Plancina and Piso would have Tiberius's blessing for their disruptive activities.

It is highly unlikely that this letter commanded or urged the couple to kill Germanicus. Livia was a crafty old witch of a woman who had more sense than to incriminate herself, in writing, in Rome's most notorious murder. But the contents of this letter were still embarrassing enough for Piso to consider it weighty ammunition if he had to pressure the emperor to save his neck in the event the Senate convicted him of the prince's murder. The letter's contents also were embarrassing enough for Tiberius to want to retrieve the letter, and not just to save his mother's reputation. Such a letter could have been construed as imperial authority for Piso and Plancina to put Germanicus's life in danger. Had the contents been made public it could have been enough to lose Tiberius his throne, and his head, in an uprising of both the people and the legions.

Did Tiberius either order or condone Piso's "suicide"? He had two motives to want Piso dead. One was an almost frantic desire to retrieve that embarrassing letter. The other was to put a cap on the whole Piso trial affair. While Piso lived, and continued to plead his innocence, some would believe him and would point the finger at Tiberius—most notably the friends of Germanicus and Agrippina. And the way the trial had been heading, Piso may well have been acquitted by the

Senate for lack of evidence on the murder charge. With Piso dead, and with his supposed suicide note in hand—a note that was merely a plea for leniency for his sons, not an admission of guilt or a declaration of intent to take his own life—Tiberius was able to wrap up the trial by immediately finding Piso guilty as charged. That does not mean that Tiberius ordered the death of Piso. But the death of Piso conveniently closed the case with a scapegoat dead and buried.

That leaves just one original suspect. Was Praetorian Guard commander Sejanus behind the murder of Germanicus? Later generations thought so, after the accusation came to light that Sejanus had combined with Drusus the Younger's wife to murder Drusus. It seemed a natural extension. And Sejanus then went on to convince Tiberius to remove Nero Germanicus and Drusus Germanicus from the picture, as he set his sights on claiming the throne for himself. Sejanus probably was just as nervous about removing Germanicus as Tiberius had been. As later history would show, within forty years the legions of the Rhine would march on Rome and defeat the Praetorian Guard to usurp one emperor, Otho, and install another, Vitellius, on the throne. And Vitellius did not have the hero status that Germanicus possessed. Such a possibility—of the Rhine legions creating an emperor of their choosing—also was very real during Germanicus's time. And the astute and patient Sejanus, who seemingly did nothing without weighing the consequences, would have known that only too well.

Sejanus was given the inspiration and the courage to begin his campaign for the throne once Germanicus was out of the way. He set out to profit from Germanicus's death by murdering Drusus the Younger and then removing the other heirs to Tiberius's throne one by one, clearing the way for his own bid for ultimate power. There is no reason to believe that he knew in advance that Germanicus was going to be murdered, nor that he knew the identity of his murderers at the time of Germanicus's death. But a case can be made that Sejanus was later approached by one of the murderers, who confessed to his or her part in the crime in the hope of winning Sejanus's and Tiberius's favor. The likelihood is that Sejanus did not entirely believe that confession, for reasons that will shortly become clear. On the other hand, it is quite likely that Sejanus orchestrated Piso's "suicide," on his own initiative, to help his master, Tiberius. Sejanus had the motive, the opportunity, and the capability to order the Praetorian Guard to carry out Piso's murder and then make it look like suicide.

So if none of these five suspects was involved, who was Germanicus's murderer or murderers?

An accumulation of evidence, from clues left over a period of forty-
six years, leads to a figure whom many may consider, at first, to be a
surprising guilty party. The man who masterminded the crime was
none other than Lucius Annaeus Seneca, the same Seneca who became Nero's tutor and later his chief secretary—and whose ambition
to himself take the throne of Rome from Nero—ironically in another
Piso plot—finally led to his downfall and suicide, as we have seen.
Seneca was not alone. He had help on the inside, from an even more
surprising source.

The key reasons for concluding that Seneca was one of the two
people behind the murder of Germanicus, and was in fact the motiva-
tor for and inventor of the crime, are these. To begin with, Seneca
possessed the two key elements that a criminal investigator looks for
when considering murder suspects: Seneca had a motive—self-
advancement—and he had opportunity—he was in the East when
Germanicus was murdered.

Seneca spent a number of years in Egypt before permanently coming back to Rome in A.D. 31. We are told that in A.D. 16, when he was
a young man, Seneca's aunt Marcia took him to live in Egypt, where
his uncle was the province's new governor, because the aunt believed
Egypt's climate would improve Seneca's poor health. Seneca's uncle
Gaius Galerius became prefect of Egypt in A.D. 16. His was an imperial
appointment, not a senatorial appointment, made by the emperor Tiberius personally. Being an imperial appointment, it was open-ended—
Galerius could spend many years in the post, as opposed to appointees
of senatorial postings, whose tenure was for just one year. In fact, Tiberius kept most of his provincial governors, such as the prefect of Judea, Pontius Pilatus (the Pilate of the Christian Gospels), in their posts
for ten years or more. And so it turned out to be in Galerius's case.

Seneca relocated to Egypt with his aunt and uncle early in A.D. 16,
or his aunt took him there within months of her husband taking up his
appointment in the spring of A.D. 16. Seneca was at that time in or
very close to his nineteenth year. Like all Romans, he had come of age
at the end of his fifteenth year. Like all young Roman members of the
Equestrian Order, his schooling at Rome would have been completed
by age seventeen, when he joined the Collega Junena, Rome's young
men's association, a cross between the YMCA and the Hitler Youth

fostered by Augustus. In this association for the sons of the elite, youths were trained to ride and to use weapons. The next step for a young man of eighteen or nineteen at Rome who was a member of the Equestrian Order, as Seneca was, took the form of six months' mandatory military service with one of Rome's legions as a *tribunus angusticlavius*, a tribune of the thin stripe. In republican times tribunes had commanded cohorts and entire legions of the Roman army, but by the imperial era the thin-stripe tribunes were mere officer cadets who served on the staffs of legion commanders.

Shortly after completing his service as a junior tribune, the young Equestrian Order member could be posted to the first of several Roman army auxiliary units he would command over the next eight years or so, with the rank of prefect. By the age of about twenty-seven, he would then either return to Rome to take up a civil service career, or, if he had shown promise with the army, he could be promoted to the rank of tribune of the broad stripe, or "military tribune." In this latter capacity he became second in command of one of the twenty-five legions maintained by Rome at the time Germanicus became commander in chief on the Rhine. At age thirty the young tribune became eligible to join the Senate. He might serve as quaestor to a consul or provincial governor, after which he automatically joined the Senate. Or he was accepted into the Senate with the emperor's approval, and could receive command of a legion as a "legate" or brigadier general. Within several years he could expect promotion to the rank of praetor, and then hope for a consulship from the qualifying age of thirty-seven. This was the normal promotional ladder for an ambitious young knight such as Seneca. But Seneca did not follow this route.

Seneca never served as an officer cadet, never commanded auxiliary units, never served as a military tribune with a legion, never commanded a legion. It was only after winning favor at the Palatium on his A.D. 31 return to Rome that he was made a quaestor that same year, and subsequently made a praetor in A.D. 49. Seneca's career path was quite different from that of the usual ambitious Roman of Equestrian rank. In going to Egypt in A.D. 16 at about age nineteen, he avoided military service as an officer cadet, almost like a latter-day draft dodger. And remaining in Egypt until he was thirty-four, he did not follow the normal military or civil service promotional ladder. This was why Seneca was living at the governor's palace in Alexandria when Germanicus was in the East between A.D. 17 and 19.

Seneca, who served on his uncle Gaius's staff, would almost certainly have traveled up to Daphne with Galerius to pay his respects to Germanicus and Agrippina when they arrived there in A.D. 17. Germanicus, as Roman commander in chief in the East, was the superior of Seneca's uncle, and like other senior Roman officials in the East, Galerius would have wasted no time going to Daphne to introduce himself to his new chief and give a personal report on the situation in his province. Seneca, being a knight of the Equestrian Order like his uncle, also would have been expected to pay his respects to the prince. In addition, Seneca would have been at the Alexandrian palace when Germanicus came to Egypt in the summer of A.D. 19 to initially implement measures to ameliorate the Egyptian drought and then to play tourist. There is no suggestion that Seneca was at Daphne when Germanicus died. So obviously, as he could not have been on the spot to poison Germanicus, someone else had to administer the poison Seneca procured. That is where the insider was to come in. More on that subject shortly.

What would have been Seneca's motive for murdering Germanicus? By that time, A.D. 19, Seneca had been sidelined at Alexandria with poor health for three years. But he was anxious to make his mark at Rome now that his health had improved in the Egyptian climate. A chance remark or two would have started his excellent mind working on how he could leapfrog into the favor of the emperor and create a scintillating career for himself. The murder plan may have begun to take shape in Seneca's mind in the summer of A.D. 19, after Tiberius's angry reaction to Germanicus's visit to Egypt. This was the first time that Tiberius had publicly admonished Germanicus in the Senate. More than illustrating Tiberius's displeasure with his adopted son, this admonishment was like a green light to Seneca—surely, he would have thought, the emperor would be grateful to a man who rid him of Germanicus's annoying presence?

Was Seneca capable of planning and carrying out the murder of a prince at age twenty-two? As his later exploits show, for all his admirable philosophical writings, there was nothing that Seneca would not stoop to. His boundless ambition had him in bed with Germanicus's daughters Julia and Agrippina the Younger soon after his return to Rome. Seneca quite deliberately ruined men such as Germanicus's quaestor Suillius as an act of revenge. Seneca had threatened to send in the military to force British tribes to repay his loans. He had no scruples about sanctioning and indeed encouraging Nero's murder of his mother, Agrippina the Younger, Seneca's former lover. Prior to that, Seneca had known about the murder of Claudius and had penned Nero's speech to the Praetorian Guard, although aware that Claudius was already dead, while Rome waited for news of the emperor's condition. He guided Nero's hand for eight years as his chief secretary, during which time he made himself fabulously wealthy at the expense of countless others. And in the end he was prepared to allow Nero's assassination so he could become emperor of Rome. As all these instances make clear, temptation and Lucius Seneca were well acquainted throughout his life.

Then there is the matter of poison. Their critics pointed out that Piso and Plancina were connected with the poisonmaker Martina. This was a diversion. In fact, it is probable that Martina had absolutely nothing to do with the murder. She was merely a tawdry friend of Plancina's who gave weight to the suspicions raised about Plancina and Piso. Just as Martina was quite unconnected with the murder, Seneca had nothing to do with her. It is likely that Seneca procured the poison that killed Germanicus from another source, in Egypt. Tacitus tells us that on the day of his own suicide, Seneca asked his doctor to give him a poison "which he had some time previously provided for himself." It was a poison, said Tacitus, that was commonly used to execute criminals at Athens. Here is graphic proof that Seneca not only had a working knowledge of fatal poisons but also had in the past procured one such deadly poison, which is likely to have been belladonna or hemlock.

Tacitus's wording could be taken to mean Seneca had actually prepared the poison himself. Not that this matters—it would been easy enough for Seneca to have one of his freedmen buy the poison from an apothecary. Tacitus does not explain when or why Seneca had previously procured that poison. Was Tacitus talking unwittingly about the murder of Germanicus? Even if he was not, this evidence indisputably links Seneca with the type of poison used to kill Germanicus.

So how did Seneca plan and execute the murder of Germanicus? And who was his accomplice?

# XXI

# HOW THE MURDER WAS CARRIED OUT

S eneca was a handsome, highly intelligent, charming, and witty young man of twenty when he first met Germanicus and his wife, Agrippina the Elder, at Daphne. Seneca and his uncle the prefect Galerius actually may have arrived at Daphne and introduced themselves to Agrippina before Germanicus arrived from the north after his kingmaking mission to Armenia. Seneca also probably attended later banquets held by Germanicus, such as the banquet for the king of Nabataea at which Piso made such a fool of himself by railing against luxury.

Tacitus does not mention that Agrippina accompanied Germanicus on his trip to Egypt in the summer of A.D. 19, yet many historians believe that she almost certainly went with him to Alexandria, based on the fact that they had been inseparable for years. Certainly there was absolutely no reason for her to stay behind in Syria. And just as Agrippina had visited Actium with Germanicus, to view the site of the famous battle between their grandfathers, it is unlikely that anything would have prevented her from visiting Alexandria, where Antony and Cleopatra had died and where their remains were entombed, and where her grandfather Augustus had finally secured control of the Roman Empire.

It is almost certain, therefore, that Agrippina did travel to Alexandria with Germanicus. But with Tacitus quite adamant that Germanicus went up the Nile alone, without even a single bodyguard, this suggests that Agrippina was forced to wait for her husband at Alexandria, where

Seneca would have had the opportunity to spend time in her company. Perhaps, with so much to see in Alexandria, Seneca acted as her guide in the famous city, which he had made his home.

It is probable that the marriage of Germanicus and Agrippina had actually become quite rocky by this stage, and this prompted Germanicus's solo trip up the exotic Nile. We know from her past and future actions that Agrippina was hugely ambitious, for herself and for her children. She had grown up expecting one of her brothers to succeed Augustus as emperor, and then, with each of them removed from the line of succession, she had seen her husband become the popular favorite to succeed Augustus. When Germanicus, a man of rock-solid morals, had refused to allow his legions to make him emperor instead of Tiberius in A.D. 14, Agrippina must have been livid. How, she would have reasoned, could anyone reject the throne when it was offered to him by the army, and when the Roman people so obviously wanted Germanicus to succeed Augustus?

Not only did this refusal to take the throne involve Germanicus's own future, it also prevented his sons, Agrippina's sons, from rising in the line of succession to become emperor after him. And that, to Agrippina's mind, must have been tantamount to wantonly depriving them of their birthright. For the next five years, proud Agrippina had to suffer the humiliation of bowing and scraping to Tiberius and his mother, the haughty Julia, when she could so easily have been Rome's empress, with the world bowing and scraping to her. Over the five years subsequent to the events of A.D. 14, Agrippina would have continued to push Germanicus to take the throne and eject Tiberius—if not for his own sake, then to guarantee the succession of their eldest son, Nero Germanicus, who was also Agrippina's favorite son by later accounts, once the boy was old enough to take the throne. Still Germanicus had steadfastly refused to oppose his "father," Tiberius. But in holding his moral ground, Germanicus was alienating his greatest ally. Heaven help anyone who stands between a mother and her ambitions for her children.

It is obvious now that, waiting at the governor's palace at Alexandria while Germanicus frittered away many weeks playing tourist, an unhappy, frustrated Agrippina formed a relationship with Seneca. He offered a sympathetic ear as she complained about her husband's lack of ambition for the throne and fretted that he was also denying her children their rightful opportunity to one day succeed him as emperor.

It is not impossible that Seneca and Agrippina had a tempestuous love affair there at the vast palace of the Ptolemys while Germanicus was away. There is no suggestion in any classical source that Agrippina was ever unfaithful to Germanicus, but judged by her later actions, an adulterous affair with a witty younger man was not out of the question. Seneca would go on to seduce two of Agrippina's beautiful daughters, and in decaying middle age still would be able to win an attractive young woman as his wife. So, an affair there in Egypt with a bitter and disillusioned Agrippina the Elder cannot be ruled out.

Not that an affair was necessary for what was soon to transpire. It may have been that Seneca and Agrippina merely became close without being physically involved. It could have been a closeness born of ambition on both their parts. And as Agrippina poured out her heart to Seneca about how Germanicus was denying her the future she felt she and her children deserved, the young man had an idea. There was a way to guarantee that her sons became emperor of Rome, even if her husband did not want the throne.

Seneca convinced Agrippina that if her husband were out of the way, then Tiberius's fear of being dethroned by Germanicus would evaporate and he would accept Germanicus's sons as his legitimate heirs. Yes, Germanicus's adoptive brother, Drusus the Younger, Agrippina's brother-in-law, would become next in line to the throne on Germanicus's death. But, Seneca would have told Agrippina, his own elder brother Junius Gallio at Rome was very close to Sejanus, and Sejanus was in turn close to Drusus's wife, who had confided to him that Drusus had no desire for the throne. If Agrippina were to follow his advice, said Seneca, Tiberius would make her sons his heirs.

This scenario, which had Drusus being superseded by Tiberius's grandsons as heirs to the throne, was not some impossible fantasy. For years, Augustus had groomed his three eldest grandsons—Agrippina's brothers, Lucius, Gaius, and Postumus—to be his heirs, sidelining Tiberius, his stepson. Only when two of those grandsons were dead and the third was imprisoned on an island had Tiberius come to be considered a legitimate heir by Augustus. In the same way, so Seneca's argument would have run, Tiberius could be expected to groom his grandsons Nero Germanicus, Drusus Germanicus, and Caligula to eventually replace him. Indeed, this was exactly what would transpire once Germanicus was dead, even while Tiberius's own son Drusus the Younger was alive.

There also was another scenario that the silver-tongued Seneca would have described for Agrippina. While the first scenario required Agrippina to wait for some years after the death of Germanicus, until Tiberius died, before one of her boys became emperor, this second scenario put Agrippina's boy Nero Germanicus on the throne within months of his father's death. That scenario was simple. If Germanicus were to be murdered, the finger of blame could be pointed at Tiberius. Passions could be raised—the passions of the Roman public, and those of the Roman military. The legions on the Rhine still adored Germanicus, and Germanicus's old friend Silius still commanded the four legions of the Army of the Upper Rhine. Sparked by the accusation that Tiberius had ordered the murder of Germanicus, public anger could create a revolution that could sweep Tiberius from power and install the son of Germanicus in his place—Nero Germanicus was already fifteen years of age; legally, he would achieve manhood at the end of his fifteenth year and could rule as an adult, with his mother's advice. Through her son, Agrippina could rule the empire.

According to Seneca's plans, one way or the other, short-term or long-term, Agrippina would have a son in the Palatium. But for the second, much swifter scenario to be realized, it must be plainly obvious to the entire world that Germanicus had been murdered, so the means of securing his death was crucial. It must be clearly a case of homicide, but those responsible must be beyond implication. To achieve this, Germanicus would have to be poisoned. Here, Seneca was at his most cunning. A man whose knowledge seemed boundless in his own time, he knew that many poisons were undetectable—a person killed with one of these appeared to have died from natural causes. To make it obvious that Germanicus had been poisoned, Seneca proposed to use belladonna, a poison with a calling card.

The governor of Syria, Piso, and his haughty wife, Plancina, also played into Seneca's hands, making themselves ideal and obvious scapegoats. They had gone out of their way to cause difficulties for, and show their dislike of, Germanicus and Agrippina. Seneca would have realized that it would not take much to convince most Romans that this pair had been involved in Germanicus's poisoning. It would then only remain for gossip and innuendo to do the rest and for the public to accuse Tiberius of putting Piso and Plancina up to Germanicus's murder. The attitudes and activities of this arrogant couple were gifts for Seneca and played right into his hands.

This, then, was Seneca's plan, to which Agrippina agreed. Perhaps that agreement came with tears and self-loathing, but it came nonetheless. Some would suggest that Agrippina was much too devoted to Germanicus to even contemplate his murder. Perhaps, when Agrippina and Germanicus were younger and his star was on the rise, that may have been the case. But ambition is a cruel, demanding master. It cannot be denied that Agrippina was driven by ambition, and that following Germanicus's death she lived for just one thing: to see a son of hers become emperor. And knowing her ambitious nature, which a critical Tacitus said made her more like a man than a woman, she must have become incredibly frustrated that Germanicus would not as much as contemplate taking the throne, when it was his for the taking until the day he died.

The murder plan went forward once Germanicus and Agrippina returned to Syria at the end of the summer of A.D. 19. Using one of his freedmen, Seneca sourced a quantity of belladonna in Alexandria. This would be his apprenticeship in poisons; as Tacitus tells us, by the time of his death he was not only learned on the subject, but also had experience procuring the type of lethal poison used to execute criminals. Agrippina may have traveled back to Daphne with the poison in her baggage, or Seneca may have sent it to her shortly after. Either way, it was not long after Germanicus's return to Syria, in the early fall, that he fell ill for the first time.

It was Agrippina, someone totally above suspicion, who personally added the poison to Germanicus's food or drink. After the first dose failed to kill her husband, she gave Germanicus a second, larger, lethal dose, which probably had to be sent to her from Alexandria by Seneca—this would account for the weeks of delay between the first bout of poisoning and the second bout. Of course, while extraordinary precautions were taken against poisoning by those around Germanicus following the first attempt on his life, no one suspected his own apparently devoted wife, and she was able to administer the final dose unnoticed—perhaps the very water she gave him to quench his thirst as he lay in increasing agony was laced with the poison. And then the deed was done: the prince was dead.

While they were together in Alexandria, Seneca would have schooled Agrippina on what she must do to capitalize on Germanicus's death. She must put his body on public display in Antioch, to highlight the cyanosis. She must conduct his cremated remains back to

Rome. She must make a grand entry into Brindisi, first pausing at Corfu to build expectation in Italy before landing in southern Italy. She must lead a funeral cortege all the way from Brindisi to Rome to stoke public grief and anger. It was crafty Seneca who wrote this script for Agrippina's dramatic return to Rome. Seneca also would have told Agrippina, in a message before she left Syria for Rome, to have her staff kill Martina the poisonmaker before she could absolve Plancina and Piso of the murder in a court of law at the capital. And that was how and why Martina had perished, while being kept under guard at Brindisi, at the hands of Agrippina's own staff. It is conceivable that Seneca even sent Agrippina more poison to achieve the removal of Martina before she left Syria.

Once Agrippina was back in Italy, with Seneca remaining behind in Egypt, she was on her own. Subsequently alone and without clever Seneca to guide and encourage her, the widow floundered as time went by. As was to be later shown, Agrippina did not even have the guile to cover up her suspicion that the apple offered to her by Tiberius at the Palatium banquet was poisoned.

To the disappointment of both Agrippina and Seneca, Seneca's second scenario failed to come to pass. Neither the Roman people nor the Rhine legions rose in revolt against Tiberius and dethroned him, despite widespread public unrest following Germanicus's death. Once Agrippina had returned to Rome and the death of Piso took the heat out of the public demands for vengeance, Agrippina had no choice but to wait for Tiberius to die, with the hope that Seneca's first scenario would one day come to pass.

Seneca himself waited at Alexandria like a guest locked out of a party. It had been his intention that Agrippina would send for him once there was a revolution that overthrew Tiberius and put Germanicus's son on the throne. When that revolution failed to eventuate, Seneca, impatient to further his ambitions at Rome with high-level backing, was not prepared to wait for years, as Agrippina must now do. Seneca knew that opportunity, like virginity, can never be regained once it has been lost. The opportunity to profit from his crime still lay before him like an open door. For a man as ambitious, and by now as frustrated, as Seneca, it would have seemed insane not to seize that opportunity.

The door to power via Agrippina may have been closed to Seneca by the outcome of the Piso trial, but he could see another door standing open before him. Seneca would have quite rightly figured that the most influential person at Tiberius's Palatium was now the Praetorian Guard commander Sejanus. And, potentially, Seneca had access to Sejanus via his brother at Rome, Junius Gallio Jr., whose adoptive father was a friend of Sejanus. It is probable that Seneca decided to send a message to Sejanus at Rome, via his brother Gallio. In that message, Seneca would reveal to Sejanus that he had masterminded the murder of Germanicus. The purpose of this revelation was a hope that he would be called to Rome to be rewarded by the Praetorian commander with an appointment that set him on the road to power and influence.

This was, of course, a very dangerous option. In his later years, a wiser, less impatient Seneca might not have ventured to attempt such a hazardous thing. In those later years, Seneca would himself say of Sejanus, "It became just as dangerous to be a friend of his as it was to cross him."[1] But the twenty-three-year-old Seneca, dreading the thought of spending his days in obscurity in Egypt, powerless, comparatively poor, and with his talents unrecognized, was prepared to take the gamble. He had, after all, just the previous year risked all by planning and executing the murder of Germanicus Caesar. What was the point, he would have thought, of committing such a heinous but fiendishly clever crime without achieving the goal that had prompted that crime? So close to the prize, and possessed of both the rashness and naïveté of youth, he had to make one last grab for that prize.

Not that he would have failed to weigh the risks against the potential outcome of communicating with Sejanus and revealing his complicity in the murder. Seneca was a dedicated student of Roman law and would later become as famous in his own lifetime for his successful legal defenses at Rome as for his writings and his speeches. As he languished there in Alexandria, he knew that the Roman legal system would actually work in his favor. In the Roman way of doing things, if you were not at Rome you were nowhere. It was as if you did not exist. For example, to be nominated for and elected to office at Rome you had to be physically in Rome. In the same way, if a legal prosecution was to be undertaken against a Roman knight or senator, it had to be at Rome, no matter where the crime had taken place. Letters or written statements from witnesses could not be presented as evidence in trials at Rome; accusations had to be supported by personal testimony. That was why it had been essential that Martina the poisonmaker appear personally at Piso's murder trial. Witnesses had to appear in court, in Rome, and give voice to their evidence. As long as Seneca remained in Egypt and did not turn up at Rome to accuse Sejanus or anyone else of complicity in or knowledge of the murder of Germanicus, his claim could not be tested in court. Neither could his letter be presented in evidence—against Seneca himself or anyone else. Only if Seneca turned up at Rome and gave personal evidence could he be heard in a Roman court of law.

Seneca sent the message to Sejanus in the late spring or early summer of A.D. 20, after news of the death of Piso and the termination of his murder trial had reached Alexandria. That year's northward sailing season had begun by that time, and Seneca would have sent a trusted freedman from his own staff to Rome bearing the all-important letter. The freedman would have gone as a paying passenger aboard one of the many Alexandrian grain ships—"round ships," the Romans called these tubby, sail-powered cargo vessels—that sailed from Egypt to Pozzuoli (Roman Puteuoli) and Ostia on Italy's western coast every year laden with the grain that kept the capital fed. That freedman carried the sealed letter from his master with instructions to pass it to Gallio, who, once he received it, passed it, sealed still, to Sejanus.

It would appear that Sejanus, on receiving this message from this comparatively unknown young man in Egypt, had not been convinced that he should believe Seneca's claim. It would have seemed incredible. An obscure twenty-three-year-old knight, the son of a famous rhetorician, suffering from a serious illness, living like an exile in far-off Egypt, now claiming to have been behind the most notorious murder in Rome's history? Sejanus could not know that he and Seneca would have much in common, that this same Seneca would one day run the Roman Empire as an emperor's right-hand man, just as Sejanus did, and would even come very close to himself taking the throne, as Sejanus also did.

Sejanus did not give Seneca credit for the murder of Germanicus. Yet, whether or not he believed that Seneca was telling the truth, he certainly did not want him turning up at Rome telling his story. Least of all, Sejanus did not want to be connected with Seneca or his claim, whether it was truthful of not. That connection could be fatal—sufficient to have Sejanus torn limb from limb by a vengeful populace if it ever became public that Seneca had been responsible for the murder of Germanicus and Sejanus was aware of it. In Italy, Seneca could be dangerous to Sejanus, even if, as he no doubt believed, Seneca's claim was the fabrication of a foolish or deranged mind. In provincial Egypt, on the edge of the empire, Seneca was no threat. Via Seneca's freedman, Sejanus sent a reply to Seneca in Alexandria—if ever Seneca set foot in Italy, the Praetorian commander would make sure that he did not live to tell his ridiculous story about the murder of Germanicus.

So although Seneca's brilliantly conceived crime remained a secret, his scheme failed to rapidly advance his career as he had hoped. He was forced to bide his time in Egypt for the next eleven years, in self-imposed exile, in fear of Sejanus should he ever venture to Rome. When, finally, Sejanus's rule was terminated by his denunciation, overthrow, and execution in A.D. 31, there was no longer any reason for Seneca to stay away from Italy. Without delay, he ended his exile and departed from Alexandria with his aunt, rushing to Rome to start his long-delayed career.

He immediately ingratiated himself with the mother and children of Germanicus, hopeful that Tiberius would now free Agrippina. Her imprisonment had, after all, been engineered by Sejanus, so logic would have suggested that Tiberius would end the exiles for which the now dead man had been responsible. This would allow Seneca to restart his relationship with Agrippina when she returned to Rome and to influence. But while some exiles were recalled to Rome by Tiberius, he did not relent as far as Agrippina was concerned; she remained a prisoner on Pandateria. As time slipped by without any sign of a change of heart from the aged and increasingly vindictive emperor and as Agrippina ran out of hope, taking her own life, Seneca decided to make the most of his connection with the family of Germanicus. Agrippina might not be of any use to him, but Seneca knew that Antonia, Germanicus's mother, was still close to the emperor, and he used her to open the way to his delayed career. Taking his opportunities as the road to influence appeared before him, he ended up in the beds of Agrippina's two daughters, Julia and Agrippina the Younger.

Did Suillius, Germanicus's former quaestor, know that Seneca had an affair with Germanicus's wife? As previously related, while defending himself in the Senate, Suillius had accused Seneca of polluting the bedchambers of Germanicus's ladies. This remark was taken at the time, and has been since, to mean that Suillius believed that Seneca had affairs with Julia and Agrippina the Younger. Yet the accusation also could be taken to include Germanicus's wife, Agrippina the Elder, among those "ladies." It is possible that Suillius was referring to mother and daughters, but there is no way of knowing for sure.

As for Seneca, if his countless wisdoms and philosophical catchphrases that have been quoted over and again down through history were all that were known about him, it would be impossible to contemplate that such a man could have been capable of planning and carrying out the murder of Germanicus Caesar. Yet we know so much more about Seneca and the mendacious life he led. As so many commentators have observed down through the ages, Seneca was a man who spectacularly failed to practice what he preached. He spoke against luxury, yet became one of the richest men in Rome. He advocated the concept of share and share alike, but he shared his wealth and power with no one, least of all the common man. He declared gladiatorial contests a barbarity, yet he counseled wars that resulted in thousands of nameless deaths, and he helped Nero engineer the deaths of others—or at the very least looked the other way while Nero did away with them.

It became clear that to secure and maintain power, throughout his career there was no crime from which Seneca would shrink. He himself wrote that the best way to cover up a crime was by committing more crimes. He wrote of the virtues of honesty, yet lived a life of dishonesty, for the pragmatic Seneca operated on the Roman maxim that honesty is praised, then is left to starve. We know that he committed adultery with one and almost certainly two daughters of Germanicus, yet he denied it. We know that he was linked to the murder of Claudius, if only in writing Nero's first speech as emperor while continuing the lie that Claudius still lived. We know that Seneca counseled the eventual murder of Agrippina the Younger, if he did not actually conceive the plan to kill her. He certainly did not try to save her. We know that he wrote the lying letter from Nero to the Senate in which he claimed that Agrippina had been plotting to kill Nero and that that was why she had herself been killed. And we know that Seneca knew about the plot to murder Nero but said nothing, waiting instead for the deed to be done in the expectation that he himself would be offered the throne by the Praetorians, and denying this, too.

Seneca may have mellowed in his last, retiring years, but for the vast majority of his life he was fueled by a desire for power that, combined with a brilliant mind and great oratorical powers, drove him relentlessly forward toward his objectives of wealth, influence, and notoriety. Emotionally and intellectually, he was perfectly capable of the murder of Germanicus. He had the opportunity and the motive, and he knew about poisons. Coldly and deliberately, Seneca conceived the murder of Germanicus, procured the poison that killed him, and seduced Agrippina into administering it.

Seneca little cared that the murder of Germanicus would set off a fatal domino reaction, acting as catalyst to the murder or unnatural death of numerous other members of the family of Germanicus— Germanicus's adoptive brother, Drusus the Younger; Germanicus's sons, Nero Germanicus, Drusus Germanicus, and Caligula; Germanicus's wife, Agrippina the Elder; Germanicus's daughters Julia and Agrippina the Younger; Germanicus's brother, Claudius; and possibly Germanicus's grandson Nero. It could be argued that none of them would have been murdered, or forced to take their own lives, had Germanicus lived to a ripe old age.

Ironically, Seneca achieved his goals of power and wealth not because he murdered Germanicus but despite the fact that he murdered him. Yet, in the end, the ambition that had driven him to murder was his undoing.

And consider this. The demise of Nero marked the end of the family of the Caesars. Seneca, in murdering Germanicus Caesar, had started the chain of murders or unnatural deaths that eliminated the wife, children, brothers, and grandson of Germanicus, and in doing so terminated the Caesar bloodline. After the Caesars, the Roman Empire descended into chaos, relieved briefly by the emperors Vespasian and Trajan, both of whom added Caesar to their names to give some stature to their reigns. Following Trajan's death, Hadrian began a contraction of the empire that could not be reversed; the decline once more gathered pace until the fall of Rome became inevitable. Blame for far more than just a single murder can be laid at the feet of Seneca. It can be argued that by murdering Germanicus, Seneca not only had the blood of the Caesars on his hands but also was responsible for causing decades of turmoil from which Rome could never recover, and for sending the Roman Empire down the road to ruin.

# NOTES

## I. The Murder of Germanicus Caesar

1. Tacitus, *Annals*, II, 73.
2. Tacitus, *Annals*, IV, 31.
3. Suetonius, *Lives of the Caesars*, IV, 4.
4. Josephus, *Jewish Antiquities*, 18.6.8.
5. Suetonius, *Lives*, IV, 5.
6. Tacitus, *Annals*, II, 82.
7. Ibid.
8. Suetonius, *Lives*, IV, 6.
9. Ibid., 3.
10. Cassius Dio, writing two hundred years later, stated that these were found at Germanicus's palace. He was almost certainly using Tacitus as his source, as was Robert Graves in the fictional *I, Claudius*, and both made the same error. Tacitus, at *Annals* II, 69, does not specify exactly where this material was found. As Piso and Plancina had by this time left Syria, it would have been their palace, the provincial governor's palace at Antioch, that was searched for evidence, as would be expected, not Germanicus's palace at Daphne. At *Annals* III, 13, Tacitus writes of the sorcery and horrible sacrifices made by Piso and Plancina—he is saying they personally made these sacrifices, an impossibility at Germanicus's palace at Daphne, which was occupied by Germanicus, his family, and, even when they were away, their loyal staff. In contrast, this would have been entirely possible, and logical, at their own Antioch palace.
11. Tacitus, *Annals*, II, 70.
12. Macinnis, *Poisons*; Mellan, *Dictionary of Poisons*; Thompson, *Poisons and Poisoners*.
13. Tacitus, *Annals*, II, 71.
14. Ibid.
15. Ibid., I, 33.
16. Ibid., II, 72.
17. See note 12.
18. Tacitus, *Annals*, II, 72.
19. Ibid.
20. Dio, *Roman History*, LVII, 18.

## II. The Immediate Aftermath

1. Josephus, *Antiquities*, 18.6.8.
2. Suetonius, *Lives*, IV, 5.
3. Josephus, *Antiquities*, 18.6.8.
4. Suetonius, *Lives*, IV, 5.
5. Ibid., 6.
6. Dio, *History*, LVII, 18.
7. Tacitus, *Annals*, II, 73.
8. Suetonius, *Lives*, IV, 1.
9. Josephus, *Antiquities*, 18.2.5.
10. See chapter I, note 12.
11. Tacitus, *Annals*, II, 76.
12. Ibid.
13. Ibid., 79.
14. Ibid.

## III. The Return to Rome

1. Tacitus, *Annals*, II, 81.
2. Ibid., 83.
3. Ibid., III, 1.
4. Suetonius, *Lives*, IV, 1.
5. Graves, *I, Claudius*, 20.
6. Tacitus, *Annals*, III, 1.
7. Ibid., 2.
8. Suetonius, *Lives*, IV, 4.
9. Dio, *History*, LVII, 18.
10. Tacitus, *Annals*, III, 3.
11. Ibid., 5.
12. Ibid., 3.
13. Suetonius, *Lives*, IV, 6.
14. Tacitus, *Annals*, III, 4.
15. Ibid.
16. Ibid., 6.
17. Ibid.
18. Ibid., 7.

## IV. Piso Returns

1. Tacitus, *Annals*, III, 8.
2. Ibid.

3. Ibid.
4. Ibid., 9.
5. Ibid., 8.

## V. Motives for Murder

1. Suetonius, *Lives*, IV, 2.
2. Plutarch, *Lives*, Mark Antony.
3. Suetonius, *Lives*, IV, 8.
4. Tacitus, *Annals*, I, 3.
5. Suetonius, *Lives*, III, 22.
6. Tacitus, *Annals*, II, 59.
7. Ibid., 59–61.
8. Ibid., 61.
9. Dio, *History*, LVII, 19.
10. Ibid.
11. Suetonius, *Lives*, IV, 6.
12. Ibid., 2.
13. Tacitus, *Annals*, I, 13.
14. Ibid., II, 54.
15. Ibid., 55.
16. Ibid.
17. Suetonius, *Lives*, IV, 2.
18. Tacitus, *Annals*, II, 57.
19. Ibid.
20. Ibid.
21. Dio, *History*, LVII, 18.
22. Tacitus, *Annals*, I, 33.
23. Graves, *I, Claudius*, 3.
24. Tacitus, *Annals*, I, 3.
25. Suetonius, *Lives*, III, 22.
26. Tacitus, *Annals*, I, 3.
27. Dio, *History*, LVII, 19.
28. Graves, *I, Claudius*, 21.
29. Tacitus, *Annals*, VI, 7.

## VI. The Murder Trial Begins

1. Tacitus, *Annals*, II, 28, and V, 11.
2. Ibid., III, 10.
3. Ibid.

4. Dio, *History*, LVII, 18.
5. Tacitus, *Annals*, III, 11.
6. Ibid.
7. Ibid., II, 21.
8. Carcopino, *Daily Life*, IX, 1.
9. Tacitus, *Annals*, I, 13.
10. Ibid., IV, 20.
11. Ibid., III, 15.
12. Ibid., 16.
13. Ibid.
14. Suetonius, *Lives*, III, 68.
15. Tacitus, *Annals*, III, 12 (entire speech).

## VII. Prosecution and Defense

1. Tacitus, *Annals*, III, 13.
2. Martial, VI, 35.
3. Tacitus, *Annals*, III, 13.
4. Ibid.
5. Ibid., 14.
6. Ibid., 15.
7. Ibid.
8. Ibid., 13–14.
9. Ibid., 15.
10. Ibid.
11. Ibid., 17.
12. Pliny the Younger, *Epistles*, II, 9, 23.
13. Tacitus, *Annals*, III, 14.
14. Ibid.
15. Ibid., 16.
16. Ibid.
17. Ibid.
18. Ibid.
19. Ibid.
20. Ibid., 17.
21. Ibid.
22. Ibid., 19.

## VIII. Destroying the Family of Germanicus

1. Tacitus, *Annals*, III, 29.
2. Ibid., IV, 7.

3. Ibid., 11.
4. Ibid., 12.
5. Ibid.
6. Ibid.
7. Ibid.
8. Suetonius, *Lives*, II, 86.
9. Tacitus, *Annals*, I, 33.
10. Ibid., IV, 12.
11. Ibid., 15.
12. Ibid., I, 69.
13. Ibid.
14. Ibid., IV, 17.
15. Ibid., 18.
16. Ibid., 19.
17. Ibid., 39.
18. Ibid., 53.
19. Ibid.
20. Ibid. Tacitus said that he found the story of this incident in the memoirs of Agrippina's daughter, Agrippina the Younger.
21. Ibid.
22. Tacitus, *Annals*, IV, 70.
23. Dio, *History*, LVIII, 1.
24. Tacitus, *Annals*, IV, 70.
25. Ibid., V, 3.
26. Ibid.
27. Ibid., 4.

## IX. The Downfall of Sejanus

1. Suetonius, *Lives*, III, 64.
2. Dio, *History*, LVIII, 3.
3. Ibid.
4. Ibid.
5. Ibid.
6. Tacitus, *Annals*, VI, 8.
7. Dio, *History*, LVIII, 10.
8. Suetonius, *Lives*, II, 65; Dio, *History*, VII, LVIII.
9. Josephus, *Antiquities*, 18.6.6.
10. Ibid.
11. Dio, *History*, LXV, 14.
12. Josephus, *Antiquities*, 18.6.6.
13. Suetonius, *Lives*, II, 65.

14. Ibid.
15. Dio, *History*, LVIII, 11.
16. Tacitus, *Annals*, V, 9.
17. Josephus, *Antiquities*, 18.6.6.
18. Dio, *History*, LVIII, 11.
19. Tacitus, *Annals*, VI, 3.
20. Josephus, *Antiquities*, 18.6.4–6.7.

## X. The Germanicus Emperor

1. Tacitus, *Annals*, VI, 24.
2. Suetonius, *Lives*, III, 61.
3. Tacitus, *Annals*, VI, 25.
4. Suetonius, *Lives*, III, 66.
5. Tacitus, *Annals*, VI, 31.
6. Suetonius, *Lives*, IV, 10.
7. Philo, *Embassy to Gaius*, 40.
8. Suetonius, *Lives*, IV, 12.
9. Philo, *Embassy to Gaius*, 38.
10. Tacitus, *Annals*, VI, 50.
11. Suetonius, *Lives*, IV, 13.
12. Ibid., 14.
13. Ibid.
14. Ibid., 22.
15. Ibid., 51.
16. Philo, *Embassy to Gaius*, 61.
17. Suetonius, *Lives*, IV, 24.
18. Ibid., 53.

## XI. The Murder of Caligula

1. Tacitus, *Annals*, I, 32.
2. Josephus, *Antiquities*, 19.1.13.
3. Ibid.
4. Ibid., 19.1.14.
5. Suetonius, *Lives*, IV, 58.
6. Josephus, *Antiquities*, 19.1.14.
7. Suetonius, *Lives*, IV, 58.
8. Josephus, *Antiquities*, 19.1.14.
9. Suetonius, *Lives*, IV, 58.
10. Ibid.
11. Josephus, *Antiquities*, 19.1.14.

12. Suetonius, *Lives*, IV, 58.
13. Josephus, *Antiquities*, 19.1.14.
14. Dio, *History*, VII, LIX.
15. Josephus, *Antiquities*, 19.3.1.
16. Suetonius, *Lives*, V, 10.
17. Josephus, *Antiquities*, 19.3.1.

## XII. The New Germanicus Emperor

1. Josephus, *Antiquities*, 19.3.1.
2. Ibid., 19.3.2.
3. Suetonius, *Lives*, V, 10.
4. Josephus, *Antiquities*, 19.2.4.
5. Josephus, who names Lupus (whose name means "wolf," incidentally) at *Antiquities* 19.2.4, says that he was a tribune. The less reliable Suetonius, at *Lives* IV, 58, says he was a centurion.
6. Josephus, *Antiquities*, 19.1.20; Dio, *History*, LIX, 31.
7. Suetonius, *Lives*, IV, 60.
8. Josephus, *Antiquities*, 19.2.2.
9. Suetonius, *Lives*, V, 10.
10. Josephus, *Antiquities*, 19.4.3. Josephus, in error, refers to him as Marcus Minucianus.
11. Ibid., 19.4.5.
12. Dio, *History*, LX, 3.
13. Suetonius, *Lives*, V, 7.

## XIII. The Murder of Claudius

1. Dio, *History*, LX, 3.
2. Tacitus, *Annals*, XII, 2.
3. Ibid., XI, 12.
4. Ibid., XII, 3.
5. Suetonius, *Lives*, V, 26.
6. Dio, *History*, LX, 8; LXI, 30.
7. Suetonius, *Lives*, VI, 7.
8. Josephus, *Antiquities*, 20.18.2.
9. Tacitus, *Annals*, XII, 42.
10. Ibid.
11. Ibid., XIII, 12.
12. Dio, *History*, LXI, 33.
13. Dio, *History*, LXI, 10.
14. Tacitus, *Annals*, XII, 65.

15. Ibid., 67.
16. Dio, *History*, LXI, 34.
17. Ibid.
18. Tacitus, *Annals*, XII, 67.
19. Gibbon, *Decline and Fall*, I, 1.
20. Tacitus, *Annals*, XII, 69.

## XIV. The Murder of Britannicus

1. Tacitus, *Annals*, XIII, 2.
2. Dio, *History*, LXII, 11.
3. Tacitus, *Annals*, XIII, 13.
4. Dio, *History*, LXI, 34.
5. Tacitus, *Annals*, XIII, 14.
6. Ibid., 16.

## XV. The Claims of Germanicus's Quaestor

1. Tacitus, *Annals* XIII, 43.
2. Ibid., 42.
3. Ibid.
4. Dio, *History*, LXI, 10.
5. Ibid.
6. Tacitus, *Annals*, XIII, 43.
7. Dio, *History*, LXI, 10.
8. Tacitus, *Annals*, XIII, 43.
9. Ibid.
10. Ibid.

## XVI. The Murder of Nero's Mother

1. Plutarch, *Lives*, Galba.
2. Tacitus, *Annals*, XIV, 1.
3. Ibid., 2.
4. Ibid.
5. Suetonius, *Lives*, VI, 34.
6. Dio, *History*, LXII, 12.
7. Tacitus, *Annals*, XIV, 3.
8. Dio, *History*, LXII, 12.
9. Tacitus, *Annals*, XIV, 3.
10. Ibid., XV, 51.
11. Dio, *History*, LXII, 13.

12. Tacitus, *Annals*, XIV, 4.
13. Ibid., 5.
14. Ibid.
15. Ibid., 7.
16. Ibid.
17. Ibid.
18. Ibid.
19. Ibid.
20. Seneca, *Agamemnon*, 116.
21. Tacitus, *Annals*, XIV, 8.
22. Ibid.
23. Seneca, *Octavia*, 957.
24. Tacitus, *Annals*, XIV, 8.
25. Seneca, *Octavia*, 956.
26. Tacitus, *Annals*, XIV, 9.
27. Dio, *History*, LXII, 14.
28. Suetonius, *Lives*, VI, 34.
29. Tacitus, *Annals*, XIV, 9.
30. Ibid., 10.
31. Suetonius, *Lives*, VI, 34.
32. Tacitus, *Annals*, XIV, 10.
33. Ibid., 11.
34. Ibid.

## XVII. Death for Burrus and Octavia

1. Suetonius, *Lives*, VI, 34.
2. Dio, *History*, LXII, 18.
3. Ibid.
4. Tacitus, *Annals*, XIV, 51.
5. Seneca, *Octavia*, 853.
6. Dio, *Lives*, LXII, 13.
7. Seneca, *Octavia*, 593–594.
8. Ibid.
9. Tacitus, *Annals*, XIV, 61.
10. Ibid., 62.
11. Seneca, *Octavia*, 859–860.
12. Ibid., 872–881.
13. Ibid., 918.
14. Tacitus, *Annals*, XIV, 64.
15. Ibid., 54.

## XVIII. The Plot to Murder Nero

1. Tacitus, *Annals*, XV, 41.
2. Ibid., 53.
3. Ibid., 66.
4. Ibid.
5. Ibid., 60.
6. Ibid., 65.
7. Ibid., 61.
8. Ibid., 62.
9. Ibid.
10. Ibid.
11. Ibid., 63.
12. Ibid.
13. Dio, *History*, LXII, 25.
14. Suetonius, *Lives*, III, 73.
15. Dio, *History*, LXII, 25.
16. Tacitus, *Annals*, XV, 64.
17. Ibid.

## XIX. The End of Nero

1. Suetonius, *Lives*, VI, 49; Dio, *History*, LXIII, 29.
2. Suetonius, *Lives*, VI, 50, 57.
3. Tacitus, *Histories*, II, 8.
4. Suetonius, *Lives*, VI, 57.
5. Tacitus, *Histories*, II, 8.
6. Suetonius, *Lives*, VI, 57.

## XX. Unmasking Germanicus's Murderers

1. Tacitus, *Annals*, I, 33.

## XXI. How the Murder Was Carried Out

1. Seneca, *Letters*, LV.

# GLOSSARY

ACTA DIURNIA  Rome's *Daily News*, the world's first newspaper. Handwritten daily by the Palatium at Rome and sent around the empire. Founded by Julius Caesar in 59 B.C.

ACTA SENATUS  Official record of the proceedings of the Roman Senate, kept in the *Tabularium*.

AFRICA  The Roman province of Africa occupied today's Tunisia in North Africa. Gnaeus Calpurnius Piso was governor there in 3 B.C. Piso's eldest son, Gnaeus Piso, was later also governor of Africa, under the emperor Caligula.

AQUILIFER  Standard-bearer who carried the *aquila*, the legion's eagle. Eagle-bearer.

AUXILIARY  Noncitizen serving in Roman army. Light infantry and cavalry. Recruited throughout empire. In Imperial times served twenty-five years. Paid less than legionary. From the first century A.D., granted Roman citizenship on discharge. Commanded by prefects. The troops of the German Guard were auxiliaries.

BAETICA  The Roman province of Farther Spain, roughly corresponding with modern-day Andalucia, where Seneca, his father, and his brothers were born and where Gnaeus Calpurnius Piso was governor for a time.

BASILICA  Roman meeting hall, used for court sessions and other public business. Once the Roman Empire officially became Christian, churches followed the basilica design.

BATAVIAN  Native of Batavia, a former German kingdom subjugated by Julius Caesar. The Batavian lands today form part of the Netherlands.

BATAVIAN HORSE  Elite auxiliary cavalry unit of Roman army. Recruited in present-day Holland. Its troopers were famous for being able to swim rivers with their horses in full equipment. By the third century A.D. the unit had become the emperor's household cavalry unit.

BOLT  Large metal-tipped arrow fired by archers and scorpio catapults.

CAMPAIGNING SEASON  Traditionally, in the imperial era, early March to October 19, when legions conducted military campaigns, after which they went into winter quarters. The October 19 date originally marked the date of the ancient Festival of the October Horse, when Rome's soldiers came home from the army to conduct the harvest. The terms "seasoned campaigner" and "seasoned soldier" derive from Roman times, denoting soldiers who have served one or more campaigning seasons in the army.

CASTRA PRAETORIA  Massive castlelike Praetorian barracks at Rome, built early in the first century by its then commander Sejanus, in the city's northeastern fourth Precinct. Torn down by the emperor Constantine in the fourth century after he abolished the Praetorian Guard.

CENTURION  Legion, Praetorian/City Guard and Marines officer, fifty-nine to an imperial legion, in eleven grades. Equivalent to first lieutenant and captain. Enlisted man promoted from ranks, although there were some Equestrian Order centurions in late republic/early empire.

CENTURY  Legion subunit made up of ten squads. In republican times, of a hundred men. In imperial times, of eighty men. Commanded by a centurion.

CHIEF CENTURION  *Primus pilus* (first spear). A legion's most senior centurion.

CITY GUARD  A military unit made up of former slaves that served as the police force and fire brigade of Rome and manned the city gates. Comprised four cohorts of fifteen hundred men each. The City Guard and the Night Watch both reported to the city prefect of Rome. In early imperial times, one cohort of Rome's City Guard was permanently stationed at the Gallic city of Lugdunensis (Lyon, France), to guard the official mint there, and another was stationed for a time at west coast ports in Italy.

CIVIC CROWN  Crown of oak leaves, military bravery award for saving the life of a Roman citizen in battle. Rarely awarded, highly prized. Julius Caesar was a recipient.

COHORT  Battalion. Ten to a legion. In Caesar's time, of 600 men. In imperial times, cohorts 10 through 2 had 480 men, the senior first cohort, 800.

COLONEL  See TRIBUNE and PREFECT.

CONQUISITOR  Roman army recruiting officer.

CONSUL  Highest official at Rome; president of Senate. Two held office annually. Also commanded Roman armies, with equivalent rank of lieutenant general.

The minimum age in the republic, forty-two; in the empire the minimum age was thirty-seven, except for members of the imperial family.

CONTUBERNIUM   Legion subunit; the squad. In the republic, of ten men. In the empire, of eight men.

CRUISER   Midsize warship, taking in the *bireme, trireme,* and *quinquereme* classes. The latter was 120 feet long, had a beam of 17 feet, with a crew of 270 oarsmen at 3 banks of oars, 30 sailors, and 160 marines.

CURIA   Senate House at Rome.

CURILE CHAIRS   The seats of the two current consuls in the Senate House.

*CURSUS PUBLICUS VELOX*   Literally, "the state's very fast runner." Imperial Rome's courier service. Founded by the emperor Augustus with runners on foot; soon expanded to wheeled vehicles and mounted couriers. Horses were changed at way stations, checked by inspectors, every 6 to 10 miles. Covered up to 170 miles per day. Compare with the nineteenth-century U.S. Pony Express, which covered 180 miles per day. It was a capital offense to interfere with *cursus publicus* couriers or their load. *Cursus publicus* carriages only carried passengers who had the personal permission of the emperor to ride in them.

DECIMATION   Literally, to reduce by a tenth. Legions were punished for mutiny or cowardice by one man in ten being clubbed to death by their comrades after drawing lots. The 9th Legion, later the 9th Hispana, was the only legion on record to be decimated twice.

DECUMAN GATE   The main gate of a legion camp and of Rome's Castra Praetoria. Faced away from the enemy.

DECURION   Legion cavalry officer. Equivalent of a second lieutenant. Four to each legion cavalry squadron. Also, senior elected civil official of a Roman town.

DICTATOR   Supreme and sole chief of Rome. An ancient appointment, made by the Senate in emergencies, intended to last a maximum of six months. Sulla used the position to make himself ruler of the Roman Republic. Julius Caesar appropriated the title with several temporary appointments before becoming dictator for life in February 44 B.C.

EAGLE   The *aquila,* sacred standard of a legion; originally silver, later gold.

EQUESTRIAN   Member of Roman order of knighthood. Qualified for posts as tribune, prefect, procurator, and Senate membership. Required net worth of 400,000 sesterces. In imperial era served mandatory six-month legion cadetship as junior tribune at age eighteen or nineteen.

EVOCATI   In the imperial era, militia corps of retired legion veterans, serving behind their old standards in emergencies. Controlled by their provincial governor.

FASCES   Symbol of Roman magistrate's power to punish and execute, an ax head protruding from a bundle of wooden rods. Carried by lictors. Denoted rank: quaestors had one, legates five, praetors six, consuls and most emperors twelve. Dictators and some emperors used twenty-four lictors.

FIRST-RANK CENTURIONS   *Primi ordines;* a legion's six most senior centurions.

FORUM   Open space, usually rectangular, in all Roman cities and towns where law courts, meeting halls, temples, markets, and speakers' platforms were located. There were several forums at Rome.

FORUM ROMANUM   Original and main forum at Rome.

FREEDMAN   A former slave, officially granted freedom.

FRIGATE   Liburnian; light, fast warship. Its length was 108 feet; beam, 12 feet. It had a crew of 144 rowers, 10 to 15 sailors, and 40 marines.

FURLOUGH FEES   In camp, one legionary in four could take leave by paying a set fee to his centurion. The state took responsibility for paying centurions these fees in A.D. 69.

GEMINA LEGION   "Twin" legion formed by merger of two existing legions.

GERMAN GUARD   Elite bodyguard unit of emperor; handpicked German auxiliaries. Comprised 10 cohorts, each of 480 men. Four cohorts were based at Rome at any one time, at the Palatium, with the remainder stationed in towns outside Rome on rotation.

GLADIATORS   Professional fighters used in public shows throughout the empire. Usually slaves. Gladiatorial contests originated as funeral rites. Sometimes used as soldiers in civil wars, but usually without success, as they lacked unit training and discipline.

GLADIUS   Roman legionary sword, twenty inches long, double-edged, with a pointed end. Known as the Spanish sword because the best were made in Spain.

IMPERATOR   Title. Literally, "chief" or "master." Highest honor for a general. Became reserved for emperors, after their armies' victories. Title "emperor" grew from *imperator*.

IMPERIAL   Relating to the period of Roman history from 27 B.C. to the fall of the empire.

IMPERIAL PROVINCE "Armed" front-line province bordering unfriendly states, administered by the Palatium. Garrisoned by at least two legions plus auxiliaries. Governed by a propraetor (lieutenant general), a former consul whose appointment, by the emperor, was open-ended. A propraetor commanded all troops in his province, could wear a sword and uniform and levy recruits, and had capital punishment power.

JUVENA COLLEGA Young Men's Association. Ancient guild for sons of Roman nobility in Italy. Fostered by Augustus. Boys joined at age seventeen. Learned horsemanship, weapons skills, manliness, etc., as a prelude to entering the army at eighteen as officer cadets.

LEGION Regiment. Main operational unit of the Roman army. From *legio* (levy, or draft). In 10 cohorts. Republican legion nominal strength, 6,000 men, imperial, 5,185 enlisted men and 72 officers, including own cavalry unit of 124 officers and men. At the beginning of the first century there were 28 legions. At the end of the war of succession, A.D. 69, there were 32 legions. By A.D. 102, 30; and 33 in A.D. 233.

LEGIONARY Soldier of a legion. Mostly a draftee. A Roman citizen (with very rare exceptions). Most were recruited outside Italy in the imperial era. Republican recruits aged seventeen to twenty, served sixteen years; imperial, minimum age twenty, served twenty years from late in Augustus's reign.

LICTORS Unarmed attendants of senior Roman officials, carrying their fasces.

LUSTRATION The Lustration Exercise, a religious ceremony performed by legions in March. Standards were purified with perfumes and garlands prior to each new campaign.

MANIPLE Company. Legion subunit, of 160 men in imperial times. Three to a cohort.

MANTLET Wooden shed, on wheels, used in siege works by the Roman army.

MARCHING CAMP Fortified camp built by legions at the end of every day's march.

MARINE Soldier serving in the Roman navy. Freedman. Served twenty-six years, paid less than an auxiliary. Commanded by centurions. Organized by cohorts; unit titles unknown.

MURAL CROWN Crown of gold awarded to first Roman soldier over an enemy city wall.

NAVY Prior to the emperor Augustus, Rome relied on its provinces and allies to provide its battle fleets. The imperial Roman navy had two battle fleets: the Tyrrhenian Fleet, based at Micenum, with a squadron also at Fréjus in southern

France; and the Adriatic Fleet, at Ravenna. Other, smaller fleets were the Classis Britannica, at Boulogne; the Classis Germanica, on the Rhine; the Classis Moesica, on the Lower Danube; the Classis Pannonica, on the Upper Danube; and the Classis Pontica, with part based in Pontus, and forty vessels based at Kersh on the Crimean Peninsula to cover the Black and Azov seas.

NIGHT WATCH   Nighttime police force and fire brigade at Rome; established by Augustus. Made up of ex-slaves. In seven cohorts of a thousand men each, stationed throughout the city. Reported to the city prefect.

OPTIO   Sergeant major. Deputy to centurion and decurion. Unit records and training officer. One to a century, four to legion cavalry units.

OVATION   Lesser form of Triumph. Celebrant rode on horseback through Rome in a ceremonial procession.

PALATIUM   Origin of the word "palace." Residence and military headquarters of emperors at Rome. First established by Augustus on Palatine Hill, from which its name derived. All emperors' headquarters were thereafter called the Palatium, even when new palaces were built by other emperors, including Tiberius, Caligula, Nero, and Domitian. Domitian's vast new palace, the Domus Augustana, which incorporated Augustus's old residence, known as the Old Palatium, would serve as the Palatium of many later emperors.

PALUDAMENTUM   General's cloak. Scarlet in republican times. In imperial times, legion commanders wore a scarlet cloak, commanders in chief, a purple cloak.

PILUM   A Roman legionary's javelin. Metal-tipped, weighted end, six to seven feet long.

PRAETOR   Senior Roman magistrate and major general. Could command legions and armies. Entitled to five lictors.

PRAETORIAN GATE   Gate of a legion camp and Praetorian barracks that faced the enemy.

PRAETORIAN GUARD   Elite unit founded in the republic to guard the praetors of Rome. Reformed by Mark Antony and made his bodyguard. Became an elite military police force in imperial times. Recruited exclusively in Italy, Praetorians were paid more than legionaries, served less time (sixteen years from late in the reign of Augustus), and received a larger retirement bonus (20,000 sesterces, as opposed to the legionary's 12,000). For centuries the Praetorian Guard was, along with the German Guard, City Guard, and Night Watch, the only military unit stationed in Italy.

PRAETORIUM   Headquarters in a Roman military camp.

PREFECT  Commander of auxiliary units, Praetorian Guard, City Guard, and naval fleets. Usually a citizen of Equestrian Order status. Prefects governed Egypt and, between A.D. 6 and 41, Judea.

PROCONSUL  Literally, "as good as a consul." See SENATORIAL PROVINCE.

PROCURATOR  Provincial official of Equestrian Order rank, deputy of governor, superior to prefect. Financial administrator and tax gatherer. Sometimes governed small provinces and subprovinces (e.g., Macedonia and Judea). Had capital punishment power. In imperial era had an annual salary of 60,000 to 100,000 sesterces.

PROPRAETOR  Literally, "as good as a praetor." See IMPERIAL PROVINCE.

QUADRIGA  Roman chariot drawn by four horses. A ceremonial golden *quadriga* was used in Triumph parades.

QUAESTOR  "Investigator." Lowest-ranking Roman magistrate. Assistant to consul and provincial governors. Served as quartermaster in republican field armies. In imperial times responsible for treasury matters, military recruiting, and special commissions.

RANK AND FILE  Enlisted men of a legion.

ROSTRA  Speakers' platforms in the Forum at Rome.

SARDONYCHIS  Emperor's personal seal, introduced by Augustus in 27 B.C., when he was granted his title. Used by most subsequent emperors. Bore image of Augustus cut by the artisan Dioscurides. For three years prior, Augustus's seal carried the image of a sphinx, celebrating his victory in Egypt over Antony and Cleopatra, and probably in emulation of Julius Caesar's seal, which bore the Caesar family's emblem, the elephant. The sphinx was briefly replaced, according to Suetonius, by the head of Alexander the Great. The *sardonychis* seal was possibly named for the superior-quality wax used, resembling onyx. Also the Palatium's outbound correspondence department, so called because the *sardonychis* seal was last thing added to outgoing letters.

SATURNALIA  Festival of Saturn. Originally on December 17, extended to four days, then five, then seven. Slaves could dress like their masters, dice playing was legal, and patrons gave their clients gifts. Origin of Christian Christmas festival and of Christmas gift-giving.

SCORPION  *Scorpio*, quick-firing artillery piece, using metal-tipped bolts. Each legion was equipped with fifty of them, plus ten heavy stone-throwing catapults.

SENATE  Rome's most powerful elected body. Members, needing a net worth of 1 million sesterces, qualified for legion commands, praetorships, and consulships.

Minimum age thirty in imperial times. In Caesar's time, some 350 to 400 members. At the start of the reign of Augustus, 1,000 members; he subsequently limited it to 600 members.

SENATORIAL PROVINCE   In the imperial era, a province with a governor appointed by the Senate for one year, by lot, from its members. With the rank of proconsul, the senatorial governor had capital punishment power but couldn't wear a uniform or a sword, or levy troops. His province had a garrison of auxiliaries (except in Africa, where one legion was stationed). Asia and Africa were the most highly prized, best-paid appointments—up to 400,000 sesterces per year.

SIGNIFER   Literally, a signaler; the standard-bearer of legion subunits and Praetorian Guard cohorts.

SPATHA   Roman cavalry sword. It had a round end and was longer than the *gladius*.

TABULARIUM   Official archives at Rome. Built in 78 B.C., on the northern side of the Forum Romanum, at the foot of the Capitoline Mount. The building was incorporated into the Senate Palace that stands on the site today.

TESSERA   A small wax sheet on which was inscribed the legion watchword for the day.

TESSERARIUS   Legion guard/orderly sergeant. Distributed the *tessera* to his men.

TESTUDO   "Tortoise" formation. Legionaries locked shields over their heads and at their sides.

TORQUE   Neck chain of twisted gold. Among the Roman army's highest bravery awards.

TREASURY OF SATURN   Rome's main treasury, in the basement of the Temple of Saturn. Managed by former praetors with a staff of some thirty-six clerks in early imperial times. Separate and distinct from the military treasury, which was incorporated into the Palatium.

TRIBUNAL   Reviewing stand in legion camp, built in front of tribunes' quarters. In a legion marching camp, it was built from "bricks" of turf. From here the commander addressed assemblies of his troops, and his adjutant announced daily orders each morning.

TRIBUNE   Legion, Praetorian Guard, and City Guard officer. Six of equal rank in republican legions shared command. In imperial legions, a "thin stripe" junior tribune was officer cadet serving a mandatory six months; five to a legion. One "broad stripe" senior tribune (so-called Military Tribune) per legion was a full colonel and legion second-in-command. From the reign of Claudius, for promotion purposes, twenty-five military tribunes were appointed annually, but not all were given legion or Guard posts. Ten tribunes of the plebeians also were elected at Rome, sitting in the Senate; their republican power of veto over Senate votes was absorbed by the emperor.

TRIREME  Midsize Roman warship with three banks of oars. The most common ship in Roman fleets.

TRIUMPH  Parade through Rome in a gold *quadriga* by a victorious general, followed by his soldiers, prisoners, and spoils. He also received triumphal decorations, a statue in the Forum, and a large cash prize. Initially granted by the Senate, later by emperors, and usually only to generals of consular rank.

TRIUMPHAL DECORATIONS  A crimson cloak, crown of bay leaves, laurel branch, and statue in the Forum for generals celebrating a Triumph; and in lieu of a Triumph.

VEXILLUM  Square cloth banner of auxiliary units and legion detachments.

WATCH  Time in Roman military camps was divided into watches of three hours, at the end of which sentries changed, on a trumpet call. The officer of the watch was a tribune.

WATCHWORD  Password in a Roman military camp and at Rome. Daily, just prior to sunset, the tribune of the watch presented the most senior officer in camp with a register of the number of men fit for duty, and in return was given the watchword for the next twenty-four hours. This was distributed to the sentries by the guard cohort's *tesserarii*. In imperial times, the tribune commanding the Praetorian Guard's duty cohort at Rome obtained the Guard's watchword from the emperor.

WINTER CAMP  A permanent base where a legion usually spent October to March.

# BIBLIOGRAPHY

Abbott, F. F., and A. C. Johnson. *Municipal Administration in the Roman Empire*. Princeton, N.J.: Princeton University Press, 1926.

Appian. *Appian, Roman History*. Translated by H. White, 1889. Revised by I. Robison. London: Loeb, 1913.

Arrian. *History of Alexander, and Indica*. Translated by P. Brunt. Loeb series. Cambridge, Mass.: Harvard University Press, 1976.

Aurelius, M. *Meditations*. Translated by G. Long. Chicago: Encyclopaedia Britannica, 1952.

Azzaroli, A. *An Early History of Horsemanship*. London: E. J. Brill, 1985.

Birley, A. *Marcus Aurelius*. London: Eyre & Spottiswoode, 1966.

Birley, E. *Roman Britain and the Roman Army*. Kendal, U.K.: Titus Wilson, 1953.

Boardman, J., J. Griffin, and O. Murray. *The Oxford History of the Classical World*. Oxford, U.K.: Oxford University Press, 1986.

Bouchier, E. S. *Spain under the Roman Empire*. Oxford, U.K.: B. H. Blackwell, 1914.

Boyne, W., with H. Stuart Jones. *A Manual of Roman Coins*. Chicago: Ammon, 1968.

Brogen, O. *Roman Gaul*. London: Bell, 1953.

Broughton, T. R. S. *The Romanization of Africa Proconsularis*. New York: Greenwood, 1968.

Buchan, J. *Augustus*. London: Hodder & Stoughton, 1937.

Caesar, J. *Caesar: Commentaries on the Gallic and Civil Wars*. Translated by W. A. McDevitte and W. S. Bohm. London: Bell, 1890.

————. *The Civil War*. Translated by J. F. Gardner. London: Penguin, 1967.

————. *The Commentaries of Caesar*. Translated by W. Duncan. London: Dodsley, 1779.

————. *The Conquest of Gaul*. Translated by S. A. Handford, 1951. Revised by J. F. Gardner. London: Penguin, 1967.

————. *The Gallic War and the Civil War.* Translated by T. Rice Holmes. London: Loeb, 1914–1955.

Caracalla. *Historia Augusta.* Loeb series. Cambridge, Mass.: Harvard University Press, 1923.

Carcopino, J. *Daily Life in Ancient Rome.* London: Pelican, 1956.

Casson, L. *Ancient Egypt.* Alexandria, Va.: Time-Life, 1965.

Cave, W. *Lives, Acts, and Martyrdoms of the Holy Apostles.* London: Hatchard, 1836.

Chevalier, R. *Roman Roads.* Translated by N. H. Field. London: Batsford, 1976.

Cicero, M. *Letters of Cicero.* Translated by L. P. Wilkinson. London: Hutchinson, 1949.

————. *Letters to His Friends.* Translated by W. Glynn Williams, M. Cary, and M. Henderson. Cambridge, Mass.: Harvard University Press, 1912–1958.

Colledge, M. A. R. *The Parthians.* Leiden: E. J. Brill, 1986.

Collingwood, R. C. *Roman Britain.* Oxford, U.K.: Oxford University Press, 1932.

Cottrell, L. *The Great Invasion.* London: Evans, 1958.

Croft, P. *Roman Mythology.* London: Octopus, 1974.

Cunliffe, B. *The Celtic World.* London: Bodley Head, 1979.

————. *The Roman Baths at Bath.* Bath, U.K.: Bath Archeological Trust, 1993.

————. *Rome and Her Empire.* Maidenhead, U.K.: McGraw-Hill, 1978.

Dando-Collins, S. *Caesar's Legion.* New York: John Wiley & Sons, 2002.

————. *Cleopatra's Kidnappers.* Hoboken, N.J.: John Wiley & Sons, 2005.

————. *Mark Antony's Heroes.* Hoboken, N.J.: John Wiley & Sons, 2006.

————. *Nero's Killing Machine.* Hoboken, N.J.: John Wiley & Sons, 2004.

Delbruck, H. *History of the Art of War.* Translated by J. Walter Renfroe Jr. Lincoln: University of Nebraska Press, Bison Books, 1990.

Depuy, R. E., and T. N. Depuy. *The Encyclopedia of Military History: From 3500 B.C. to the Present.* London: Military Book Society, 1970.

Dio, C. *Cassius Dio, the Roman History: The Reign of Augustus.* Translated by I. Scott Kilvert. London: Penguin, 1987.

————. *Dio's Roman History.* Translated by C. Cary. London: Loeb, 1914–1927.

————. *Romanarum Historiaum.* Geneva: Estienne, 1592.

Duff, J. D. *Lucan.* Cambridge, Mass.: Harvard University Press. 1977.

Ehrenberg, V., and A. H. M. Jones. *Documents Illustrating the Reigns of Augustus and Tiberius.* Oxford, U.K: OUP, 1967.

Emile, T. *Roman Life under the Caesars.* New York: G. P. Putnam's Sons, 1908.

Forestier, A. *The Roman Soldier.* London: A. & C. Black, 1928.

Frank, T., ed. *An Economic Survey of Ancient Rome.* Peterson, N.J.: Pageant, 1959.

Frere, S. S. *Britannia: A History of Roman Britain.* London: Routledge & Kegan Paul, 1987.

Frontinus, S. J. *Stratagems. Aqueducts of Rome.* Translated by C. E. Bennet and M. B. McElwain. London: Loeb, 1969.

Furneaux, R. *The Roman Siege of Jerusalem.* London: Rupert Hart-Davis, 1973.

Gardner, J. F. *Family and Familia in Roman Law and Life.* Oxford, U.K.: Oxford University Press, 1998.

Gibbon, E. *The Decline and Fall of the Roman Empire.* Chicago: Encyclopaedia Britannica, 1932.

Grant, M. *The Army of the Caesars.* Harmondsworth, U.K.: Penguin, 1974.

―――――. *Gladiators.* Harmondsworth, U.K.: Penguin, 1967.

―――――. *The History of Rome.* Harmondsworth, U.K.: Penguin, 1978.

―――――. *The Jews of the Roman World.* Harmondsworth, U.K.: Penguin, 1973.

―――――. *Julius Caesar.* Harmondsworth, U.K.: Penguin, 1969.

―――――. *The Roman Emperors.* Harmondsworth, U.K.: Penguin, 1985.

―――――. *Roman History from Coins.* New York: Barnes & Noble, 1995.

Graves, R. *I, Claudius.* London: Arthur Barker, 1934.

Haywood, R. M. *Ancient Greece and the Near East.* London: Vision, 1964.

―――――. *Ancient Rome.* London: Vision, 1967.

Highet, G. *Juvenal the Satirist.* Oxford, U.K.: Clarendon, 1954.

Home, G. C. *Roman London.* London: Eyre & Spottiswoode, 1948.

Horace. *Satires, Epistles, Ars Poetica.* Translated by H. R. Faircloughs. London: Heinemann, 1955.

Jimenez, R. *Caesar against the Celts.* Conshohocken, Pa.: Sarpedon, 1996.

Jones, A. H. M. *Augustus.* New York: W.W. Norton, 1972.

Josephus, F. *The Complete Works of Josephus.* Translated by W. Whiston, 1737. Republished as *The New Complete Works of Josephus.* Grand Rapids, Mich.: Kregel, 1999.

―――――. *De Bello Judaico.* Oxford, U.K.: Typographeo Academico, 1837.

―――――. *The Jewish War.* Translated by H. St. John Thackery, R. Marcus, and L. H. Feldman. London: Loeb, 1926.

―――――. *The Jewish War.* Translated by G. A. Williamson. London: Penguin, 1959.

Keppie, L. *Colonisation and Veteran Settlement in Italy, 47–14* B.C. London: British School at Rome, 1983.

―――――. *The Making of the Roman Army: From Republic to Empire.* Totowa, N.J.: Barnes & Noble, 1984.

―――――. *Roman Inscribed and Sculpted Stones in the Huntorian Museum, University of Glasgow.* London: Society for Promotion of Roman Studies, 1999.

Ker, W. C. A. *Martial*. London: Loeb, 1919–1920.

Laking, G. F. *A Record of European Armour and Arms through Seven Centuries*. New York: A. M. S., 1934.

Macinnis, P. *Poisons: From Hemlock to Botox and the Killer Bean of Calabar*. New York: Little, Brown, 2005.

MacMullen, R. *Soldier and Civilian in the Later Roman Empire*. Cambridge, Mass.: Harvard University Press, 1967.

Mannix, D. P. *Those about to Die*. London: Mayflower, 1960.

Marsden, E. W. *Greek and Roman Artillery*. Oxford, U.K.: Oxford University Press, 1969.

Mattingly, H. *Roman Coins from the Earliest Times to the Fall of the Western Empire*. London: Methuen, 1927.

Mellan, I., and E. Mellan. *Dictionary of Poisons*. London: Owen, 1958.

Mommsen, T. *The Provinces of the Roman Empire*. Edited by T. R. S. Broughton. Chicago: University of Chicago Press, Phoenix Books, 1968.

Napthali, L. *Life in Egypt under Roman Rule*. Oxford, U.K.: Clarendon, 1983.

Parker, H. D. M. *The Roman Legions*. New York: Barnes & Noble, 1958.

Payne-Gallwey, Sir R. *The Crossbow: Mediaeval and Modern, with a Treatise on the Ballista and Catapults of the Ancients*. 1903. Reprint, London: Holland Press, 1995.

Peterson, D. *The Roman Legions Re-created in Color*. London: Windrow & Greene, 1992.

Petronius Arbiter, G. *The Satyricon*. Translated by M. Heseltine. London: Loeb, 1913.

Philo Judaeus. *The Works of Philo*. Translated by C. D. Yonge. Peabody, Mass.: Hendrickson, 1993.

Plato. *The Dialogues*. Translated by B. Jowlett. Reprint, Chicago: Encyclopaedia Britannica, 1952.

Pliny the Elder. *Natural History*, Edited and Translated by H. Rackman. London: Loeb, 1938–1963.

Pliny the Younger. *The Letters of Pliny the Consul*. Translated by W. Melmoth, 1746. Revised by W. M. Hutchinson. London: Loeb, 1915.

————. *Pliny's Letters*. Translated by A. J. Church and W. A. Brodribb. Edinburgh: Blackwood, 1872.

Plutarch. *The Lives of the Noble Grecians and Romans*. Translated by J. Dryden, 1683–1686. Reprint, Chicago: Encyclopaedia Britannica, 1952.

————. *Plutarch's Lives*. Translated by B. Perrin. London: Loeb, 1914–1926.

————. *Plutarch's Lives of Illustrious Men*. Translated by J. and W. Lanhome. London: Chatto & Windus, 1875.

————. *Plutarch's Lives of Illustrious Men*. Translated by T. North, 1579. Reprint, New York: Southworth-Anthoensen Press, 1941.

Polybius. *Histories*. Translated by W. R. Payton. London: Loeb, 1922–1927.

————. *The Histories of Polybius*. Translated by E. Shuckburgh. London: Macmillan, 1889.

————. *The Rise of the Roman Empire*. Translated by I. Scott-Kilvert. London: Penguin, 1979.

Raven, S. *Rome in Africa*. London: Longman, 1969.

Robertson, D. S. *Greek and Roman Architecture*. Cambridge, U.K.: Cambridge University Press, 1943.

Robinson, H. R. *The Armour of Imperial Rome*. Oxford, U.K.: Oxford University Press, 1975.

Romer, J. *Testament: The Bible and History*. London: Michael O'Mara, 1988.

Rossi, L. *Trajan's Column and the Dacian Wars*. London: Thames & Hudson, 1974.

Rostovtzeff, M. I. *The Social and Economic History of the Roman Empire*. New York: Biblio & Tannen, 1957.

Rowe, G. *Princes and Political Cultures: The New Tiberian Senatorial Decrees*. Ann Arbor: University of Michigan Press, 2002.

Salway, P. *Roman Britain*. Oxford, U.K.: Oxford University Press, 1981.

Seager, R. *Tiberius*. London: Eyre Methuen, 1972.

Seneca. *Four Tragedies and Octavia*. Translated by E. F. Watling. London: Penguin, 1966.

————. *Letters from a Stoic*. Translated by R. Campbell. Harmondsworth, U.K.: Penguin, 1969.

————. *Octavia*. Leipzig: Teubnes, 1902.

————. *Octavia*. Translated by W. Bradshaw. London: Swann Sonneschein, 1902.

————. *Seneca's Moral Epistles*. Edited by A. L. Motto. Wauconda, Ill.: Motto, 2001.

Sherwin-White, A. N. *The Roman Citizenship*. Oxford, U.K.: Oxford University Press, 1939.

Simkins, M. *Warriors of Rome*. London: Blandford, 1988.

Smith, F. E. *Waterloo*. London: Pan, 1970.

Starr, C. G. *Roman Imperial Navy, 31* B.C.–A.D. *324*. Ithaca, N.Y.: Cornell University Press, 1941.

Statius. *Collected Works*. Translated by J. H. Mozley. Cambridge, Mass.: Loeb, 1928.

Strabo. *The Geography of Strabo*. Translated by H. L. Jones. Cambridge, Mass.: Loeb, 1924.

Suetonius. *De Vitae Caesorum*. Leipzig: Teubnes, 1907.

————. *Lives of the Twelve Caesars*. Translated by F. Etchells and H. Macdonald. London: Etchells and Macdonald, 1931.

——. *Lives of the Twelve Caesars*. Translated by P. Holland, 1606. Reprint, New York: New York Limited Editions Club, 1963.

——. *Lives of the Twelve Caesars*. Translated by J. C. Rolfe. London: Loeb/ Heinemann, 1914.

——. Translated by A. Thompson, 1796. Reprint, Williamstown, Mass.: Corner House, 1978.

——. *The Twelve Caesars*. Translated by R. Graves, 1957. Revised by M. Grant. London: Penguin, 1979.

Sulimirski, T. *The Sarmatians*. New York: Praeger, 1970.

Syme, R. *History in Ovid*. Oxford, U.K.: Oxford University Press, 1979.

Tacitus. *Agricola et Germania*. London: Macmillan, 1869–1872.

——. *Annals*. Translated by D. R. Dudley. New York: Mentor, 1966.

——. *Annals*. Translated by M. Grant. London: Penguin, 1966.

——. *Annals and Histories*. Translated by A. J. Church and W. J. Brodribb. Reprint, Chicago: Encyclopaedia Britannica, 1952.

——. *Annals and Histories*. Translated by W. Petersen. Loeb Series, 1914–1937. Reprint, Franklin, Pa.: Franklin Library, 1982.

——. *History*, Translated by A. Murphy. London: Dent, 1900.

——. *Tacitus*, Translated by H. Mattingly and S. A. Handford. London: Penguin, 1948.

——. *Tacitus*. Translated by C. H. Moore and J. Jackson. London: Heinemann /G. P. Putnam's Sons, 1913.

Thompson, C. J. S. *Poisons and Poisoners: With Historical Accounts of Some Famous Mysteries in Ancient and Modern Times*: New York: Barnes & Noble, 1993.

*Times* of London. *Concise Atlas of World History*. London: *Times*, 1982.

Todd, M. *The Early Germans*. Oxford, U.K.: Blackwell, 1992.

——. *The Northern Barbarians, 1000 B.C.–A.D. 300*. New York: Blackwell, 1987.

Trench, C. C. *A History of Horsemanship*. Garden City, N.Y.: Doubleday, 1970.

Vernam, G. R. *Man on Horseback*. Garden City, N.Y.: Doubleday, 1964.

Warmington, E. H. *Nero*. Harmondsworth, U.K.: Penguin, 1969.

Warry, J. *Warfare in the Classical World*. London: Salamander, 1989.

Watson, G. R. *The Roman Soldier*. Ithaca, N.Y.: Cornell University Press, 1969.

*Webster's New Twentieth-Century Dictionary of the English Language*. Cleveland: World, 1953.

Weigall, A. *Nero, Emperor of Rome*. London: Butterworth, 1930.

Wheeler, R. M. *Rome beyond the Imperial Frontiers*. London: Bell, 1954.

White, K. D. *Greek and Roman Technology*. Ithaca, N.Y.: Cornell University Press, 1983.

Wightman, E. M. *Roman Trier and the Treveri*. New York: Praeger, 1970.

# INDEX